Bonfires at  Heaven's Gate

DR. DAVID HYATT

LILLIAN HYATT

Bonfires at ᘒᘒᘒᘒᘒᘒᘒ Heaven's ᘒᘒᘒᘒ Gate

A Biography of Dr. David Hyatt

ᘒᘒᘒᘒᘒᘒᘒᘒᘒᘒᘒᘒᘒᘒᘒᘒᘒᘒᘒ

The Seabury Press • New York

1983

The Seabury Press
815 Second Avenue
New York, NY 10017

Printed in the United States of America

Library of Congress Cataloging in Publication Data
Hyatt, Lillian L.
  Bonfires at heaven's gate.
    1. Hyatt, Dave. 2. National Conference of Christians and Jews—
Biography. 3. Catholics—United States—Biography. I. Title.
BL43.H9H9 1983 261.2′6′0924 [B] 82-17013 ISBN 0-8164-2354-7

Used by permission:
Front cover photo: Ellis Photographers
Frontispiece: Blackstone Studios
Illustration on epigraph page: © 1979, Geyer Studio, Inc.
Page 68: Ellis Photographers
Pages 69, 70, 71, 72: Religious News Service/Camera Arts

This book is dedicated to David Hyatt, the subject of Bonfires at Heaven's Gate. *It is his inspiration in my life that I wish to share with others.*
It was his way, when he prayed to his God in the chapel of the Catholic church near our home, to light one candle after another. I used to call it "lighting bonfires at heaven's gate."
It is clear to me that his life is a bonfire which will serve others as a beacon to a better world.

July 30, 1982

Acknowledgments

The author wishes to thank the many people who combined their vision, generosity, and talent to make this book a reality.

Mr. Edward J. Bermingham, Jr., President of Seabury Press, encouraged the creation of *Bonfires at Heaven's Gate*.

A unique band of gifted, dedicated women from Union Theological Seminary gave unstintingly of their skills and knowledge.

My deep gratitude also goes to Joyce Glover for her sensitive editing, and to Mary Holland for her research skills.

The following persons ensured the outreach of *Bonfires.*

Mr. Nathan Ancell
Mr. Leonard P. Aries
Mr. Robert L. Beda
  Cleveland Chapter, NCCJ
Dr. Robert Blaine
Marcus and Bertha Coler
  Philanthropic Fund—
  Jewish Communal Fund
Mrs. Miguel Elias
The Reverend Edward Flannery
Dr. Eugene J. Fisher,
  Executive Director
  Secretariat for Catholic-
  Jewish Relations, National
  Conference of Catholic Bishops
Estate of Helen and Joseph Friedland
Mr. Robert N. Getz
Mr. and Mrs. George V. Goulder

Rabbi Paul L. Hait,
  Executive Director
  The New York Board of Rabbis

Mr. Emanuel Hettlemen

Archbishop Iakovos
  Greek Orthodox Archdiocese
  of North and South America

Mr. Henry Kirschenbaum

Mr. Harold M. Lane, Sr.

Mr. Philip Lax,
  President, International Committee,
  B'nai B'rith

Sally and Nat Lefkowitz Foundation

Rabbi Irving Lehrman

Mr. Lester S. Levy

The Honorable John L. Loeb, Jr.
  U.S. Ambassador to Denmark

Mr. William F. May

Dr. Peter Mellette

The Very Reverend James Parks Morton
  Dean of the Cathedral
  of St. John the Divine

Bishop Francis Mugavero,
  Bishop of Brooklyn and
  Episcopal Moderator of the
  Secretariat for Catholic-Jewish
  Relations, National Conference
  of Catholic Bishops

Dr. Allyn P. Robinson

Mr. Arthur Rubloff

Mr. Bernard Schapiro

Mr. King D. Shwayder

Mrs. V. J. Skutt

The Honorable Herbert Tenzer

Mrs. Norman Weil, Sr.

Contents

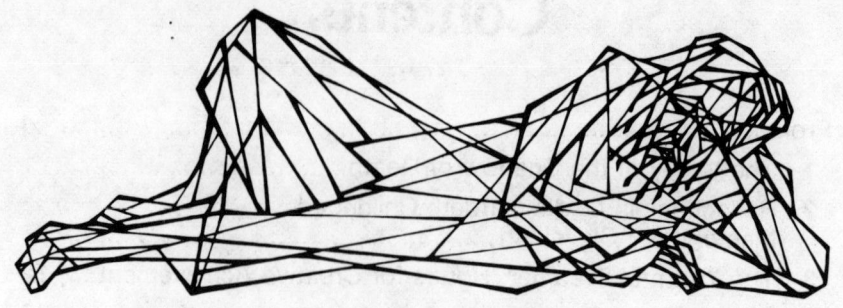

The only thing necessary for the triumph of evil is for good men to do nothing.

—EDMUND BURKE

This is the story of a good man who did something to combat the evil of one race against another, one religious group fighting another. He succeeded in his time, and did all one man could do in a lifetime.

"It is not for us to finish the work, but we must not desist from doing it."

—*Rabbi Tarfon,*
2nd century

Prologue

It was a typical cold, rainy day in early November 1965, a sharp contrast to the cosy comfort of the Braniff Room on the fourth floor of the national headquarters building of the National Conference of Christians and Jews (NCCJ). The staff streamed into the room where they were greeted by a tall man with a warm, expansive personality and glowing blue eyes set in a tanned, ruggedly handsome face. To take literally the old adage that the eyes are "the windows of the soul," David Hyatt's eyes gave a glimpse of a reflective soul, one concerned with the hopes, fears and dreams of other human beings. He had been in Pakistan on a two-year leave of absence from the Conference, but people there remembered him as a man who could be trusted to give direction to the agency then in the throes of the same sharp divisions as those plaguing the entire United States that year.

The Vietnam War had left a confused, angry generation of young people—who were no longer sure that their country was right to intervene in the internal affairs of another country and support one side against another in what they perceived as a civil war. In the Black, Hispanic, and other minority communities, the high expectations of the mid-fifties and early sixties were seen as tarnished dreams, promises never fulfilled. Turbulence prevailed throughout the country, with angry demonstrations staged by minorities, students, women, and anti-war groups. Their voices filled the streets, newspapers, and airwaves. With Martin Luther King's assassination, despair, bitterness, and disappointment replaced hope for far too many people. King's followers considered non-violence as a way of effecting social change to be a failed dream. In that troubled time David Hyatt was recalled to serve as Executive Vice-President of the NCCJ.

In his personal life there were many forces that could have pulled him away from the direction for his life implicit in leaving Pakistan

to return to the United States and this new post. But he had no
doubts or questions about his decision to return to the work he
loved. He had embarked on a journey of the heart, and it would
shape the rest of his life. He was giving up a promising diplomatic
career, but he had made a similar choice in 1954 when he gave up
a flourishing financial career, to the dismay of his family and friends,
to accept the post of National Director of Public Relations at the
NCCJ. He would now pursue his dream that in later years he characterized movingly as "creating a unified America." The burning idealism which had motivated him to risk his life in the African desert
with the British Eighth Army as an ambulance driver in the American Field Service made the later decision inevitable. In the desert,
called by the Arabs "God's Garden," the man called David McKinley Hyatt found the beginning of a passionate love affair—not with
a woman, but with an ideal and an idea that was to shape the rest
of his life: that people of all creeds, colors, and social backgrounds
could indeed come to regard each other as partners in creating a new
world.

His great conviction gave him confidence about accomplishing his
goal, and the representation at NCCJ from the diverse ethnic, racial,
and religious groups forming the mosaic of his native land made this
organization the place best suited for him to work out his conception
of the Deity's plan for his life. His own words, written at the age of
twenty-six as he despaired at the sight of dead and wounded all
about him, their life blood ebbing into the desert sands, express
cogently David Hyatt's beliefs:

> War is 90% boredom, and the rest of it is simply obscene. But out
> of it somehow something wonderful is growing. I feel now, for the
> first time, it is possible not only to win the war, but the peace as
> well. For these men I'm here with aren't fighting for themselves
> alone; but they have fought together expressing their mass deter-
> mination to stop Hitler's slavery and slavery all over the world.
> I can begin to believe that if this same oneness of all men for others
> persists in peace as it now exists in war, a new world will really,
> actually, come out of it—a world without hunger, a world without
> slavery, a world without boundaries, where all men are brothers.

In the assembled group that November day was a serious young
woman, quite new to the staff. She and David Hyatt in future years
were to have a tremendous impact on each other's lives. Years later
David Hyatt remembered quite vividly his first impressions of Lili,
a striking, dynamic, blue-eyed blonde who expressed in every way
a lively awareness and alertness.

As Lili stood there that day, she was filled with boundless curiosity about the new Executive Vice-President whose glowing reputation had preceded his arrival. For over a year, ever since joining the staff, she had heard the repeated refrain, "When Dr. Hyatt comes back, everything will be all right." As she admitted to David years later, her response was skeptical; having experienced the limitations of mortal beings, she wondered exactly what miracle could be produced by that pleasant-looking man standing there in the center of a knot of people. But, as she also said later, this skepticism was quite diminished and her usual poise somewhat shattered by the unexpected warmth of his greeting expressing genuine interest and knowledge about her work at NCCJ. This gave her a clue to his capability for easing the problems at NCCJ. Much later she admitted to David her unexpected self-consciousness at this first meeting, and her recognition of it long after the fact as the first sign of a love that was to find fulfillment after years of separation and tragedy in both their lives.

David's first day at the Conference created a mood of guarded optimism in the usually cynical staff. His closing words helped the disillusioned staff members to start finding their way back to the reasons for their own involvement in the NCCJ and to the purpose for which NCCJ had been founded:

> You all share with me the hope and prayer, I know, of the late, great theologian and philosopher, Father Pierre Teilhard de Chardin, S.J., who said, 'Some day, after we have mastered the winds, the waves, the tides and gravity, we will harness for God the energies of love: and then, for the second time in the history of the world, man will have discovered fire!

As Lili listened she was reminded of a tribute paid to Bertha Pappenheim by Martin Buber:

> I not only admired her but loved her, and will love her until the day I die. There are people of spirit and there are people of passion, both less common than one might think. Rarer still are the people of spirit and passion. But rarest of all is a passionate spirit. . . .

From that day Lili continued to see in David that passionate spirit which moved others to follow where he led and inspired them to attempt to share his dream.

From that momentous day of his return to the National Conference of Christians and Jews David Hyatt was unwittingly fulfilling a prophecy expressed by a former professor, Bergen Evans, Chairman of the Department of English at Northwestern University. At the time David entered law school at the university, Dr. Evans said:

> *Hyatt is something between Huck Finn, Booker T. Washington, and Abe Lincoln in Illinois. He's had a hard life and slugged his way up—the American Way—until he collapsed from overwork and malnutrition—also the American Way. He's got a lot of brains in a wild sort of way, tremendous vigor in everything he does, and a considerable dramatic flair. Endless roaring humor coupled with a continually-raging sense of social injustice and a wild determination to do something about it. He's got demons. He'll never stop fighting—never. The greater the odds, the more excited he'll get, that's all.*

The man Lili saw in 1965 was no longer the raging, roaring, wild character that Bergen Evans had described 24 years earlier. This was a man who had focused his spirit and energy in a way that gave him an aura of mission and destiny, a man on fire, a man who had spent the better part of his life contending with a vision that had bent him to its own configuration. It was this vision, a vision of unity, which enabled him to fulfill the leadership role for which his entire life was a preparation.

1

The Valley
of the Shadow of Death

〰

The waiting was the worst of it. All through that hot Egyptian
summer they had waited—and the heat was unbearable. Nothing
moved. Squads of flies seemed to hang suspended in the hot waver-
ing air, mercilessly irritating. And everywhere the desert stretched
outward from El Alamein.

After the turmoil and traumas of Tobruk, the wait was at first a
kind of respite. But, all too quickly, the inactivity and the boredom
shortened tempers; inconsequential, routine matters became explosive issues, triggering anger, irritation, and uncertainty. Nightfall
brought little enough relief; in the morning it started all over again—
the oppressive and relentless heat, the flies, the waiting, the rumors.

El Alamein was not a town, not even a small village. It was a
camping place in a hellish eternity of desert sand. It was from here
that the Allies had determined to mount their defense of Cairo,
Alexandria, and the Suez Canal. For eight weeks the British Eighth
Army waited—in a site with no diversion, neither brothel nor bazaar, not even a bar where a Tommy might quench his thirst. Even
the Bedouins avoided the place on their way across the desert. The
only activity a man could enjoy was speculation. Rumors were in-
cessant, and ultimately as oppressive and irritating as the flies. The
same questions circulated over and over and over: Where was Auchinleck? Where was Rommel? Would the Allies be able to with-
stand another attack? Could they defend the Suez? Would Cairo
fall? The men would have traded anything to end the uncertainty
and the inactivity. They all knew that, if they had to retreat through
Cairo, all Africa would be lost, and the way would be open to the
oil fields of Arabia.

David Hyatt was 26 that year. Incensed by the Nazi juggernaut across Europe, he had enlisted in the British Eighth Army through the American Field Service, joining before the United States had entered World War II. Now, as an AFS driver, as well as a frontline correspondent for the North American Newspaper Alliance, David found himself woven into the fabric of the war being waged by the Allies against the Desert Fox, General Rommel of the German High Command.

He had been in law school when the war intervened. He came to understand what was at stake in Germany and other parts of Europe under Nazi domination after reading *Not Peace But a Sword* by Vincent Sheehan. This book described the box-carloads of Jews being shipped to concentration camps in Germany. He could barely absorb the enormity of what was happening. Then he saw a film called *The Mortal Storm*, one of many powerful movies exposing Hitler's persecution of the Jews. David found himself deeply outraged, and that anger and sorrow began to take shape as a decision to leave school and serve with the British.

In a way, this was the only religious belief that David had at that point in his life; all his sympathies and his passion and his moral idealism were kindled into flame by the brutal murder of Jews, the enslavement of entire populations, the crushing of the unprotected and defenseless by Hitler's armies. But his convictions were the raw substance of genuine faith, and they were tempered in the desert by terror and despair. There are moments when a man makes his peace with death because he has no other choice, only to find that he has passed through its shadow to be reborn. In the year of El Alamein, David's life was changed. During the second half of the war, he wrote about the experience:

"That morning I moved out with my section, out into the desert, out to El Alamein. I was serving with a Regimental Aid Post. We waited for hours. It was quiet except for occasional salvos and a light air raid.

"In the morning of the second day, the horror began. I picked up six men from a shelled outpost half a mile to the north. One had the head of his penis cut off and his back splattered with shrapnel. He screamed, 'Oh Jesus, Jesus!' While three of us held him down the Doctor administered morphine. He died as I loaded him into my ambulance.

"In the afternoon, after a raid, a pilot crashed. I rushed over to the burning plane, but there was nothing to pick up. There were pieces of the pilot all over the desert, and one big hunk, like meat wrapped in burnt cloth, was the remains of his trunk. I don't know why, but I felt no sorrow. I guess there was nothing to feel sorry about; it was simply grotesque. Later that night I was spent and exhausted.

"No rest. All through the night the Allies attacked. The artillery cleared the way, the infantry went in; then behind them in three lines the vehicles and guns of the artillery moved forward three miles under cover of darkness. By daybreak, the men in my section and I hauled the wounded back as fast as we could. They were everywhere. Small clusters of men stood beside the hurt ones and waved for us to come and help them. There was no time to think or feel, or we would have been horrified by the men mangled by shrapnel, men with bayonet wounds, and those with dismembered limbs.

"Mobs of prisoners were being forced back on foot from the fighting area. Around the Regimental Aid Post, the shelling continued in full fury. We had to go along the edge of a minefield far beyond the lines to pick up six wounded Jerries. The Germans cheered as we drove up. Two New Zealanders lay dead beside a dead German. I got out of there as soon as we were able to load the wounded. I was helped by the Germans who were wounded, but not as badly as their comrades.

"I got back and was assigned to take a wounded man, that had been brought in, to the temporary carpost, a makeshift medical station half a mile from the front. As I finished, I stopped to talk with a striking-looking New Zealand captain who had just driven up with a truckload of wounded German prisoners. We both heard the planes. We looked up and the sky was filled with white spurts of smoke. Explosions shattered the air and mushrooms of dust and fire rose where bombs hit the earth. Directly above me a plane dove down. I jumped into a nearby slit trench and pressed my face into the sand. There were ready-built trenches all around us, for this had been a battlefield. I pressed my body closer into the sand, but I could tell by the screech of the plane and the whistle of the wings cutting the air and the savage drive of the plane's big engine that it was charging to the ground, that 'this was it.' Then I heard bombs being released with an earbreaking scream, and the scream seemed to cut into my flesh and I felt myself rise to the scream and come down with it. I tightened and shrunk deeper into the earth. The bombs zoomed down toward me, and I lay there and waited for the inevitable. Now I was beyond fear. This was it, this was the finish. In a second it would all be over. I'd be torn to bits, done for, beyond even salvage for burial.

"Then the bombs hit, five yards away, another fifteen, and the whole earth shook around me, the dirt from the trench collapsed over me, pieces of shrapnel hit the walls of the trench; and I waited for the steel to drive through my flesh, I waited for Death.

"Then the dust whirled, and there were sounds; and then only dust. I could hardly believe I was alive, for by every right I should have been dead. I had a sense, as I lay there covered with dust and half-buried by sand, that I had been saved by a miracle. There was no time to think. Voices of stunned men, not hit but seemingly unable to move from the shock, yelled, "Stretcher! Stretcher!" for the wounded. The captain's middle and leg and hip lay wide open, and it was the first thing I saw when I scrambled out of the earth. I rushed over to him and loaded him on a stretcher; and while the Doctor was giving him morphine, I loaded on another man whose lung had been punctured. As I turned to put the captain in the carpost ambulance, he came to and recognized me. He tried to joke, and passed out cold. Then I heard someone down below yelling, "Ambulance! Over here!" As I ran, I remember thinking that he would be dead when he reached the dressing station. There was not a chance that he would survive the hour and a half trip in the jouncing ambulance. Not many poor devils wounded that badly made it."

Later, at war's end, David was to put his feelings into words, in a poem he called *The Ones Who Cry War*.

> *How can we tell them what pain really is?*
> *Jaws shot away*
> *Spinal columns severed,*
> *Arms torn to shreds,*
> *Eyes turned to yellow,*
> *Vitals sheared off,*
> *The moans of death when dying yourself.*
> *Let them see a man thrash in the bushes*
> *Like a wounded animal,*
> *And then lie very still.*
> *Let them watch a man lurch forward*
> *Before a stream of fire,*
> *Then collapse face down,*
> *The opening of the back of his head*
> *Pink where brains seep out on the sands.*
> *Let them see the shoes of men with the feet still in them,*

But nothing else remaining.
Let them pick up these men,
By the hundreds and thousands,
Until the sight breaks their hearts
And the sheer, empty weariness of burying the dead
Exhausts them completely.
Their strident voices will become choked whispers.
Their throats will ache.
They will no longer talk war.

"There was no more time to think, the confusion was getting worse. I hurried as fast as I could back to my car, and when I got there I saw that a big piece of shrapnel had ripped into the front end, torn through the dashboard, and wrecked the steering wheel. The whole inside was peppered with holes and the seat was burning. I yelled to one of the other drivers, twenty yards away, to head down there; and turned the extinguisher on the flames. I had to cut out the burning seat with a knife because my extinguisher was exhausted.

"When dusk settled, we towed the wrecked car back beyond shelling range. I was left in a vast open spot in the desert, out of sight of the vehicles. I knew I would have to stay there until the salvage crew arrived. I sat on the back step and simply stared ahead of me, too grateful to be alive to think any coherent thoughts. I was flooded with a surging warmth, an all-encompassing physical conscious-ness. I was still alive, I could still feel the air in my lungs, sense the flesh on my bones, see with my eyes, feel life in my groin; and though the bomb still screamed in my ears, I could hear. I remember calling my own name and feeling so grateful to be able to hear my own name come back to me. I felt privileged to be alive!

"As the dusk grew grayer, I felt as though the desert waste was lifeless. I knew I would have to find a way to distract my mind from the screaming of the bombs that still churned in my head. I opened the glove compartment beside the wrecked dashboard. There, cov-ered with sand debris, lay the small Bible which I read occasionally. The passage on the page I opened to read shocked and amazed me 'Yea, though I walk through the valley of the shadow of death, I will fear no evil, for thou art with me.' I read the words again.

"I was not one to believe anything easily, but I could not deny that I felt as though my life had been saved by a miracle. I had not touched that Bible in months, and I could not deny that the words I read explained that miracle for me. Alone in the desert, now dusky and grey, vast and seemingly infinite, the sands stretching beyond sight to the edge of oncoming night, I found it logical to believe that I had just been the beneficiary of an amazing miracle. I had somehow been saved and was still alive. But why? Why me? Was there some reason for this? Why was I spared? The psalm seemed to have spoken to me: 'Yea, though I walk through the valley of the shadow of death, I will fear no evil: for thou art with me.' "[1]

While the experience was not an epiphany in the strictest sense, it was certainly, for David, the beginning of a new way of thinking that was to shape many of his actions in the years to come. In the furnace that was the Egyptian desert and in the holocaust which devoured other men, the soul of a warrior was forged. His armor would be Truth, his shield Justice, and his sword Compassion. His goal: justice and equality for all men and women. His enemy: all those who sought to enslave others, deny them religious liberty, refuse their right to life's opportunity because of race, creed, or color.

2

Reflections in God's Garden: Childhood Memories of Cleveland

❦

As David waited out the hours before the arrival of the salvage crew, the recent encounter with the waste and horror of death in war inevitably led him to examine his past life and to scrutinize closely his conclusions about what was really built into the rafters of the universe. David mused that there was no better place than this, "God's Garden," for such reflection.

Past and present intermingled as he lay there. Vivid images of the young German boys taken prisoner by the Allies as his unit retreated from Tobruk saddened him and reminded him how very different his own childhood had been from the frightful desolation surrounding him.

He pictured the large comfortable house, set in the midst of green lawns and trees in Cleveland, where he had lived with his adored mother, Rose Miller Hyatt, the lovely granddaughter of William Gray Rose, former Mayor of Cleveland; his father, Harry Hyatt; and his older brother, Hudson, commonly known as Hud. His dad's official job title was City Forester, but his actual function as assistant to the Mayor and host to official visitors to Cleveland meant that he was always busy with visiting dignitaries. (Harry Hyatt had also been appointed at the age of 28, in 1918, to serve as secretary to the Cleveland City Planning Commission.) David's beloved grandmother, Evelyn Miller, also helped to create his secure child's world, and he recalled the way she used to regale him with stories of the Hyatts who had ventured out west to California. David especially identified with Uncle Ed Hyatt, founder of the California junior college system.[2] Another favorite recollection centered on the adventures of his grandfather, Charles Miller, whom David remembered as a prominent Cleveland attorney, but who in his youth had fought along with Teddy Roosevelt in the Spanish-American War. Grandma Miller had related some awe-inspiring stories to David about her uncle, William McKinley, twenty-fifth President of the United States. All these tales, together with the books his Grandma Miller provided, fired his already active imagination.

When David had left for the Middle East, he packed his boyhood diaries. There in the desert he recalled rereading entries which clearly depicted his boyish enthusiasms. The one for August 24, 1926 read, "I went to Cleveland today with Grandpa Hyatt, and he took us to Grandma Miller's house and I brought home the life of William Mckinley, and the Southern Mountains, and the Iron Brigade, and the American Boy, which my Great Grandma Rose wrote." Another entry, on the following day: "I read fifty pages in the life of William Mckinley, my second cousin." The misspelling of the family name always brought an inner chuckle.

Memories of the next period of his life still brought pain. His secure world had vanished overnight when his mother was taken away to a mental hospital. He knew that this wound would never really heal. It was a cataclysmic event in the life of a child of six. His Grandma Miller, despite her valiant efforts, could neither fill the void nor control the two Huckleberry Finns, David and Hud. In addition to these concerns, she was heavily burdened with caring for the welfare of her sick daughter. David's father, crushed by the weight of his wife's illness and burdened by his work, increasingly left his two young sons to their own devices.

As David reflected on this period of profound unhappiness, he remembered setting fire to a dry grassy field next to his home. He had spread paraffin, used in jelly-making, on the field, lit a match, then hid when he heard the fire engines. When he realized that his actions had brought out the entire Cleveland Fire Department, he was completely terror-stricken. About the same time his family discovered that he was not attending school but instead was spending his days in the local blacksmith's shop—when he was not in the gravestone sculptor's shop.

A family conference, called to review both the fire episode and the truancy, decided that both David and Hud would fare better on a farm outside of Cleveland under the supervision of the Reynolds family, who provided a foster home for youngsters in circumstances like those of David and Hud. (In 1923 the charge to parents for this care was $1.00 per child per day!)

David still thought with nostalgia of life on the Reynolds farm. His affection for Uncle Fred and Aunty, as he and Hud called Mr. and Mrs. Reynolds, was undimmed by the intervening years. Evenings spent by the Reynolds' glowing hearth while Mrs. Reynolds read from Dickens, Shakespeare, and a host of other writers, left their profound impression on David's sensitivities. Also, because they were deeply religious, the Reynolds made sure that David heard his share of Bible readings. These served to develop his love of language and poetry. Once again, David felt a surge of gratitude that he and Hud had spent their formative years with such a loving, literate, and sensitive couple.

The psalms learned with Mrs. Reynolds' encouragement reechoed now. If his memory served him correctly, each one learned was worth a nickel. He had never forgotten the one beginning, "The heavens declare the glory of God and the firmament showeth his handiwork." He thought, How strange that the power and beauty in men should show itself so brightly in the midst of all the obscenities of war. It was curious that, in many cases, when men faced death, they did not think of themselves. How often it happened that the men somehow became bigger than themselves. David wondered by what name to call that phenomenon. Selflessness? God's light within men? Brotherhood? He knew now it was one of the deepest impulses in man, in all men he was sure—something sacred and holy and a part of God.[3]

David's battlefield revery about the Reynolds farm brought to mind the hours of hard work, and going to bed many nights too tired to write more than one line in his diary. One entry, on July 19, 1926, bears this out: "We made hay all day, hauled five loads." Another time still vivid in David's memory there on the battlefield was recorded on June 18th: "It rained today in the evening. We needed it bad enough. If it hadn't rained pretty soon, the farmers would be in the poorhouse before fall."

The fun on the farm came from such experiences as the cooperative efforts of all the farmers during the threshing season, when relaxation came to the huge tables set out with bountiful food. David thought warmly of the trips with Mr. Reynolds into Cleveland's "Little Italy" to market grapes and into Ashtabula to sell milk and produce. It was a kind of remarkable fate, David thought, that had allowed him to acquire a set of foster parents who could give him a firm set of values and a sense of stability, both mental and spiritual, to prepare him for later trials such as those he was presently enduring in North Africa.

Ruefully David recalled that these benefits from life with the Reynolds did not always stop him from joining other young rascals in some pretty earthy pranks, such as turning over the school out-houses on Halloween. These were temporary aberrations, however. He studied by himself, became an Eagle Scout, and wrote poetry and stories. Sadly, he remembered that it was in this period that his father remarried, and consequently saw less and less of his sons. His new wife, Else, looked upon them as real nuisances who interfered with her nomadic, carefree life with Harry. Hotels, she felt, were no place for two lively little boys, and their father's "home" was usually a hotel.

When the depression took firm hold on the country, Harry lost his job. Soon he could no longer afford to pay even the dollar per day required for the boys' care. As David remembered hearing Uncle Fred and Aunty telling his father, "Pay when you get a job again," he felt tears come to his eyes. The Reynolds knew this was an almost non-existent prospect in the troubled economy of 1930, but they cared so much about David and Hud.

David recalled another ugly manifestation of those years—the growth of the Ku Klux Klan. He first encountered it at the funeral of the sexton of the local church in Austinburg, Ohio, when he noticed with astonishment two rows of hooded figures dressed in white bedsheets. On his next visit to Cleveland he asked his grand-mother what it all meant; she told him that these men hated Jews, Catholics, and Blacks. His bewilderment was complete for he knew from observation that the number of Jews, Blacks, and Catholics was very small in that town. His discussions with his fair-minded grand-mother had no doubt shaped his present feelings. He was no longer so bewildered; now he felt anger about the prejudices which had contributed to the horrible carnage in the world in this year of 1942.

For a moment in the peace of the desert, immense and seemingly isolated from the turmoil, he found it hard to be angry and bitter. But just for a moment. The muffled sounds of the big guns reaching his ears—sometimes sounding closer, sometimes sounding farther away—told him the fighting was not far off. He could not help wondering how the battle was going; even more acutely he won-dered whether his own people would find him. Or would he be picked up by a German patrol? As he pondered his possible fate, Cleveland and his boyhood seemed very remote.

Contemplating this situation, he heard in his mind the advice from Mr. and Mrs. Van Arnam at Austinburg High School to "write about what you know." There his interest in creative writing had resulted in a short novel. That and his involvement in dramatics had shaped his college career. Now these years in the desert had certainly provided him with much very familiar material. He could write several novels and plays, but the sobering thought passing through his mind was, Would he live to "tell the tale"?

3

The Youthful Dreamer: Hopes for Creative Achievement

❧

Daylight was fading. A chill came into the air, creeping in with the twilight. Although it was summer and the drop in temperature at nightfall was not severe, the cold that covered the desert by night always took him by surprise. He had never really adjusted to the extreme temperature changes. He watched the desert changing. It was turning slowly from hot scorched amber to silvery blue. He shivered. "Where the devil is that salvage crew?"

Impatience was fruitless, he knew, so he settled back against the wrecked ambulance and let his mind meander to the time when he and Hud were wild with excitement over an invitation to go to California. The invitation had arrived the spring before Hud finished Austinburg Grammar School. It was to be a graduation present for Hud, but David had been asked to come as well.

The boys, long deprived of a family of their own, were overjoyed at the prospect of seeing their grandmother Maudie Cleve Hyatt, their grandfather Harry Hyatt, Sr., and their father's sister, Hazel Hyatt. Hazel had been recently widowed, and that prompted her parents to move to California from Cleveland to be near her. When he retired, Grandpa Hyatt built an additional room on to Hazel's modest cottage. They all felt that the boys would be comfortable there on their summer visit. While these plans were being formulated, tragedy struck again. Grandma Hyatt was stricken with peritonitis, brought on by a ruptured appendix, and died.

Unwilling to disappoint the boys, and despite their own bereavement, Aunt Hazel and her father decided to take the boys, as previously planned, on a sightseeing trip the length of California. David would never forget his first glimpse of California—Yosemite, Lake Tahoe, the redwoods, Big Sur, the huge lemon and orange groves of Riverside and Orange Counties, the vineyards of the Napa Valley, the vast irrigated farmlands from Sacramento to Fresno and on to Bakersfield, Death Valley, and the Mohave Desert. The trip opened up new worlds for the two boys, who at twelve and fourteen had never been out of Ohio.

The entire experience had such an effect on David that when Grandpa Hyatt offered to come to Cleveland to take the boys back to California for another summer visit, this time as a present for Hud on his graduation from Austinburg High School, David determined to stay on in California when Hud left for Western Reserve—where he had been given a scholarship. David remembered wanting to start a new life in California. Austinburg High School, with its small student body of ninety and its limited curriculum, was too confining for him. Corona High School, he knew, had four hundred students and offered courses in drama and journalism. Moreover, his Aunt Hazel, a teacher at Corona, in talking about the school, had whetted his appetite for the new experience.

Aunt Hazel was a college graduate, rare for a woman in her day, and a brilliant language teacher. It was this woman who was to awaken in him his love for the theater. Her wide interests were reflected in her conversations with him, and her charm and loveliness, coupled with her affectionate ways, captivated the lonely boy of seventeen who had been without a mother for eleven years. Hazel had never had a child, although wanting one, so it was inevitable that the two should become very close. She took him often to Los Angeles, to concerts and the theater, to see performances by the greats and near-greats of the time.

David remembered with gratitude that his grandfather, unlike his father, had time to spend with him. In Harry Sr., a graduate engineer, David found a walking encyclopedia of information about plants, rocks, trees, and a host of other subjects. Although his professional life had been spent as the superintendent of the Otis Steel Works, his many varied interests made him a real Renaissance man. He loved wood carving, gardening, and talking with David. A close tie was forged between the youth and his grandfather, so close that by the end of the summer it was clear to David's father that David should be granted permission to remain in Corona with his rediscovered family. Once more his father arranged to pay one dollar a day for his room and board. He was careful to do so because Grandpa

Hyatt was retired, there was no Social Security in 1933, and Hazel's entire salary for a year of teaching language amounted to $1600.

David remembered the two years that followed as a contented period in his life. His only uncomfortable memory from that time came from his encounter with prejudice in his schoolmates. For reasons which he could not quite understand, the "in" clique at Corona High School reacted with resentment to him as a new student. His friends claimed that his academic achievements and easy rapport with others threatened the clique. When David decided to run for student body President, this group of young people was determined that the boy from Austinburg, Ohio, was not going to win. To ensure this, they blocked his name from the ballot. His friends, hearing of this, were angered and upset. David smiled when he realized that the clique had reckoned without the knowledge that David carried within him the genes of a very successful politician, his grandfather William Gray Rose. They also did not take into account an additional edge, an unexpected edge, that David had. Out of his innate enthusiasm for people, David had come to know all sorts of his fellow students, not just the Big Men on Campus and the popular girls. Since he was blocked out of appearing on the ballot, his friends got enough signatures on a petition to enter him on the ballot. So that no one could forget that David was running for office, they painted posters and distributed handbills and badges, all marked "Let's Go Higher with Hyatt." But the faithful band of followers went even further than that, he recalled with a smile. He arrived at school one morning and found the slogan painted in huge letters, in tar, on the circular driveway leading to the front entrance of the school. He remembered his enjoyment when, in a fair election, he won the office of student body President. Strangely enough, neither David nor his opponent, whom David admired as a "good guy," relished this sort of competition. In fact, all through their senior year at Corona High they remained warm friends.

That spring, while finishing up high school, David worked in the orange groves with a crew of twenty Mexican-Americans and learned firsthand about their incredibly poor housing conditions and paltry pay. Even now he shuddered to think about it.

The following year, he recalled, he was chosen to be a "cherub," as aspirants for a drama scholarship were called at Northwestern University. With encouragement from both his Aunt Hazel and his grandfather, he took the scholarship and left Corona for Evanston, Illinois.

David's years in college were governed, he remembered all too clearly, by two overriding factors. One was his economic situation, precarious to say the least; the other, his love of the theater, very constant. He took care of the economic situation by maintaining his academic work; all he had to do for that, he recalled ruefully, was to be first in his class each year! His scholarship provided only tuition expenses. There were other financial considerations to be met, such as where to find the money for meals, a room, and books.

To earn his meals he became a delivery man for the Hoos Drug Store in Evanston, Illinois, where he worked from 1935 to 1938 on a schedule of fourteen hours every Sunday, three hours every Saturday, and lunch hour every weekday. In return, he got all of his meals, served at the well-equipped lunch counter and soda fountain which was basic to every drugstore in those years. Here in the desert he surely could use one of those meals right now. Bully beef, day after day, had lost its charm. He paid for those drugstore meals in full measure, he recalled. Sometimes he was so tired, on his long Sunday, that in the thirteenth hour he would go into the drugstore bathroom just to sit on the commode to rest. One cold Sunday night, when the wind off the lake brought a temperature of thirty below zero, he set out on his bicycle to deliver some containers of hot coffee to a sorority house. He remembered, still with amusement, arriving at his destination with half a dozen frozen coffee popsicles!

Another source of income he developed was from editing and writing for the college paper. That assignment brought him $300 a year. It paid for lodging at the college dorm, and later at a modest rooming house.

Despite all the rigors of providing for himself, David managed to have fun and still keep up the academic work in the Drama department which enabled him to win the freshman, sophomore, and junior class scholarships. Proud memories came to him of his lead roles in plays by some of the greats, like O'Neill, Chekhov, Lillian Hellman, and, of course, Shakespeare. In addition to all of this he still found energy to be a part of the varsity fencing squad.

In the summer of 1937 he joined the Old White Arts School and Colony in White Sulphur Springs, West Virginia, as one of the Old White Players.

Recalling that summer was bittersweet because that was when he fell in love with Phyllis Campbell. She was a beautiful, self-contained young woman from his home town, Cleveland. He thought, "It was like a script from a B movie; he fell in love during rehearsals of Romeo and Juliet. Well, corny as it sounded, it was exactly what happened." The devil of it was she still haunted him, despite his laconic dismissal of the depth of his feelings. Miles separated them, and months had gone by, but he still ached whenever he thought of the way they had said goodbye. She had made sure that he understood that there would be no question of anyone waiting for him when he returned.

When he had packed away his scrapbook from that golden summer, he had taken the trouble to look at one particular photo that froze a moment in time, that told the whole story of their relationship. The positions of the figures told the tale, so that "even he that runs may read." David was standing on a stairway looking up at a lovely girl several steps above him. He laughed aloud at that. Her father had expressed disapproval of David in his gentle, well-bred way. As an actor, playwright, and author, David was a young man whose head was filled with dreams of being a novelist like Thomas Wolfe, a playwright like Eugene O'Neill, and an actor-director-producer like Lawrence Olivier. His vagabond existence did not help to alter the picture of a young man with no solid economic base. Case in point, what was he doing here in North Africa while other men were building careers in banking and engineering? He could almost hear Phyllis's parents saying that. David had to admit that any young woman's parents could make a case by saying, "Look, my dear, he is, we admit, handsome, wild, reckless and daring and romantic; but he shows no visible means of being able to support a life partner." As a matter of fact, they might point out, and be right, that he was barely able to support himself, even in the most Spartan manner.

Well, he could not blame Phyllis or her parents; he really had to get done what he had set out to do. He was determined, through his writings, to express his deep conviction about society's ills. His dream was to write and produce plays like Maxwell Anderson's *Gods of Lightning,* and *Winterset;* Gorky's *The Lower Depths;* Ibsen's *An Enemy of the People.* He wanted to write novels like Zola's *Nana* and Steinbeck's *Grapes of Wrath,* and above all works such as Zola's essay, "J'Accuse"—works of deeply emotional social conviction. He had to admit that a dream like that did not leave room for a nine-to-five job as a clerk in an office hoping to work himself up to being president. Dreams. What was life anyway? It would have been wonderful if Phyllis had wanted to share his dream, but, like most women, she dreamed another dream, of a career in the theater, becoming another Katherine Cornell. Eventually, if the fates allowed, she wanted a secure home, a loving and attentive husband and children. It would be a very long time before he could offer that to Phyllis or anyone.

David's reverie deepened with the coming of night, as he recalled how his soul had been offended when, in his freshman year, there was an upheaval in the dormitory due to the presence at Pearson Hall of two Black students. Some students with southern backgrounds may have begun the ruckus about the two Black men being housed in "their dorm," but they were joined immediately by many young men who had been born and brought up in the North. The rehabilitated building was no palace, but they confronted the resident faculty advisor on several occasions as though their own particular castle had been invaded by a noxious enemy army. David was especially distressed by the fact that, at the conclusion of the affair, the two Black men were consigned to a back room, close to an outside back stairway, so they could not be observed from the street when they entered and left the building.

David recalled that these two decent young men survived this shameful indignity and eventually became good friends with their erstwhile tormentors. This, David felt, was a tribute to their ability to forgive inhuman treatment and subhuman behavior, a fact that was not lost on David. His esteem for the young men was enhanced as his disgust for the white men who had created the issue mounted. He could not help making a comparison with the Nazi behavior towards the Jews, as he sat pondering in the middle of the desert. Perplexed and angry, he cried out to the empty desert, "Why?" The U.S.A. was a civilized country, populated by decent people; and Germany was considered by many people to be a leader in the scientific and medical fields, and by all standards had produced great poets, philosophers, and writers, and some of the greatest musicians the world had ever known. Where did the whole thing go wrong and allow insane behavior to become the norm?

His thoughts continued in the same vein as the night deepened and the stars came out overhead. In his junior year at Northwestern, he remembered, he was befriended by two young Jewish men who for reasons not clear to David at the time saw fit to stay together and not mix very much with their classmates. One of them had a friend, also Jewish, who was an excellent student; and his plan was to go to medical school upon graduation. In the spring of that year he applied to thirty-five medical schools. To his dismay he was turned down by all of the schools, including Northwestern. It was clear that his scholastic record was not at fault, so he tried an experiment. He changed his name. His name had been obviously Jewish and he changed it to one that was just as obviously Gentile. He reapplied for admission and was accepted on a full scholarship at a top Canadian medical school. The hostile reception he had received in the U.S.A. made him happy to study outside his native land. This story was told to David when the three young men met him to have a few beers and conversation on a Saturday evening.

David wondered what had become of that young man. He was glad he had persevered. What a waste of good medical talent it would have been if he had not had the guts to fight the system. David wondered too what damage had been done to this man whose major crime seemed to be that he was born a Jew. Again David could not help seeing the parallel in the situation he had been reviewing in his mind to the one that had developed from just such seeds into bitter, bitter fruit, in Germany and Austria and throughout Europe.

The injustice and irrationality of man's apparent inhumanity to man left him with a passionate sense of outrage. "When this war is over," he promised himself, "I'll do something about it. I'll write some plays, I'll get them produced. I must make people understand how wrong and insane all this sort of action and thinking is."

He felt confident that with the good training he had gotten at Northwestern from people like Alvina Krause, who coached him as he learned his acting craft from 1936 to 1938; and from Garrett Leverton, who headed the Theater department at Northwestern; and from Bergen Evans, who had labored with him as he learned to be a writer, he would be able to express himself with power and conviction and fulfill that promise.

He was grateful, recalling those wonderful people who had befriended and helped him, each in a different way, seeing in him the potential to make a contribution to the world. The first year he worked with Alvina Krause, he somehow found the money. The second year she learned of his financial circumstances and put him on an informal scholarship arrangement. She was convinced that he was a talented and serious student, though poor. Garrett Leverton had seen the dedication and talent too, and knew the young man would have difficulty in finding the money to see the cultural events that Leverton felt were essential for his growth as a serious contributor to the theater. Therefore, Leverton frequently provided opportunities for David to see plays, go to the opera and hear the Philharmonic. Bergen Evans taught David through freshman English, Advanced English, and Advanced Composition. While this was going on, he was learning about the character of the young man under his tutelage. When David decided to go the Northwestern Law School, he consulted with Bergen Evans, who encouraged him.

If Evans had the gift of prophecy, then his future was assured. In his letter requesting scholarship aid for David he had written: "He speaks well, with turbulent impetuosity. I think if he could be harnessed, he'd be valuable. He needs financial aid desperately, and I hope there are a few hundred somewhere that can be thrown his way. They won't be wasted."

4

Rescue in the Desert

§

He was awakened by the first light coming through the open rear doors of the ambulance. He was grateful the vehicle was still in good enough shape to sleep in. He was really getting worried; surely the salvage crew should have arrived by this time. It was futile to worry, he thought, and besides he was hungry. Better to tackle a concrete problem he could do something about than to worry about something he could not control. He set to work and made a small fire by pouring a little gasoline into a hole in the sand. Then he lit a match and heated water for the strong sweet tea he had learned to enjoy from his comrades, the Tommies. Opening the inevitable can of bully beef, he settled back to eat while he waited.

In fixing his meal he thought of the Forestal's well-stocked kitchen. It was a far cry from the rude equipment he was using to prepare his breakfast today. His thoughts drifted back to the way the Forestal family had come into his life. He remembered the day in June in 1939 he had graduated from Northwestern and climbed into his forty-dollar Model A Ford "flivver" and driven to Pasadena, California. He chuckled to himself as he recalled the way he had solved the problem of the cracked block on the Ford. Regular oil simply poured away as soon as it was put into the motor, at the rate of four quarts every hundred miles. He discovered that if he asked for crankcase oil, which was the discarded oil from other cars, it held the car together like glue; the car ran like a top and got him where he wanted to go. The other advantages were that he only had to replace the oil every three hundred miles, and it cost him nothing when he bought his ten-cents-a-gallon gasoline. Very important considerations for a poor young man!

He recalled arriving in Pasadena in time to begin attending the public tryouts for roles in the three theaters of the Pasadena Playhouse. He spent the summer and fall of 1939 and the winter and spring of 1940 playing in ten shows and writing three plays. One play, *Men in Darkness*, portrayed life in a mining camp, and *White Thunder* the life and difficulties of Dr. Oscar Semmelweis, who was driven from his hospital post in Vienna because he insisted that child-bed fever could be prevented if doctors would wash their hands between patients and disinfect their clothes. The third play was a light farce written in a Noel Coward style. Happily for the budding playwright and actor, he had saved enough money to concentrate on his acting and writing all summer, but when fall came it was clear that he had to have a job or he would not be able to continue at the Pasadena Playhouse.

The job that materialized was with the Forestal family, who became very fond of David and shared his interests. They often came to applaud him when he performed at the Playhouse. Mr. Forestal had been an actor as a young man, touring with Fay Bainter and with the senior Douglas Fairbanks before he became a great silent film star. He encouraged David and was most helpful to him. David remembered that the family had provided him with a base that was vital to him at the time. It gave him an opportunity to perfect his craft and pursue his dream. He did not need much money, nor did he spend much; his expenses amounted to little more than gas for his car and admission to an occasional movie.

His fifteen dollar a month stipend from the Forestals was supplemented by a room of his own, bath, and board. The job, however, carried with it many responsibilities. For nine months he plowed through a dizzying schedule which included serving the Forestal family as a gardener, butler, cook, and general houseman. He was asked to prepare breakfast for Mr. and Mrs. Forestal and their two children, a young man and woman attending junior college. Every morning he was required to sweep the sidewalks and do whatever light gardening was needed. Monday he was responsible for doing the family wash and hanging it out to dry. Tuesday he did the ironing. All the sheets, pillow cases, tablecloths and napkins had to be run through a mangle. Wednesday he was expected to do a thorough cleaning of the downstairs. Thursday was his day off, and Friday he cleaned the upstairs. Saturday was for mopping and cleaning the dinette and kitchen. Every noon he made lunch for the family and cleaned the kitchen afterward.

At 1:30 P.M. he was off to the Pasadena Playhouse in his Model A Ford for play rehearsals or to the library to write. At five he returned to the house to prepare dinner under Mrs. Forestal's direction, and at six he donned a white coat and served dinner. While the family ate in the dining room he ate his own dinner in the kitchen, washed the dishes, and by 7:30 P.M. was off in his Ford runabout to the Playhouse for more rehearsals or a performance. When there were no activities at the Playhouse, he was at the library writing.

Nine months of this routine called for a change, even for a dedicated artist. He landed a paying position as an actor in the summer of 1940, in a Pilgrimage Play which promised six weeks of employment. The play concerned the life of Christ. He doubled in brass, playing the part of a Roman soldier and a follower of Jesus. He was able to play both characters by putting a long flowing white robe over his soldier's uniform.

The summer was soon over and a job offer came from the Santa Fe Civic Theater. The salary was $100 per month, and his enthusiasm for the job ran high because he would have an opportunity to direct as well as act. His living accommodations were in an old abandoned church in the Mexican section of Santa Fe, which he rented for $30 per month. The main hall was adapted for a rehearsal hall, and he lived in the sexton's quarters. His dedication had to be complete, he recalled with a smile, because that left him with exactly $70 per month for food, clothing, and all his other needs. This was the way life went in the fall, winter, and spring of 1940-41.

Later that spring he applied for scholarships at the law schools of Northwestern and Western Reserve and was awarded tuition scholarships at both institutions. In the fall of 1941 he accepted a full scholarship at Western Reserve and began law school. Once in Cleveland, needing cash and missing his first love, the theater, he got a job at the Cleveland Playhouse, playing in *Saint Joan*. His role was Dunois, the Bastard of Orleans. The money earned from the Cleveland Playhouse was not enough to keep body and soul together, so he worked at the college bookstore to earn more money.

News of the war, going badly for the Allies, made him increasingly restless. He was disturbed by what was happening to freedom-loving people all over Europe and especially by the internment of Jews in concentration camps in every Nazi-occupied country. One day he read an article in the *Cleveland Plain Dealer*, written by a man who had served with the American Field Service in World War I and was now recruiting young men to serve as ambulance drivers with the British in North Africa. After training they would be attached to the British Eighth Army, then commanded by General Auchinleck. Everyone who signed up was asked to serve without pay, and required to buy his own uniform. The American Field Service paid the passage over and the British Eighth Army provided room and board and "issue" clothing after arrival in the Middle East.

One morning David woke up and decided he could not face another day of reading and studying torts, or researching another case in the library. He decided he was finished with law school. He would forfeit his scholarship and go to North Africa and join the British as an ambulance driver for the AFS.

Once the decision was made, he quickly implemented the plan. He sold everything he owned except for his battered old typewriter. He needed that to establish himself as a war correspondent; he would need to earn enough money to buy a few beers. His suits fetched ten dollars each; three suits, thirty dollars. His relatives were not going to be helpful, he knew, because they felt they would be encouraging him to throw away his life.

Because he knew that the $200 amassed from selling his belongings would not last long, he paid a visit to Paul Bellamy, publisher of the *Cleveland Plain Dealer*, and asked him if he would buy any article he might write from the frontlines of North Africa. He recalled Bellamy saying, "I like your spirit. If the articles are good, I'll buy them; if they are not, I can't." Bellamy obviously wanted to help him because, after he delivered his warning, he leaned forward in his chair and said, "Look, if your articles are good, they ought to be syndicated. I'll send John Wheeler, who heads the North American Newspaper Alliance, a letter about you, and you go and see him when you get to New York."

Wheeler, David recalled, was a tough man, who also told the young aspiring war correspondent, "If your stuff is good, we'll be glad to use your articles. That's all I can promise." Well, David now thought, Wheeler would get an article about this adventure, and he hoped the one he had sent from Tobruk would also be used. He needed the $25 from Bellamy and the $25 from Wheeler.

David was to learn, several months later, that he had managed to launch his career as a war correspondent in style. His articles on the Tobruk campaign had been delayed in reaching home due to the slow mail delivery from North Africa. Therefore they arrived in the States when Tobruk had fallen. Because all the major newspapers subscribed to the North American Newspaper Alliance, including the *New York Times* and the *San Francisco Chronicle*, David was to have his proudest moment as a budding war correspondent. The *New York Times*, that grand dame of all newspapers, printed his article on page 3 and gave him a byline. That pleased him even more than knowing that the articles had run in the one hundred and twenty papers that subscribed to Wheeler's North American Newspaper Alliance. They also had appeared with his byline on the editorial page of the *Cleveland Plain Dealer* as feature stories.

Now David heard the motor of a lorry in the distance. He fervently hoped it did not mean trouble. As the truck came over the dune, he let out a hissing breath of relief. It was his own people. Feeling impatient, he didn't wait for the motor to be cut off before he asked, "What happened to you guys?" The larger man shrugged. "We couldn't get through because of the minefields, mate. There's a hundred blokes out there we couldn't get to. You're lucky." David had to agree with them. He watched gratefully as they assessed the damage to his ambulance. "It's useless," the large man said to his companion. "This one won't roll again." He turned to David and said, "You better climb in and let's get out of here before the Jerries find us." David climbed wearily onto the back of the truck, glad to be going back to where there would be some company. What next, he wondered?

The next few days were filled with confusion as the battle continued to rage. David was assigned to another ambulance, sharing it with a new recruit. He was shortly sent to Baalbek, in Lebanon, for a brief rest, and was there assigned to drive an ambulance—first being posted in Tripoli, Lebanon and later in Damascus, Syria. Both were Aid Stations of the British Eighth Army, which was occupying Lebanon and Syria.

A few months later he was again reassigned to the North African desert and moved with General Montgomery's frontline forces back to Tobruk, then to Bengasi, to Homs, and finally Tripoli, the coastal capital of Libya.

At Tripoli, along with his fellow drivers in the American Field Service, and all the British Eighth Army who had advanced into Tripoli, he joined in a huge celebration of their desert victory over General Rommel and the Afrika Korps. The dramatic two-hour parade was viewed by Winston Churchill, who had flown in for the event.

A few days after the completion of his second "hitch" with the AFS, David decided it was time to return home and join his country's forces.

5

The Naval Lieutenant Becomes a Civilian

𝄞

Cleveland seemed very quiet after the celebration at Tripoli and the noisy atmosphere of the Middle Eastern cities. David found himself thinking how good it was to be home after a year and a half of desert heat, poor food, and strange languages. He realized he had been homesick for a long time without knowing it. He hadn't much time to reflect, however, because he was due to enlist in the U.S. Navy before the week was out. So he spent his time enjoying the summer weather in that July of 1943. He looked up family and friends, visited the Cleveland Playhouse, and savored the experience of just being back in his own country.

It was going to be a different war for him, he was sure. Serving with the U.S. Navy would be a far cry from his chaotic life as an ambulance driver with the British. Since he was seeking a commission, he anticipated much more theoretical work, training and study. He was right. When his orders came through, he found he had been appointed an ensign and committed to six weeks of officer training at Quonset, Rhode Island, without even the groundwork of boot camp. Those six weeks felt like being in college all over again, at heightened intensity and urgency—cramming for exams, aptitude tests, tests for skills—and never enough sleep. After combat, much of it seemed infuriatingly academic and juvenile, and some of it downright unnecessary. The program required 14 hours a grueling day of training and indoctrination. When it was over at last, he had his assignment: he was to train night fighter pilots in radar interception at Vero Beach, Florida.

He was totally unprepared for the wet heat at Vero Beach. He often found himself on a 100° evening putting on a heavy, padded flight suit to prepare for icy weather 30,000 feet aloft. Far worse, the men were so green that maneuvers were hazardous business; men could be lost needlessly. He was beginning to realize that this assignment was in many ways more hazardous than his service with AFS in the desert war. There he was responsible only for his own skin. In this situation he had the men under his command on his mind constantly. He felt personally responsible for them. One mistake in judgment in the air and he would have a lot to answer for.

At that time, planes were directed by radar borne by a ship in the Naval fleet. One of the skills David was trying to teach was flight at 200 or 300 feet, with the objective of avoiding enemy radar. This involved each man's using his own radar to focus on a target ship in which David was the observer. David began to wonder about the actual capacity of aircraft radar, and, gradually, an idea took shape in his mind. Suppose a mother plane could be used to direct the planes instead of a ship in the fleet. If the planes were directed from 30,000 feet in the air instead of at sea level, the planes could operate miles beyond the line of sight. This would give the U.S. Naval forces a great advantage. He planned on a few days' leave to get up to Quonset again to talk with the Brass. He was sure that this was an idea worth investigating. In early March he was able to get a leave. He spent the time in Quonset, staying up late into the night assembling the technical data he would need to develop and present his idea to his commander. He left that memo with a prayer, knowing how conservative Navy Brass could be.

His leave was nearly over now, but the work had actually gone faster than he had anticipated. With time remaining he decided to go to New York to visit Phyllis Campbell, his college sweetheart. As many times as she had told him that it was no use, they had remained warm friends; and somewhere, deep down, he still hoped. He knew that she was appearing in *Harriet* with Helen Hayes, an actress David much admired both on stage and on the screen. Phyllis was playing one of her twin daughters.

David arrived at Grand Central just in time to make the curtain. He had called Phyllis before he left Quonset, and they were planning to go out after the show.

Seated in the dark theater, David watched with lively curiosity the beautiful young woman playing the *other* twin. She had been made up to look exactly like Phyllis. It was quite uncanny. He found himself intrigued by gestures and inflections that differentiated her from the original. He was taken with her grace and skill, and he much approved of the way she delivered her lines: there wasn't a false note among them. She was not only good to look at; she was a very good actress as well.

He went back stage to see Phyllis and was delighted to discover that she had invited four of the cast members to go out with them. The young woman who had played Phyllis' twin was one of them. Before long, David and Ricky, as she was called by her friends, were chatting and exchanging theater experiences. David found himself more and more drawn to her; in fact, she was as interesting and beautiful off-stage as she was on. He learned that before she had appeared in *Harriet*, she had been a model for *Vogue* and *Harper's Bazaar*. That accounted for her style and presence.

On their second meeting he learned that her real name was not Ricky at all, but Lenore Wade Moerschelle, and that she was half-Irish and half-Alsatian. She hated her given name because people had teased her so as a young girl, calling her "the lost Lenore." David was also surprised to find that he was falling in love. He had carried such a large torch for Phyllis for eight years that it hadn't occurred to him that that was possible. It felt like a new experience. This time he saw that his love was reciprocated. In fact, Ricky made no secret of her lively interest in the tall young ensign from Cleveland.

The war left little time for the niceties of peacetime courtship. When young lovers said goodbye in wartime, they rarely knew when or if they would meet again. Promising to write, they each went back to their respective lives, he to Vero Beach and she to continue with the Broadway run of *Harriet*. In July David managed to return to New York, and after five days, he and Ricky were engaged. They continued to correspond, and the phone bills mounted. When the play closed and left on tour, communication became more difficult. Nonetheless, David was determined that they should marry. In December of 1944, David managed six days' leave, and they met in Cleveland where *Harriet* was playing as a road show. They were married by a Justice of the Peace, with a reporter from the local paper serving as maid of honor and official witness. David and Ricky had actually been together for only seven days out of an eight-month period, but that sort of courtship was common during the war. David figured that they'd get to know each other better later. After all, he was 28 and she was 23. They had a whole lifetime—with luck. After their marriage, Ricky, who had a run of the play contract, continued with *Harriet* until it reached San Francisco in May of 1945. David returned to his night fighter radar training duties at Vero Beach.

They were no sooner reunited in June in Vero Beach, after *Harriet* closed, than David was dismayed to receive orders to go overseas as of July 5, 1945. They had an idyllic four weeks together at Vero Beach; then he had to leave for San Francisco, en route to joining the fleet at Pearl Harbor.

A bout of mumps delayed him for three weeks; and then, abruptly, the war, which had seemed endless, came to an end with the bombing of Hiroshima and Nagasaki in Japan by the American forces. David could hardly believe it when he awakened one morning in San Francisco to find himself suddenly released from the Service.

It was October of 1945. Quite without warning, he was faced with an entirely new set of problems: How was he going to make a living? What kind of life were he and Ricky going to make together? Where were they to settle down? His first thought was to return to New York to the theater and to his writing. Ricky agreed.

When they arrived in New York, David located an apartment on 78th Street off Broadway—not a palace, but the plumbing worked and there was a good French restaurant on the corner. Which proved invaluable. The bride could act, but cooking was another story.

Two weeks later, David came home throwing his hat into the air, both mentally and physically: "I've made it," he said, "I've got a part on Broadway!" Ricky was as ready to celebrate as he was. It was a small part—but it was on Broadway, after all, in a play called *The French Touch*, starring Brian Ahern and Arlene Francis. So what if the landlady changed the lightbulbs back to 25 watts every time they left the apartment? Soon one of them would get that "big break," and they wouldn't have to live in a five-floor walk-up, whose woodwork they often shared with uninvited guests.

In his wild and roaring way David made Ricky laugh over their temporary discomforts and privations. He checked his pockets. He had two dollars—just enough for a meal at the little French restaurant on the corner. They ate and chattered happily about the future.

Between rehearsals, just to make sure that he wasn't dependent solely on Broadway for his big break, he wrote a mystery novelette, *Prayer for Michelle*, about a priest who hears a murderer's confession but cannot break the seal of confession. Still concerned over the unequal treatment of minority peoples, which had bothered him in college, he was also busily at work on a play about the bias system, called *Buckle My Shoe*. Now that he was beginning to work on radio shows, he was bringing home money on a regular basis. He got parts in "Gangbusters," "Dick Tracy," and "Terry and the Pirates," dreaming *Hamlet*, but the grocer didn't care where the money came from.

That summer he and Ricky abandoned the apartment for a tour in the Catskill Mountains. David was directing a small company offering Broadway hits. They played one-night stands at the "borscht circuit" hotels, such as the Concord, Grossingers, and the Neville. The old station wagon would often break down; checks were late in coming; much of the time the little band would be stranded without funds. At one point David and Ricky were about to give up and return home. It was beginning to dawn on both of them that perhaps Broadway could survive for a very long time, quite unconcerned that the two of them weren't there. David's writing was bringing in mountains of rejection slips, and Ricky found work more easily as a receptionist than she did as an actress. Even Uncle Bob Sheehan, who encouraged David for the hundredth time, saying he would make it, didn't help their spirits. Uncle Bob knew quality writing—he was a senior editor for *Fortune* magazine—but that didn't take the sting out of the rejections, or the lack of offers to play on stage or in a movie. David concluded one day that if he spent as much energy selling shoes as he did making the rounds of the theatrical agencies, he'd be a rich man.

Finally, David realized the he had to do something else if he were going to make a decent living for himself and for Ricky. But what career would draw on the rich experience he had absorbed in the theater? He decided to try his hand at teaching.

Fortunately, the people at the Cooperative Teachers Agency agreed with his decision. He was offered, and accepted, the post of Supervisor of English at the Lenox School, a very fine girls' school in Manhattan. Deciding that he had better prepare himself further for a career in education, he began work on his masters degree at Teacher's College, Columbia University.

A year at the Lenox School convinced David that he could teach. But one incident made him positive that his fate was not to teach adolescent girls. He was proctor of a study hall in the library one afternoon, busily doing some work of his own. At that time, if a student wished to leave the library for the rest room, she had to make the request by holding up her hand. Because he was preoccupied with his own work, he didn't notice that there had been an inordinate number of such requests that afternoon. When he looked up from his work near the close of the study period, the library was empty of students! Upon investigation, he discovered that all his charges were in the ladies' lounge having a party. When an offer came from Manhattan College to take a post as Instructor of Public Speaking and Director of Debate, he accepted with alacrity.

Over the next year David became a popular figure on campus and was given the affectionate title of "Mumbles Nemesis." At the time, David resembled the comic-strip detective Dick Tracy, and Mumbles was a character in that comic strip. Since David allowed absolutely no one the luxury of mumbling in his classes, his students came up with that nickname. In fact, they shared it with the entire campus by printing a cartoon in the campus newspaper showing David in the guise of the famous sleuth.

Before accepting the position at Manhattan College, David had applied for a position as Director of Public Information at Cornell. A year and eight months later David was elated to receive a call from Dean Catherwood, who headed the New York State School of Industrial Labor Relations at Cornell. David was interviewed several times and then offered an assistant professorship concurrent with service as Director of Public Relations for the school.

David and Ricky's first child was born after they were already established at Cornell. Financial pressures made it imperative that David think about a change in his career direction. He had also gained considerable experience in his work at Cornell. He began to examine the business world with great attention. When a post opened up at the Hartford Insurance Group, he accepted and remained with the Hartford until 1952.

In late 1952, he was offered a substantial raise in salary and an advantageous move to Wall Street, where he would have the opportunity to work as second in command under the senior partner for sales promotion at Merrill Lynch, Pierce, Fenner and Beane. He accepted. In this position, David wrote the investment books, working with Merrill Lynch's massive research staff, as well as the Annual Report, working with Milija Rubezanian, better known as Ruby, and the managing partner, Winthrop Smith.

After his second daughter was born in 1953, he began to feel a sense of dissatisfaction with a life centered around making money. He enjoyed his work at Merrill Lynch, loved the people there, and was learning a great deal, but he felt unhappy. He often discussed his feelings with Ricky, who was at a loss to understand why he felt dissatisfied. She told him that it was simply a mood; his future was so bright and he would surely wind up as a partner. She was very proud of his success. But his dissatisfaction deepened, and he began to look for a way to express the deep need he felt to make a significant contribution to a better world.

One day he received a call from a friend who told him about a public relations opening with a struggling organization that had as its main focus the elimination of religious bigotry and other forms of prejudice. That organization was the National Conference of Christians and Jews. He went to see the first President of the organization, Dr. Everett Clinchy, who had pioneered in the field of interreligious understanding and had written a landmark book about interreligious prejudice in the United States, called *All in the Name of God*. He spent some time with Dr. Clinchy and Dr. Sterling Brown, was drawn to the work these men were doing, and wanted to join them.

He had a long talk with Ruby at Merrill Lynch and tried to explain his feelings. To his relief, Ruby understood. With his thick Yugoslavian accent, Ruby told him that he was insane to throw away his opportunity to grow with Merrill Lynch, and then added, "David, if you were going to another outfit on Wall Street, I would never forgive the disloyalty, but for this . . ." He paused, and then went on: "For this I say, I forgive you and wish you luck. It is a fine organization." This was all David needed to come home and tell Ricky he was accepting a cut in pay and the uncertain future offered by the NCCJ. He was leaving Wall Street to follow his as yet nebulous dream by working for the NCCJ.

David could see that Ricky was dismayed and seriously upset. His friends and relatives were quick to point out that they had anticipated great success for him at Merrill Lynch. Why, they wanted to know, was he trading that in for an uncertain future with an organization in dingy rented quarters at 28th Street and Fourth Avenue? He listened to them, but could hear only the inner voice that urged him on. He arrived at his new office and saw that, even with all his zeal and dedication, he would have to paint it before he could work in it. So the first weekend after he came on board as a staff member of NCCJ, armed with a paintbrush, he rode the subway and went to work on his new career.

6

A Golden Opportunity
to Serve the Lord
at NCCJ

David was given no specifics as to what he was to do when he joined the staff, except that he was expected to work in the general area of public information and to develop the Labor-Management Program of the NCCJ. When the Supreme Court handed down its historic decision on school desegregation, known as Brown vs. the Board of Education of Topeka, in May of 1954, he saw in this development a golden opportunity for service to an ideal he passionately believed in and felt that he had personally been given another indication that he was fulfilling God's plan for his life. The court decision changed the role of the NCCJ. Previously it had sought to subtly bring Blacks and Whites and Christians and Jews together in goodwill dialogues about common concerns. When integration in the public schools became the law of the land, the NCCJ became the persuader, leading people to willing compliance with the law.

His days and evenings were filled with thinking of how he could truly help to implement the law and move civil rights ahead. Like most NCCJ staff he knew he was very much on his own and that he literally was his own boss. Because of that, he had to weigh what approaches and strategies would be most effective. One particularly thorny assignment dealt with the difficult area of discrimination in business and industry, which came under the umbrella of the Labor-Management Program of NCCJ. After a lot of research and soul searching, David set to work on three highly controversial pamphlets: *The High Cost of Discrimination, Negroes in the Work Group* and *A Fair Chance for All Americans.*

It took several months of hard labor, but with a sense of real accomplishment David saw the first copies back from the printers, ready for distribution. He felt that it would be best that this first effort should not bear his name and made a decision that through the years his work would be credited to others. Since he was doing the Lord's work, it did not matter who received credit for the final product. The important thing was that the work be done, and done well.

The pamphlets were distributed to the staff all over the U.S.A., both above and below the Mason-Dixon Line. David's phone began to ring, and he discovered he had gotten into a hornet's nest. The strong radical emphasis in the program material frightened and appalled some of the southern Directors, who immediately began a campaign to suppress the material wherever possible.

David realized that all new ideas were accepted with difficulty, but he knew that these three pamphlets were a major breakthrough in the NCCJ's publication program. Nothing had been done on equal opportunity in business and industry by the organization; indeed very little had been written anywhere on the subject. He was counting on the eminence of the people whose work he featured and edited in the pamphlets to make the publications effective.

He worked closely with Elmo Roper and was counting on his influence as a pollster and public opinion reporter of the American people to get the message across. David had read a speech that Roper had given to a group of top level business executives in New York City. He contacted Roper and asked him to expand it so that he could use it in pamphlet form as an educational tool to be distributed by the NCCJ. When it finally was worked out and appeared under the title of *The High Cost of Discrimination*, David felt they had achieved their goal. Roper pointed out that the cost of discrimination to business and industry, in loss of manpower, morale, and productivity, added up to $30 billion a year. In addition he said, "If, in 1920, I had predicted that by 1950 the forty-hour week would be in effect in all major companies in the United States, many people would have labeled me a hopeless visionary. And there will be some today who will say I am dreaming when I predict that by 1980 industrial firms will no longer even think in terms of race, religion or nationality when they hire and promote their employees."[4]

David appreciated and applauded Roper's view, and commended both his optimism and realism. Both David and Roper knew the task confronting them was not easily accomplished; nor were they going to pretend that it was. Roper stated clearly: "But the end of such practices will not come automatically. It will take hard work and determined effort. The fact that a number of industrial firms and labor unions have already established humane and practical non-discriminatory policies is most encouraging. That's why I am confident that ending discrimination in business and industry will be one of the next great strides forward in American democracy."[5]

David's inspiration for *A Fair Chance for All Americans* came when he read Frank M. Folsom's testimony, given before the subcommittee on civil rights of the United States Subcommittee on Labor and Public Welfare during hearings in February 1954 on proposed civil rights legislation. He saw that if he could use the example of a prestigious corporation like the Radio Corporation of America and its powerful chairman, Frank M. Folsom, he could persuade others to follow that example. Therefore, he asked Folsom, Ivan L. Willis, Vice-President of International Harvester Company, C. V. Martin, Vice-President of Carson Pirie Scott and Co., and M. J. Spiegel, Chairman of the Board of Spiegel, Inc., to allow him to report their successful experiences with integration in the workplace.

Feeling that there was not enough coverage of research on discrimination in the workplace, David prevailed upon one of his former colleagues, Dr. Jacob Seidenberg at Cornell's School of Industrial Labor Relations to allow him to make a digest of a research report that Dr. Seidenberg had prepared while at Cornell. Seidenberg at that time was Executive Director of the President's Committee on Government Contracts, under the Eisenhower Administration. The result was *Negroes in the Work Group*. Although he met with resistance, David was able to arrange the distribution of the pamphlets to more than 100,000 executives and supervisory personnel. He was to face a barrage of criticism from his colleagues as a result of his efforts.

David began to get a clear idea of the passionate feelings he had aroused with his work when he attended his first staff conference prior to the 1954 November Annual Meeting of NCCJ. After that meeting it was clear to him that the NCCJ was a house divided, with several vocal Southern Directors claiming that the National office was pushing the NCCJ too fast and too far into the racial issue.

The states seemed to follow the expected cultural and historical pattern: Alabama, Georgia, Louisiana, and Tennessee stood at the extreme right of the question of equal rights for all Americans, while North Carolina was not committed to blocking civil rights, although not very enthusiastic about supporting it. Texas was divided. Virginia wanted to progress along legal guidelines. The northern offices wanted to adopt the stance that Virginia advocated.

Although the question of equal rights was exhaustively discussed at the meeting by the staff and the National Board, David was unhappy to see that there was no resolution of the issue coming out of the Annual Meeting. He was relieved when he heard Robert Frehse, Sr. of the Detroit office speak eloquently to his fellow Directors as he sought to conquer the move to water down the actions that northern Directors would be allowed to take in spearheading a strong Equal Opportunity in Industry Program.

First, in order to encourage those who would listen, Bob told them a success story from his own region of Detroit. He described how he worked with the management of a major department store in Detroit on the idea of integrating the employees of the store. He had persuaded them to allow him to address all of the employees on the main floor of the store, after hours, about a plan to accomplish integration of the store's work force. The employees were willing to cooperate after Bob said to them: "This is the way our Founding Fathers originally planned this country to be—a country where everyone was equal—and it did not matter if they were foreigners, or of a different color. The whole idea was that we were all to be equal in this new land. We have not achieved it yet, but this one store could be an example for businesses all over the country to follow. Will you help?"

Bob went on to tell how integration was accomplished peacefully, and with wonderful cooperation from all the employees and the management of the store. David watched intently to see what impact this statement had on them. As he heard one objection after another coming from the floor, he knew that he had heard only the opening salvo of the internal battle now being fought within the NCCJ. He was convinced of that when he heard Bob say wearily, as he faced an angry, anxious, wary group, still pleading: "Surely, we do not have to reduce the whole question to the lowest common denominator." David's heart sank. If Bob, with his gift of persuasion, had failed to carry his colleagues with him, what chance was there for him as a comparative newcomer to reach any of them?

His forebodings were well founded, as he discovered some weeks later, when the National administration told the staff in the southern offices that they did not have to use the materials he had produced with such devotion. He was consoled, however, that the pamphlets at least had served the purpose of putting the Conference on record as being committed to racial equality. In his heart he felt as though a milestone had been passed, and, despite the discouraging first round, there was hope. Soon his ebullient nature reasserted itself.

Surely with continual negotiation with the staff and the Boards of Directors throughout the country, reason would prevail.

After the meeting, David was pleased to learn that Everett Clinchy, the first President of NCCJ, and Sterling Brown, Executive Vice-President, had sent the first communication to offices in every part of the country, urging that all Boards of Directors of every region integrate as quickly as possible. The significance and hopefulness of these events helped him to feel that his life was indeed on the track that God had intended for him. And week after week was filled with rewarding, fulfilling work. He spent his time criss-crossing the country, often more familiar with Pullman berths than his own bed. He participated in talks that stretched far into the night with Vice-Presidents across the country who might be influential in changing the minds and hearts of Directors of offices and the Directors on the Boards. In time he came to know that in certain places there would be the response of tokenism, and in some places no response at all. When he returned to New York, more talks at the National Office finally resulted in the decision that to push the issue further would result in divisiveness, would be counter-productive, and might even destroy the organization. David, sadly admitting to himself the wisdom of that argument, knew he had to accept the decision, at least temporarily.

A divisional Vice-President from the South, William Tipton, told David that while he thought he was sincere, he felt David simply did not understand the workings of the southern mentality, nor did he understand the institutions in the South. David really came to value Bill's friendship when Bill invited him to accompany him on a speaking tour of the South. As they traveled, David wondered if he was there to educate the southerners he spoke to, or whether Bill had invited him there to give him an education about the South in relation to the racial equality problem. He continued to guess; he discovered that Bill was a skillful human relations practitioner, and the last thing he would do would be to make anyone feel awkward. In any case, David was finding the whole experience exhilarating. They drove thousands of miles, making stops every few hours to speak in small towns and big cities of the South.

When he returned home David felt that he had a better understanding of the problems and fears faced by the southern Directors in that time of challenge and change. But he had a deep conviction that the challenge must be met and efforts to bring about that change must be unceasing and relentless—not only in the South but in the North as well.

7

The Job Grows
in National Outreach

By the late 1950's David's job with the Conference had expanded considerably. The NCCJ program had become a source of pride to him, and he much enjoyed his position as Public Information Officer. His job necessitated his travel all over the country, interpreting the program in television discussions and personal speaking engagements, and through hundreds of press releases and articles.

By the time Dr. Clinchy was nearing the end of his term, David realized that the President was depending on him to a greater and greater extent, asking counsel of his younger colleague, relying on his judgment. A bond was developing between the two men, based on a shared vision. They both believed that there was a great need for an international educational program similar to the one developed by the NCCJ in the United States. From his war experiences, David was more than aware that Hitler had risen to power in a so-called "cultured and developed nation": Germany. He remembered with sorrow how other nations in the international community had stood by silently at Evian-les-Bains, in France, where the self-styled "Nations of Asylum" refused, in 1938, to undertake any obligations toward financing the involuntary emigration of the Jews. This stand ensured their extermination, because no Jew was permitted to leave Germany or Austria with more than 10 reichsmarks— less than $5.00. That single resolution rendered every Jew from Germany and Austria unacceptable to the "Nations of Asylum." Only Holland, Denmark, and the Dominican Republic agreed to help. This silence effectively informed the Nazis that, should they proceed with their plan to exterminate the Jews, no major, or even minor, power would interfere.[6]

Many staff members of the NCCJ were unable to appreciate the reasons for the close friendship and respect developing between Dr. Clinchy and David, and were uncomfortable with it. They felt that a newcomer was usurping their places as senior advisors to the President. David was at a loss as to how to deal with the situation. He was aware that tensions were building around his relationship with Dr. Clinchy, but his tasks, as he saw them, were clear. Finally, he decided to leave the situation to a higher Power, while he concentrated on what needed to be done.

He believed that his major task through the next few years was to build a strong Public Relations department. It was important that the public understand and support the work for equality he felt was so vital to his country's well-being and development. To that end, he enlisted the best people he could find—a press specialist, a television and radio specialist, and an expert media specialist for the greater New York area—and trained them to work with him as a team. This freed him to improve his already well-developed speaking skills, so much so that Dr. Clinchy once remarked with pleasure that David was becoming one of the NCCJ's outstanding platform stars.

David's pride in the considerable progress he was making was tempered by a deep sense of thanksgiving. Often he stopped in at a nearby church to offer a prayer of thanks to God for motivating him to train as he had—as a writer, a speaker, a journalist, and an administrator. He considered his career holy work, and his skills enabled him to motivate others in that work. He sometimes felt as though he were in possession of a spiritual bank account, from which he could draw on all the resources he required to be effective in his mission.

One cold week in February of 1955, during Brotherhood Week, he looked out at the sea of faces at the LeClaire Hotel in East Moline, Illinois, and said the words that reflected all of his deepest beliefs: "To humiliate man is to degrade God." He carried that message through the Quad Cities area that week, where he talked to any group that would listen. He talked to church groups, P.T.A.'s, and Rotary clubs. He spoke at fund-raising banquets for the NCCJ program, in synagogues, at women's and men's clubs. He went to universities and high schools. Many of his speeches drew on stories from the life and teachings of Jesus, and from the Old Testament. He also talked about the lives and works of outstanding human beings like Dr. Tom Dooley, Dr. Albert Schweitzer, or St. Therese of Lisieux, the Little Flower. He concluded, "We cannot all become

Tom Dooleys or Albert Schweitzers, but every one of us is in a position to put the principles of brotherhood into practice in our daily lives. . . . The most revolutionary idea in the world today is 'The Brotherhood of Man under the Fatherhood of God'—and it's still untried!'"[7]

Because it was his first Brotherhood Week, David's experience of the Quad Cities made a strong impression on him. In that year of 1955, Davenport, Iowa, and Moline, East Moline, and Rock Island, Illinois totalled 350,000 souls—four cities nestled together in a valley along the Mississippi in the Midwest. So in the following year, during Brotherhood Week of 1956, he was shocked to hear that 35 Jewish merchants, in the cities where he had spoken, woke to find their store windows plastered with heavily glued printed signs, reading: "This place owned by Jews—Anti-Jew Week, February 21 to 28." The signs had been put up by an outside hate movement from St. Louis.

What happened immediately afterwards, however, inspired and excited David. The whole town mobilized in support of the merchants. The police tore down the signs almost before the public had a chance to see them. Telephone operators worked overtime putting through calls of encouragement and support from Protestant and Catholic businessmen to their Jewish brothers. Speeches on the radio and on television, and editorials in the press, denounced the incident, decrying the work of the Nazi "hate salesmen." Before any fire of hate had time to get started, the entire community was fire-proofed. David knew that the quick mobilization of people of good will in the Quad Cities was no simple happenstance. Good will is a human resource, but quick response takes education and organization. And this he could credit to the work of the NCCJ: The mobilization of those networks of concerned people was the realized product of human relations workshops for teachers in the area; human relations institutes for high school and college students; programs on intergroup relations at local parishes and synagogues, and at the P.T.A., the women's clubs, the Kiwanis and Rotary clubs. He hoped that his own talks and speeches there the year before had helped, too.

David's pride in the NCCJ program grew. That year, Louis Radelet, a creative leader in the field of police and community relations, invited him to Michigan State University to observe a pioneer program in human relations training for police officers. David was aware that no group dealt more directly with the problems of racial tension than police officers. He knew they were on the firing line.

The program deeply impressed him; 250 police officers from more than 40 states and 60 major cities had come to MSU to acquire the skills they needed to avoid community conflicts in racially tense situations.

David also travelled to the Youth Conferences being held in different parts of the country. He was in great demand by regional directors, who saw how his enthusiasm for the ideals and work of the NCCJ communicated itself to the youth leaders in their communities. Young Catholics, Protestants, and Jews of many and varied racial and ethnic backgrounds attended these conferences and quickly became his friends. After his informal talks, they often asked what they could do to help in the work of the NCCJ.

In many ways, this was where David's heart was—with his work and contacts among these bright, eager young people, who were leaders among their peers in high schools and colleges across the nation. This, he felt, was the most hopeful and productive thrust of his mission: If he succeeded in helping these students to see their role as mediators and peacemakers in the troubled schools, perhaps their whole generation could be shaped into people who would live peacefully in their racially and ethnically diverse communities.

David often accompanied the well-known personalities who were sent on tour by the NCCJ to speak to youth groups all across the U.S. He was very proud to be working with these tours, and grateful for their legacy of privileged moments; perhaps the most thrilling and moving of them took place in an all-White segregated high school in Oklahoma. The tour group included Jackie Robinson, the great Black ballplayer who broke the color barrier in professional baseball. When Jackie walked into that segregated assembly of 1,200 boys and girls, every one of them stood up to cheer him. After Jackie's talk, they stood up again and cheered him even more loudly. This incident convinced David beyond all possible uncertainty that this work was his to do for the rest of his life. He knew that desegregation—peaceful desegregation of the schools—was one aspect of social change to which the Conference was making an important contribution, and he saw it as his job to tell people everywhere this fact, by voice and by pen.

He was proud of having encouraged the growth of the NCCJ's youth program. He thought: This is where we need to be—directly involved with young people, helping young Protestants, Catholics and Jews of all racial and ethnic backgrounds to learn to live together and play together and solve their mutual problems together.

David often made it his business to attend the one- and two-day conferences for community leaders in Atlanta, Savannah, Charlotte and Greensboro, Dallas, San Antonio, Louisville, and 25 other key cities in the South. At one such conference, he heard Superintendent Omer Carmichael of Louisville give the NCCJ credit for the thoughtful, sane educational workshop and institute approach, and for creating the climate of opinion that made integration of the schools in Louisville possible in 1955 without incident or trouble of any kind.

Of course, not everything was as he would have wished, particularly with respect to the Catholic Church and the NCCJ. In certain parts of the country, the Conference had difficulty getting a Catholic diocesan priest to give an invocation at an interfaith dinner. In fact, David was sensitive to the fact that the very word *interfaith* was suspect at that time to Catholics. He puzzled over that matter a great deal, thinking that attitude ironically *un*-Catholic, since the word itself means "universal."

Despite these difficulties, he was encouraged by the fact that the Conference continued its programming for interreligious understanding. He and the other staff members worked where they could. Fortunately, there were those who could and did help them. Cardinal Cushing of Boston, Cardinal Ritter of St. Louis, Cardinal Shehan of Baltimore and many others helped with the ecumenical work of the NCCJ. David quietly blessed them for their understanding and vision. He fervently hoped that the educational program of the NCCJ would result in a changed ecumenical spirit. He had always had faith in dialogue, in the person-to-person communication and encounter that leads to understanding.

An explosion at Miami's Temple Beth El on March 16, 1958, galvanized the leadership of the NCCJ, staff and lay members, to mobilize the people of decent conscience in the South—who were outraged by this act of violence. David issued the NCCJ's clarion call in every way he could, making clear that, "We see this loud and destructive violence as a threat, not only to the brethren of one faith, but ultimately as a menace to the peace and safety of the entire community, whether Protestant, Catholic or Jew." During the same period, Jacksonville, Birmingham, and Nashville were experiencing similar violence. The NCCJ served as a rallying point for community organizations, service clubs, labor unions, and commercial bodies to express their contempt for these forces attempting to undermine justice, decency, and good will. In May of 1958, David edited a memorandum going out to the field to encourage the various communities to issue "A Declaration of Conscience." Since the NCCJ had always believed that the vast majority of Americans had decent instincts but were often less vocal than the forces of hate, the Conference served as a vehicle for the expression by decent men and women in favor of a fair and equitable society. To David, that period had all the elements of a holy crusade.

He seemed to thrive and his days were happy and filled to the brim with the work he loved. Those who knew David well were astounded by the vitality and happiness that he radiated. He had always been known as a hard worker, but his prodigious output puzzled his co-workers, who watched in awe the amount of work he seemed to generate so effortlessly. David had no problem with that; he knew the Source of his energy. He believed firmly that he was doing the Lord's work, the work he had been born to do. For him, the work had a life of its own.

He remained Director of the Labor Management Program until 1956, when he turned the responsibility over to Dr. Leonard Aries. He prepared special reports for the staff people to use as inspiration for their regional Labor-Management programs. He wrote and published a bulletin every two months for business executives to read, called *Highlighting Human Relations in Business and Industry*. He worked with printers to turn out beautiful fund-raising presentations for the development arm of the Conference, so that money would continue to flow into the organization to fund the human relations programs and workshops that were burgeoning all over the country.

He continued to write speeches for himself and for NCCJ's lay leaders. He worked with and wrote speeches for Benjamin F. Fairless, Chairman of U.S. Steel; Admiral Lewis L. Strauss; John Roosevelt; and many others. When Dr. Louis Webster Jones became president of the Conference in August of 1958, David wrote many of his speeches, since Dr. Jones had little familiarity with the NCCJ program.

David was aware that many of the regional directors on the staff needed guidance and stimulation in interpreting the Conference program to the top lay leadership of the NCCJ. In order to meet the problem, he burned a lot of midnight oil. Eventually, he came up with a tool for the staff: a speech reference library, filled with sample speeches and speech source materials. This he sent to all of the 62 offices in the organization. But the midnight oil did not stop burning. He was in the midst of completing his doctorate at Columbia University, and was quite relieved when he earned the degree in 1959.

When David wasn't speaking and writing he was managing the press coverage in New York, Washington, D.C., and across the nation. One morning he found himself in the White House with President Eisenhower—who was receiving the NCCJ Board of Directors in the East Room. David had worked hard with James Hagerty, Press Secretary for the Eisenhower Administration, in setting up arrangements for the event. He was grateful for that experience when he became involved in a nationwide NCCJ campaign on television, radio, and in the press, called "Keep Religion Out of Politics." This campaign affected John F. Kennedy's presidential aspirations. In T.V. and radio spots and suggested editorials going to every media outlet in the country, the theme was "Vote for the best qualified person—not because of his religion but because of his experience and ability."

Jack Kennedy always felt he owed the Conference a special debt for the successful conclusion of that campaign, which put the first Catholic President into the White House. David felt that this was marvelous progress because the NCCJ had been founded after the Al Smith presidential campaign in 1928—when a vicious, overwhelming wave of anti-Catholic sentiment swept the country. Although he was an able and beloved political figure, Al Smith had gone down in defeat partly because of his religious affiliation and beliefs, and because the campaign had evoked such horrible hatred and bigotry.

David spoke at least one hundred times during the Kennedy presidential campaign, encouraging NCCJ lay leaders and groups of people from all walks of life to support the idea that Presidents should be elected on their merits and not on their religious affiliations. David often felt that the Lord really did provide miracles; he was doing all his work with a budget that totalled less than $50,000 for the entire year.

His forty-first birthday was coming up, and David felt he had so much to be thankful for. Ricky was so beautiful at thirty-six, and the girls were thriving. Caroline was eight and Ann five; he was so proud of them. Life was good. He had all that a man could wish for. However, he did realize that his family, living in Rye, did not see much of their buoyant, happy father during this period. Even a man serving his highest ideals and his Lord cannot create more than twenty-four hours in one day or more than seven days in a week.

His conscience gave him some misgivings, but he was unaware that anything was really wrong. Thus, he was startled one day in late September to discover the discontent in his household. He was going over his wife's account book and discovered an entry, dated September 4, 1957:

There isn't really very much compensation in living and giving. We expect a small amount of compensation. In living we expect none. And we get none.

All of a sudden there comes time when we are needed. But not noticed. And we are noticed—then we are not needed.

It would be wonderful to be really loved for just being me.*Which of course couldn't be—because* me isn't much.

He was disconcerted by what he read. He realized that he hadn't had a long talk with Ricky in months. He had been so busy. Was this a momentary low, or was she having problems she hadn't shared with him?

Now that his memory had been jogged, he began to recall all the over-long cocktail hours, the dinners of crackers and cheese instead of proper meals. He realized that it could get lonely for Ricky in the evenings after their two little girls went to sleep, and he was out on a speaking engagement or off on a trip or at Columbia studying.

He tried telling himself that she probably craved that time alone to read her beloved books. But his conscience wouldn't accept the rationalization. How could books be enough company, month in and month out, one lonely evening after another, for a pretty young woman, accustomed to attention, to fun and dates? Was she eating properly when he was away? He realized he really didn't know. Yes, they must have a talk. Perhaps he'd been selfish in not being sensitive to what she was thinking and feeling, while he was deriving all his satisfactions from his educational and career goals. He was confident he could soon put things to rights. He would spend more time with her and the children.

8

The Kennedy Connection

Offsetting David's growing inner concern for his wife's unhappiness and loneliness was the promise and excitement that attended the election of John F. Kennedy. He had been deeply involved in the Kennedy campaign, and saw his election in 1960 as proof of the powerful influence the NCCJ could exert if the forces and resources within it were mobilized for useful, positive purposes. Both interracial and interreligious problems appeared to be more manageable than in the past, and solutions unavailable before now seemed possible.

While he continued to work as hard as ever at his job, thoughts of a new challenge involving work within the Kennedy administration began to circulate in his mind. All of his experience pointed perhaps to a post in an overseas embassy. Although he was completely happy with his work and knew that everyone in management at NCCJ was pleased with his performance and obvious dedication, thoughts of that overseas assignment kept tantalizing him. And more and more those thoughts began to intersect with the more sobering realization that what he had only suspected in 1958 and 1959 was true: Ricky was increasingly troubled and unhappy.

He saw that she was withdrawing little by little from the small group of young women with whom she shared community activities. He knew that although she served as a Brownie troop leader, it was not a role she would have adopted by choice. She felt it was a duty. The whole suburban housewife routine was slowly driving her mad. She had beauty, intelligence, and a wonderful way with people. Yet the only outlets for her talents and skills were the care of her two young children, her household chores, and community work. Most of the women she met in small suburban Rye did not share her love of literature, and their conversations were too often restricted to children's problems and domestic trivia. David recalled that she had complained of this on more than one occasion. Her free time to read was curtailed because his modest salary could not pay for much in the way of domestic help—even if such help were readily available. Her days were taken up with washing clothes, sewing curtains, mending, cleaning . . . and in her account book was another disquieting entry: "You drink too much, where do you think the money comes from—trees, maybe?"

Another day he was leafing through the book where she entered her chores planned for the day or week, and read: "Clear out hall closet, clear out cabinet in den hall, cupboard in den, drawers in bar, clear out our closet, children's closet. . . ." And in larger letters appeared, "For heaven's sake, read a book."

Yes, it was more than clear: He had to do something to make her life more bearable. She had stood by him while he pursued his own career and education; now he had to exert a major effort to fulfill his promise to her in the early days of their marriage: to provide her an exciting and rewarding life. He would find a way to get that job in an embassy overseas. It would give Ricky and the girls a chance to see and experience what he had seen and experienced during his service with the British in Africa. Travel—that was a good answer. More of a partnership. We'll make a good team, he thought. She has a gift for being a good hostess; that is important in the diplomatic corps.

Because it was rare for him just to think about something without taking action, he was soon placing telephone calls to good friends in Washington and elsewhere. In early 1961 he was writing letters as well. One of them garnered the reply he had hoped for from the White House:

> *(DATED: March 25, 1961)*
> *Your letter has been received by the President. He wants you to know that your friendly expressions and words of commendation pleased him very much and that he is grateful. Your willingness to be of help is appreciated and will be borne in mind.*

It was signed: Larry O'Brien, Special Assistant to the President.

After his return home that early April evening to find the letter waiting for him, David and Ricky discussed the various possiblities. Weeks passed, and his concern for her seemed less urgent. She seemed so much brighter and happier than she had been in months and took more interest in her appearance. His excitement was contagious, and soon they were discussing ways and means, ifs and whens. They even talked about the boldest step of all—selling the house in Rye, if and when they should go overseas.

This desire of David's to work within the Kennedy administration was based in part on his affinity with John Fitzgerald Kennedy's expressed feelings and beliefs about the rights of man. When Kennedy was still a candidate for the presidency of the United States, he spoke the words that made David feel that this man was a leader with integrity and vision whom he could follow without any hesitation.

It was only for such a man that he would even for a moment think of leaving the work he loved within the framework of the NCCJ. Kennedy's words were an assurance that he could continue, in an international arena, the work he was doing in the U.S. Along with many others in the United States, David believed in Camelot. In Los Angeles, on September 9, 1960, candidate Kennedy had asserted:

> As a moral leader, the next President must play a role in interpreting the great moral issues which are involved in our crusade for human rights. He must exert the great moral and educational force of his office to . . . support the right of every American to stand up for his rights. . . . For only the President . . . can create the understanding and tolerance necessary as the spokesman for all the American people, as a symbol of the moral imperative upon which any free society is based.[8]

When Kennedy became President, David was elated to see that his words were not merely campaign promises but that he meant to keep his covenant with the people who had given him power as one of the great leaders in the democratic world. On March 6, of 1961, a few days before a letter arrived at the Hyatt household from the White House, Mr. Kennedy had ordered the creation of a "vastly strengthened machinery" to ensure that "Americans of all colors and beliefs" would have "equal access to employment" by the government and "the contractors with which they did business." He had created the President's Committee on Equal Employment Opportunity, with Lyndon Johnson as its Chairman.[9]

Along with his President, David felt it was "a time to act," a time to redress grievances long neglected. With his new goal of serving the Kennedy Administration in the back of his mind, he pushed even harder at work—to complete a task set for himself in late 1959 with the complete approval and support of Dr. Lewis Webster Jones. That task was to design, write, and edit a series of manuals and

training guides for the staff of the NCCJ. Dr. Jones' approval of this
plan stemmed from his awareness, shared with David, that NCCJ
lacked a comprehensive and unified staff training program. Because
the program was so dynamic and moved so rapidly within the
context of events all over the country, David knew it would take all
of his energy and time in the months ahead. Therefore, the training
guides were needed to motivate and encourage innovative programming. David wanted to put them into a form that could be shared
by all regions of the country in spite of their differing timetables and
approaches to the various national thrusts of the NCCJ program.

Because it was urgent to encourage the people working for NCCJ
in communities where they often met opposition or financial sanc-
tions from their neighbors, David set up a *Brotherhood Awards Manual*. Financial support was vital to the continuance of the work; so
he wrote, edited, and produced a 272-page training guide called
Building Financial Support, followed by *How to Organize and Develop
New Chapters*. Regional Directors during that period often worked
on shoestring budgets in tiny offices, and struggled for survival in
often hostile communities. Therefore, his colleagues were sometimes far from thrilled with David's constant queries on how and
what they were doing and his insistence on material coming through
quickly to supply his need for case examples from all over the
country to include in the book. When he heard the edge in a hard-
pressed colleague's voice, he would hasten to say, "Anyway, as soon
as you can." On more than one occasion he had to depend upon the
fact that he had always been so willing to help them all out when
a speaker failed to materialize a week, or even a day, before a major
fund-raiser or conference. For that reason his colleagues were loathe
to deny him a favor.

Always conscious of the importance of the media, David wrote
and developed three guides based on the use of television, the most
important form of media. They were called *Operation Understanding, New Horizons in Human Relations,* and *Rearing Children of Good
Will*. Each manual gave a Director a packaged format of a thirteen-
week TV series involving community leaders discussing human
relations problems. The series could easily be presented and "sold"
to a TV manager or producer.

Because he knew that he was more familiar with making media
contacts than most, and because he felt it would be helpful to the
Directors and Vice-Presidents, David often left New York, making
lengthy trips, just to accompany the Vice-President or Director in
making presentations to TV station managers. The effort and travel

proved worthwhile; at year's end he had successfully placed more than forty television series in various parts of the country.

His conviction that his efforts were useful for the NCCJ and for the country as a whole were borne out when he ran across an article in the Pittsburgh Press stating:

> *"Operation Understanding" is, I suspect, pretty close to the kind of thing the U.S. Government had in mind when it set aside TV channels for educational-community use. It will never have an audience like "Have Gun, Will Travel," and no sponsor would be interested, even if it were available to a commercial sponsor. And there, of course, lies its strength. It can say what it has to say, do what it feels it should do. It can experiment a little, squirm around within the medium of TV, whose commercial operations have become largely an extension of the Hollywood movie industry.*[10]

Other important outreach to the community was also of concern to David. Since most offices had very little in the way of staff, David felt the Directors had to tap the leadership in the local community to speak up for NCCJ's principles. Therefore, he wanted to encourage them to start speakers' bureaus. By 1962, *How to Run a Successful Speakers Bureau* was off the presses and out to the regional Directors all over the country.

Unfortunately, despite his resolve to spend more time with Ricky and the children, all his other duties continued as well. He was responsible for the press coverage in New York and Washington. One day he came home after a hair-raising experience at the White House, with a tale to tell about his hero, John F. Kennedy.

The Washington Director of NCCJ had been too busy with fund-raising efforts in connection with honoring President Kennedy to focus on the details of the presentation ceremony. When David arrived to pick up the award on his way to the Oval Room of the White House for the ceremony, he was horrified to discover that it had never been framed and that the local artist who had done the work had reused the back of a previous client's advertising poster. All across the back of the parchment were the words, "tick-tock, tick-tock, tick-tock," in large italics. David thought in despair, "How can we show up at the White House and hand this to the President?" He would probably turn it over and see the inscription. Quickly David dashed by cab to Woodward and Lothrop, a Washington department store, and purchased a thirty-dollar frame which fit the parchment perfectly and gave appropriate dignity and importance to an award for the President of the United States. David returned to the NCCJ office to find the entire group of top NCCJ National leaders anxiously and impatiently awaiting his arrival with the scroll. Without it, obviously there could be no presentation ceremony. Off they sped to the White House in the waiting limousines.

As the President turned on the famous Kennedy charm and, along with Kenneth O'Donnell, welcomed everyone, David relaxed. Mr. O'Donnell summoned the press photographic corps to take photos of the President accepting the scroll from the NCCJ National Co-chairman. After the ceremony David watched in great relief as the President turned over the award in his hand to stroke the velvet on the back of the frame. David thought to himself, "Thank God he can't see tick-tock, tick-tock, tick-tock." Safe at home, as he told Ricky, David chortled and rejoiced because the story was on all the major wire services and had appeared in more than 1200 morning newspapers all over the country.

The excitement over, David reflected on Kennedy's effect on him. The man said things that resonated in his soul. He was involved in arranging for Kennedy to accept an award from NCCJ in conjunction with an annual meeting of the Board held in Washington. Difficulties surrounding the acceptance turned on the usual political considerations, such as who would ask, what persons would be repaid for favors. David was grateful when an influential real estate tycoon from Philadelphia, with excellent connections in the Democratic party, turned his attention to the matter and gained Kennedy's agreement. In advance David sent the President some material about NCCJ via his good friend, the Honorable Brooks Hays, Special Assistant to JFK. David was touched and elated when he stood in the Rose Garden of the White House that gray November day at the end of 1961 to hear Kennedy say that he was

> delighted to hear that the group is committing itself to an intelligent and to a non-partisan and open discussion—continued discussion really—of the relationships between the state and religion. It, after all, was a matter which occupied our Founding Fathers, and should occupy our attention; and I am hopeful that the fact that you are discussing it will be another evidence of what an open and happy society we live in. So I welcome you here. I congratulate you for the efforts you are making in this area. You are performing a valuable function as citizens. And therefore, speaking as President, and personally, we want to emphasize how much your work is appreciated, how valuable it is, and what service you are rendering.[11]

David felt he could not have reached millions of Americans more effectively with a lesson in interreligious understanding than through the voice of the nation's chief executive. He was grateful that the President's message had received nationwide coverage; once more he felt guided by a Power greater than himself. When he prepared the NCCJ material for the President to read, he never expected the immediate and inspiring response received. He felt drawn more and more strongly to the idea of working in the Kennedy Administration. Before he left Washington, he spoke to Brooks Hays.

Brooks promised to inquire for him about the possibility of an overseas post and to be in touch soon. In early spring of 1962, things began to move—more rapidly than David could have dreamed. Forms were forwarded, filled out, returned; clearances and interviews followed in quick succession. Brooks, with his down-home humor, wrote in reply to one of David's thank-you letters:

> *Thanks for your fine letters. I think I should carry it around with me just to read if I should have a depressed feeling about anything. You are a great morale builder.*
>
> *I have seen Donald Wilson's letter and it is very encouraging. Hope you can call me when you are in Washington.*[12]

At the end of February Ricky and he went to Washington for their interviews. In the Diplomatic Corps, wives are a very important part of any position a man would be given. Ricky was really feeling much better, and anticipation over the move made her daily rounds easier to manage. David couldn't have been happier. He loved her and wanted deeply for her to be contented. It gave him joy to see her glowing again. Her problems seemed to be under better control.

It was the middle of March when David read the memo sent by Dr. Jones, President of NCCJ, to his colleagues all around the country:

> *I know you will feel the same pleasure and satisfaction that I do in Dave Hyatt's being asked to serve on Edward R. Murrow's overseas staff with the United States Information Agency. He requested a three-year leave of absence, which I was glad to grant. He has been given a very fine appointment at the rank of Consul and will probably be assigned as Cultural Affairs Officer in Western Europe or perhaps the Near East or India. . . .*[13]

The weeks flew by and one April morning in 1963, David boarded the plane to Washington, D.C. to start his training program. In the evenings during the week he missed the family, but his days were filled with classes and study about Pakistan, its culture, language, political system, and history. Three days after his arrival in Washington, he was told that he had been assigned to Karachi, Pakistan, as an A.I.D. Information Officer. (A.I.D. was governmental shorthand for the Agency for International Development.) The night after he heard this news, he was given the "Post Report" to read, to familiarize him with conditions in Pakistan. His reading distressed and disturbed him so much that he spent a very restless night. Life in Pakistan sounded like a horror story—boiled water, amoebic dysentery, cholera, malaria, and leprosy. On awaking the following morning he thought of calling Ricky and telling her that the whole idea was a mistake. He thought in despair, "This thing sounds like a disaster; what am I bringing my family into?" Fortunately, he did not act on his first impulse, but he did begin to ask some pointed questions.

Later he learned that the reports for newcomers were often more graphic and grim than necessary. There were a variety of reasons for "overwriting and overblowing" the Post Reports. One was to ensure the continuance of the "hardship allowance" which was an additional pay increment over and above the regular salary allotted in the particular grade for the work performed. When David entered the Foreign Service, the allowance for Pakistan hands was 25%, the maximum. It had recently been reduced to 20%, but the Foreign Service wasn't about to reduce it further unless conditions truly improved. Hence, the disturbing and grim reports had their basis in fact and were unfortunately true, if not diplomatically stated. The other reason was to insure that families did not have improper expectations and then suffer disappointments and consequently make a poor adjustment. David also learned that most important was how to adjust and the ability to "roll with the punches" and accommodate to the true hardships.

That weekend, when he flew home, he and Ricky had an exciting discussion about Pakistan with the two girls. They all decided it would be a great adventure and wanted to chance it despite the reports.

Once more, David realized that Ricky was being left behind in Rye to tend the home front, sell the house, and take care of the children. Only now he was watching carefully to see that she was able to handle the problems without being overwhelmed. She seemed to be cheerful and happy, and looking forward to the overseas adventure. He felt that he could devote the next few months in Washington to mastering the information and special skills needed in his new assignment.

9

Assignment: Pakistan

David watched for a while as the movers went back and forth, loading the furniture into a van. It was a queer feeling to see the house disappear, knowing that their belongings would be in transit for weeks before they reached Karachi. He had come in from Washington to help ease the transition for Ricky and the girls. They would be coming back with him to live in Washington while he completed his training. The girls in particular were clearly having some second thoughts about leaving their familiar surroundings. Ann, who was nine, was openly frightened. Caroline, with the increasing sophistication of not-quite-fourteen, was a better actress. David could sense her apprehensions as well.

He put an arm around each of them and promised them a trip to the theater once they had settled in at their quarters in Washington. They smiled up at him, their fears quelled for the moment at the thought of a good time in the immediate future. He thought: "We'll have time to adjust. The girls and Ricky are doing okay. We'll do just fine." There would be a month, while he completed the last of his four-month intensive training program, for the girls to explore the nation's capitol before they all left for Europe on August 2. He had planned the move in stages; Europe, the first leg of the long trip, would give the family a chance to experience other cultures and to enjoy themselves before they had to settle into a more alien culture halfway around the world, on the subcontinent of south Asia.

The furnished, rented house in Chevy Chase was comfortable and attractive, and the month passed very quickly. They had hardly had a chance to feel at home when it was time to pack their bags and fly to London. When David saw the amount of luggage they were carrying, he wondered whether his position as U.S.I.S. Information Officer for A.I.D. should not have been reserved to a bachelor rather than a married man with two clothes-conscious young daughters.

David decided to pull out all the stops and give his family a vacation they would not soon forget. In London he took them to the theater, and supper afterwards at the Savoy, which Ricky labeled "elegant." The next evening he took them to Claridges, which the girls promptly dubbed "more elegant." In Paris, they went sightseeing all over the city in a horse and buggy. Everyone's mood soared.

In Rome, he decided against the "budget" accommodations allowed by the State Department and they stayed at the Excelsior. Once more they took in the sights in a horse and buggy. These were memories that would hold them in good stead over the months of adjustment in their new home—memories of Buckingham Palace, the Louvre, and St. Peter's. They had obtained a sense of each of the lovely cities they had stayed in, if all too briefly, agreeing that they could have stayed cheerfully in each city for a month. David, basking in the glow of their excitement and pleasure, thought: "This was a good idea. It's just as well we didn't decide against it—simply because we may encounter a few hardships later on."

Their last stop, Teheran, Iran, prepared and initiated all of them for Karachi. The bazaars and poverty-stricken areas bore the stamp of all Middle Eastern and South Asian countries. When they at last arrived in Karachi, they were somewhat seasoned and felt more curious than frightened. They found themselves alternately amazed, fascinated, and profoundly depressed by what they saw throughout Pakistan. They were charmed by the strangeness of it, the fact that Pakistan seemed set in a different time somehow. The poverty, the disease, the beggary, the dire need for health, education, and housing facilities shattered them, unaccustomed as they were to such rigid and accepted lines of social privilege and privation. Ricky and David found it difficult to attend a reception in the exquisitely appointed home of a wealthy Pakistani and then drive home past people sleeping in the roads or curled up in the doorways of mud huts.

Ricky set to work immediately. She was suited to a diplomatic role. David was pleased to see how easily she adjusted to life as a diplomat's wife—helping out at the Embassy functions, making the required diplomatic calls. She was talented and capable. She also managed the household, settling the family into their comfortable home, and coordinating the efforts of an English-trained cook, a bearer, a driver, a laundryman, and a gardener. She arranged for the girls to attend the excellent Pakistani-American school.

Fortunately, Patrice, the cook, was familiar with the procedures that kept the family from becoming violently ill. All the water used for cooking and drinking had to be boiled. The vegetables had to be cooked thoroughly, and both meat and vegetables had to be soaked in permanganate. This last precaution made Ricky uncomfortable, but she knew that the alternatives were not pleasant. She sometimes felt that her life was becoming consumed with preventive measures; and she worried constantly about the children being exposed to cholera epidemics and to malaria. Nevertheless, David thought, she seemed to be thriving and involved, doing work in the leper colony and running the complicated household.

All of the family consistently ran afoul of local custom, but most of the incidents made for hilarious family stories. One Saturday morning, David felt the need for some exercise and swept the back porch and sidewalks surrounding the house—only to find that he had scandalized the entire household staff by engaging in manual labor. Ricky never did get used to the social boundaries established for work in the house. Rigid distinctions and categories were established not only between the *sahab* and his staff, but were adhered to by each person on the staff with regard to the other staff members. For example, the inside sweeper would have nothing to do with the outside sweeper. Ricky could never ask anyone to do the simplest chore outside what custom decreed was his proper job. She told David that the situation reminded her of a story about the household staffs in Victorian England: neither the upstairs maid nor the downstairs maid believed it within the scope of her position to do the stairs; hence, each household was obliged to hire a "tweeny"—a person who worked between the boundaries of those two separate positions and whose job it was to do all the stairs in the house.

David, meanwhile, was quickly absorbed by his position as Information Officer for A.I.D. He was involved in all facets of press and public relations—arranging and overseeing press and photo arrangements for loan treaty ceremonies, development projects, outreach programs; writing articles on A.I.D. projects for the U.S.I.S. magazine, *Panorama;* working with a U.S.I.S. Radio-Motion Picture Officer to coordinate a radio program series and a series of ten-minute movies on A.I.D. operations. A great deal of his time went into arranging and setting up press interviews with top A.I.D. officials for correspondents from *Time*, the *New York Times*, Hearst, AP, UPI, and local newspapers. The most sensitive of his assignments was to assist the Country Public Affairs Officer in composing an A.I.D. information report to Washington.

When President Kennedy was assassinated, David wrote the ambassadorial statement thanking the people of Pakistan on behalf of the American people for their moving expressions of sorrow and sympathy over the death of the President.

David himself was shocked and numbed by the Kennedy tragedy. The entire family felt as though they had lost a personal friend. Although David had met President Kennedy personally on only two occasions, the Kennedy administration had been very bound up with the family's lives. David considered JFK a great force for the progress of human rights. He felt his loss keenly.

As Information Officer, David enjoyed sitting in on top-level A.I.D. conferences at the Pakistan Mission, representing the U.S.I.S. and advising A.I.D. as to which projects would have the most psychological and public relations impact. David's major concern, of course, was to promote and get priority for those projects which would be beneficial to U.S. foreign policy in Pakistan. He felt some urgency about this. Despite the amount of money, time, and effort the U.S. government expended on behalf of the Pakistani people, the Pakistanis were antagonistic and sometimes downright hostile to the U.S. His own observations were reinforced by Pakistani journalists themselves, who often made late-night visits to his home and spoke with him over scotch and soda. They told him quite directly that the mood in the country was anti-U.S. He often joked about whether they came because they felt the need to talk freely and openly about what they were thinking about political events, or because liquor was so difficult to obtain in a "dry" Moslem state.

One man, however, he was certain about—his good friend, Azhar-Ali Kahn, editor of the *Morning News*, the leading paper of Karachi. Azhar-Ali had spent two years at the University of Michigan getting a masters degree in journalism on a Fulbright scholarship grant from the U.S., and he had a real understanding of what A.I.D. was trying to do in Pakistan. David felt comfortable with him and they talked easily. It was clear that Azhar-Ali wanted to see U.S.-Pakistani relations improve.

When David had been at his post six weeks, John Heilman, Chief of the A.I.D. Mission in Pakistan, was promoted and recalled to Washington. The A.I.D. mission had dispensed more than $1 million a day in U.S. money to improve the Pakistani economy, and to try to make Pakistan an ally of the free world. Because U.S. observers regarded Afghanistan in constant risk of a Soviet takeover, the A.I.D. mission had been attempting to create in Pakistan a shield against communism in that part of the world.

In Heilman's departure David saw an excellent opportunity to publicize the overall A.I.D. program. To that end he arranged for a

three-hour interview session between John Heilman and Azhar-Ali
Kahn. The result of that effort was a front-page story in Pakistan's
most influential newspaper, carrying a three-line banner headline,
and continuing for two full additional newspaper pages. The headline was:

> UNLESS PAKISTAN INCREASES ITS AGRICULTURAL PRODUC-
> TION AND ITS EDUCATION, IT WILL BE IN DEEP TROUBLE IN THE
> YEARS AHEAD, U.S. A.I.D. CHIEF WARNS.[14]

David was gratified to find that he was not alone in thinking that
the U.S. needed a showcase for its efforts with A.I.D. He was commended by the U.S. Ambassador to Pakistan, Walter P. McConaughy; U.S.I.S. Public Affairs Officer William King; and his own
immediate superior, U.S.I.S. Chief Information Officer, Clyde Hess.

In the ensuing months, David developed a warm relationship
with the journalists of West Pakistan; this made possible a great
increase in public knowledge in Pakistan of A.I.D.'s developmental
work. One of the most effective instruments he had for conveying
his message was the program itself: He invited major journalists
from all over Pakistan to participate in a two-week tour to view the
A.I.D. program and gain an understanding of its amazing outreach
to ninety million people.

When David had been with A.I.D. six months, he was promoted
to Press Attaché at the Embassy. His replacement at A.I.D. was
delayed, however, so that he worked for months, dividing his time
between his two offices. In his new job, he was required to attend
a daily 8 A.M. meeting, called by the Chief Political Officer, where a
few top embassy staff members shared whatever knowledge and
intelligence they had gathered the previous day that would prove
useful for the better conduct of Embassy business. He also was
charged with the responsibility of distributing selected releases from
the daily U.S. Government worldwide wire service. The wire service
reached the Karachi Embassy after midnight and was delivered to
David's home around 6 A.M. David read the 30- to 40-page text at
breakfast and, as he was being driven to the Embassy, would select
the five or six stories to be sent that day to all the Pakistani newspapers. He and his staff of 20 people also monitored all of the Pakistani
newspapers and radio broadcasts in order to prepare a daily cable
indicating the reaction of the Pakistani people to world events.
President Johnson had requested that he be kept informed by this
method. The cable had to be cleared by the Chief Political Officer

at the Embassy. Often it was marked "Top Secret," and always "Confidential."

For example, when Chou-En-Lai came to Pakistan, the Pakistani government decided on an all-out festival type of welcome for the communist envoy. They arranged for truckloads of Pakistanis to be picked up from the streets and carted to the airport to cheer the Chinese envoy's arrival. The people thus assembled in the crowd were paid 3 piasters, or 60 American cents. The whole procedure was monitored and reported to the White House because the State Department considered any Pakistani overtures to the Red Chinese a threat to the stability of the region.

Over the next two years, those journalists friendly to the U.S. did not fare well in Pakistan. Government repression had all but brought Azhar-Ali Kahn's career to an end. His discussions with David had turned to talk of leaving, and David was much saddened to realize that one of Pakistan's finest journalists might have to leave his own country for the sake of his professional development. During this period, David helped Azhar-Ali Kahn to get articles out of the country to the *Christian Science Monitor* and the *Baltimore Sun*.

In November of 1964, Ambassador McConaughy was invited to give a major address at the inauguration of the seminar on Human Rights sponsored by the Pakistan United Nations Association on the 16th anniversary of the Universal Declaration of Human Rights. Normally, the Ambassador wrote his own speeches and preferred to do so; but, in this case, he turned to David for guidance and help in writing the address. He wanted David to draw on his unique background and experience in the human rights field. David submitted a draft to the Ambassador for his approval and comments, whereupon the Ambassador requested that David prepare and complete the address.

As David became more involved with this assignment, he felt a sense of nostalgia, thinking back to the NCCJ and the work that had been so close to his heart—the complex and challenging problems in the field of human rights and human dignity. Still, he reflected, the job he was doing now intersected with those concerns and challenges. He enjoyed the hectic daily work expected of him as a Press Attaché for the U.S. Embassy. He didn't regret his choice.

David loved the weekends, when he and Ricky and the children could go down to the beach. The beach in Pakistan was beautiful; the long sandy shore and the surf of the Arabian Sea reminded him of southern California's and Martha's Vineyard's best. They always laughed to see the children climb on the camels that were brought to the beach by their drivers in order to earn the equivalent of twenty cents per ride. Ricky would always pull out the camera at this point; and by the look of the photo album in their living room, all the Hyatt family did was to ride on camels. Ricky was glowing and happy for the most part these days, and the children were doing well in school. David hated to share with them the fear he had of being moved from his post and being sent to Vietnam. He feared for his family. Families were not allowed into war zones; therefore they would be sent to another, safer location. He did not feel confident in Ricky's ability to manage on her own. Occasionally on Sundays, when the servants were not on duty to prepare meals, he noticed the return of her problem.

He decided to let that discussion rest until he came back from the Khyber Pass the next week. When he did return, Ricky looked so lovely it was as if they were back to the early days of their marriage. He really felt pleased with the way his plan to come to Pakistan had worked out. It had been good for the entire family. Life had a rhythm that he loved: Sonny Driver would drive him to work in the morning, and while he worked hard, he felt he was accomplishing something good each day. His family seemed to be so contented, and he felt this was a productive, happy period.

Then, that evening when he and Ricky were having cocktails, he noticed that she was very quiet and did not always answer his questions. He finally had to ask if anything was wrong. She looked up and told him hesitantly that she was fairly sure she was going to have another child. She seemed a little crushed and was not thrilled at the idea of having another baby at forty-three, especially in a strange country far from home. He was at a loss for words. He did try to comfort her, and gradually over the next few weeks she adjusted to the idea.

Some months later, in September, David was hospital-bound, driving down a one-way street—the wrong way—at four o'clock in the morning. Fortunately, at that hour of the morning there were no other cars about. He had phoned the fine Pakistani lady doctor who was to deliver Ricky's baby at the Seventh Day Adventist Hospital, and David knew that she would be waiting when they arrived. He glanced anxiously at Ricky; it always struck him that a grown woman at a time like this looked most helpless. "Well," he reasoned, "women have been having babies for a long time. It will come out all right." He knew he was whistling to keep his courage up. She was no longer a young girl.

The next morning at seven o'clock the baby was born—another

girl, but very small. They told him she would have to spend the next week in an incubator. David was so relieved. The baby was fine, Ricky was recovering, and he could breathe again. When he went to see the newest addition to his family in the nursery, he was gleeful and amused. She stood out as the only white baby in a room full of brown ones.

A crisis developed immediately after the baby arrived home, for no one had thought to buy diapers. The girls were instructed to go the bazaar and bring home some diapers as quickly as possible. They set off with Sonny Driver; four hours later they came home close to tears, to report that there were no diapers anywhere in the bazaar, and no one seemed to know what they were talking about. David summoned Patrice, who knew everything about any matter. He explained what they needed. Patrice was polite but puzzled. When David became more explicit and the children helped, a big smile appeared on Patrice's face. Then he laughed aloud. "Ah," he explained, "you need nappies." With one voice the girls said, "Nappies?" David doubled up with laughter. Off the girls went to the bazaar and returned triumphant, diapers in hand, or "nappies" as they were thereafter called in the Hyatt menage.

Grace, the aptly named nurse, came and joined the household to look after Ellen, the new baby. Grace had only one child left out of the ten she had borne. All the others were carried off early by disease. To David, this sweet, patient woman symbolized all that made his heart ache for the marvelous people of Pakistan. The infant mortality rate, the ignorance and illiteracy were bad enough in the abstract, but up close they were devastating. He had a genuine affection and admiration for a people who managed to survive tidal waves, poverty, hunger, disease, and a totalitarian government led by self-interested men, and still maintain dignity.

A few months after Ellen's birth a letter came for David from the President of the NCCJ, asking him to come home to assume the Executive Vice Presidency of NCCJ. A decision had to be made: Would he continue in the Foreign Service or return home to America? He pictured Ricky alone in Thailand, with a new baby and the girls, while he went off to Vietnam. He shook his head. Impossible. Moreover, he had been gone too long from his chosen mission. It was time to return to his dream.

Preparations had to be made and work done before he could leave, but he knew he was ready for a new challenge. There were passports to be obtained and updated. Ellen, the newest arrival, had to have all of her papers in order. David was also aware that the Pakistanis were increasingly hostile to the U.S. and had embarked on a harassment campaign of U.S. nationals; but he did not realize how tense the situation had become until he arrived at customs with his family.

A customs official had obviously been given instructions to be especially difficult with David and his family. He immediately refused to permit the baby an exit visa, saying that she did not have the correct immunizations. After talking with the man, David saw the message clearly: This was the harassment policy being implemented and he had gotten caught in it. Ricky and the girls were frantic because the ship was due to leave in two hours.

David kept his head and began to call some good friends who were in positions of influence within the Pakistan government and press. They would see what they could do. He also called the Embassy to report what was going on and to see if it could avert a real incident and great inconvenience for the Hyatts. Then he went back to the customs official to see if the man could be reached on a human level. After all, he was traveling with three children and his wife, and one of those children was a baby. After a short talk, the man told them in a surly tone, "You can leave now." This was an hour before the ship was due to depart.

The next morning when they were out to sea, the ship's wireless newspaper announced that Pakistan and India had declared war the night they left.

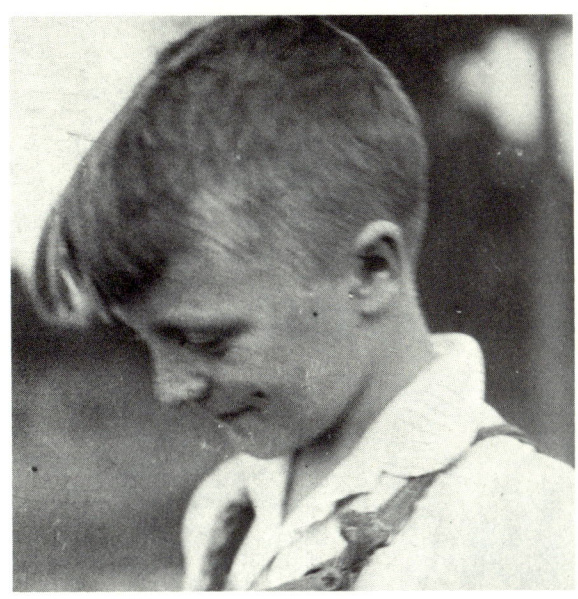

*David in his
Huckleberry Finn
period—on the farm
in Ohio.*

*Working his way through college
(Northwestern University). David
delivered for the Hoos Drugstore
and Soda Fountain.*

David in World War II, an ambulance driver with the British Eighth Army (1941-1943).

David's bride in 1944: Leonore Wade Moerschelle, known to her friends as Ricky.

David as an officer in the United States Navy air arm (1943-1945).

HYATT, DAVE
LExington 2-1100
S. S. No. 298-18-9635

TELEPHONE EXCHANGE

Leads, Straight, Heavies.

RADIO: Dick Tracy, The Telephone Hour, Time To Remember, School Of The Air, Gangbusters, 10 months with WHK, WGAR (Cleveland).

STAGE: Reiner in The French Touch starring Brian Ahern (N. Y.). Other roles: Lord Bacon in Elizabeth The Queen and Frank in Mrs. Warren's Profession at Pasadena Playhouse. Mio in Winterset and Dunois in Saint Joan at Cleveland Playhouse. Stock at Santa Fe and White Sulphur Springs.

TELEVISION: WABD (Dumont), WBKD (Chicago).

Age	29
Height	6'
Weight	160
Hair	Brown
Eyes	Blue
Voice Range	25-38

4/46

The actor's so-called "Lexington card," used by New York producers and directors in casting (1946).

David served as Press Attache for the U.S. embassy in Pakistan (1963-1965). Here he is greeting Field Marshall Ayub Khan, President of Pakistan, with U.S. Ambassador Walter P. McConaughy.

David and Lili in the early years of their marriage (1972).

Among David's colleagues in the battle for interracial justice and interreligious understanding were (left to right) Dr. Bertram Gold, *Executive Vice President, American Jewish Committee;* Vernon Jordan, *President of the Urban League;* Roy Wilkins, *Executive Secretary, National Association for the Advancement of Colored People;* Dr. John Slawson, *Executive Vice President Emeritus, American Jewish Committee.*

David in Jerusalem, talking over problems of Christian-Jewish-Moslem relations in the Holy Land with the Mayor of Jerusalem, Teddy Kollek.

Lili and David at David's inauguration as President of the National Council of Christians and Jews (1973).

David chatting with President and Mrs. Gerald Ford on the occasion of the Charles Evans Hughes Award Dinner. The President and Mrs. Ford received the award from Secretary of State Henry Kissinger (1977).

David greeting President and Mrs. Jimmy Carter in Washington, D.C. (1979). President Carter was being honored for his championship of human rights.

David presents the National Media Award to Gerald Green for his outstanding television play, Holocaust *(1979).*

David pays tribute to Sir Sigmund Sternberg for his leadership as Chairman of the 17-nation International Council of Christians and Jews. Lady Hazel Sternberg is beside him.

10

Return to NCCJ

For the Hyatt family the return voyage home proved to be an unforgettable experience. From Karachi they crossed the Arabian Sea, stopped briefly at Aden, sailed through the Suez Canal to the Mediterranean and then on to Italy. At Brindisi they got off and flew across Italy to Naples, where they spent five days. David took the girls to Pompeii before they left for New York. If David felt on the way over that he should have been a bachelor if he were going to be a Foreign Service Officer, on the way home he was sure of it. Including all the paraphernalia for the baby, the family had thirteen suitcases. His shoulders ached; his patience wore thin as he shepherded his small flock across oceans, through customs in three countries, and in and out of hotels. He concluded this was all unimportant compared to the unusual and rewarding experience for all of them. He was really elated to be going home and was looking forward to his new post at NCCJ. One thing troubled him; he would have to leave his little brood with Ricky's twin sister in Troy, New York, while he located a home. He reassured himself with the knowledge that Ricky and her sister would be so happy to be together for a month or so to exchange news. The two of them were very close. The trip to Pakistan had been their longest separation ever. "The furniture would not arrive for a month or so," he thought, "because it was coming by ship, so perhaps the timetable would work out just fine." Then he relaxed and enjoyed his family and the ocean voyage from Naples to New York. When the S.S. Independence docked at New York harbor, David was so pleased to see Dr. Sterling Brown, NCCJ's President, there to greet him. The two men had a few minutes to talk while Ricky's family surrounded Ricky and the children.

After settling the family temporarily in Troy and himself in his office, David began to hunt for a home. He found one in Scarsdale,

New York. The schools were excellent, the commute bearable, and it was a lovely spot—in some ways like an English village in the Cotswolds. The old house needed a lot of work, but the grounds were promising. It took some doing to put the financing together because, although his title was Executive Vice-President, his salary, like those of the rest of the NCCJ staff, was modest. By November of 1965, with the older girls settled in school and Ricky and the baby at home together and adjusted to a routine, David felt he could turn his full attention to his new assignment.

It was quite clear to him, even before he set foot in the United States again, that race relations had to become a paramount program priority in the years immediately ahead. Just two weeks before he left Pakistan, the Pakistan *Observer*, published in Dacca on August 16, 1965, ran a front page story on the riots in the Watts area of Los Angeles. If it was front page news in Pakistan, it most certainly was also headlined in America. Of this David was sure, even taking into consideration the extreme sensitivity of the Pakistanis about racial issues after years of British rule. Some ancient Pakistanis recalled signs posted at the Sind Club in Karachi which read, some generations back, "Dogs and Indians not allowed."

The Watts story, as it appeared in the *Observer*, was headlined,

NEGRO REVOLT SPREADS IN LOS ANGELES

The story was reported as a "revolt," not a "riot" as presented in the American papers:

> *Los Angeles, Aug. 16—One policeman was shot dead, another seriously wounded, last night as Negro rioting spread from the tightly-controlled "black ghettos" to other parts of the city, reports Reuter.*
>
> *A rampaging mob attacked police in the coastal Long Beach area, 15 miles south of the Watts Negro quarter, where armed police and National Guardsmen enforced a tight curfew.*
>
> *Police rushed to seal off a half-mile-square area of Long Beach and called on State authorities to reinforce them with troops.*

Later in the article the real dimensions of the incident were expressed.

> *The heat wave, which forced Negroes out of shanty homes into the streets and aroused tempers, has been blamed for blowing up a comparatively trivial incident into a savage street war.*

> *The trouble started with the arrest of a Negro accused of drunken driving.*

When David used blowups of the article in speaking to American audiences, he was careful to state that it was not to dismiss the seriousness of the riot that he made this point, but to stress how American responses to racial problems were reported abroad. He made the point that Watts was a blot upon a democratic society. It was very serious that 762 people were injured and 31 killed, and that the despair in the Black community was such that a trivial incident could indeed result in such bloodshed. His talk was entitled: "America's Unfinished Business."

Soon after his arrival David began to sense that not only was the country in a state of upheaval, but that all was not as it should be within the Conference. He had guessed in Pakistan that his recall a year early and the request that he serve as Executive Vice-President had something to do with his success in getting along with his colleagues and their trust in him. It also led him to speculate about the exact nature of the problems facing NCCJ. He knew that all was not well and that the struggle to elect a new president had created strains among the staff. However, after a few weeks he had to admit that the internal problems within NCCJ were more serious than he had thought possible before his return.

So were America's problems in race relations. David felt a foreboding that the United States was moving towards two societies: one Black, one White—separate and unequal. Watts was but a warning of worse things to come. How could he muster the forces for good among the religiously-motivated people of all faiths to avoid that catastrophe—that was the question. What to do, and how to do it? He pondered that question on the train home every evening and on the way to the office every morning. He was most unhappy at the violent encounters that had occurred in Birmingham, Alabama, in 1963, while he was in Pakistan. There the police had used dogs, firehoses, and cattle prods against marchers, some of whom were children. White racists shot at Blacks and bombed Black residences. Blacks retaliated by burning White-owned businesses in Black areas. One quiet Sunday morning when a bomb exploded beneath a Black church, four young girls in a Sunday school class were killed.[15] It had to be stopped, he thought. But how?

Although he understood the powerlessness and frustration felt by the minority communities, he was sure that violence was not the route to a better society. In the final analysis, mob rule and disorder, he knew from experience, only nourished repression. Again he was reminded of the chilling example of Nazi Germany where a fearful middle class supported an Adolf Hitler who promised to maintain a society free of anarchy. He was all too aware of the complexities of the racial attitudes and behavior of White Americans toward Black Americans. Yes, that was the key! Attitudes!

The NCCJ had been dealing with attitude change in the inter-religious field; surely it would be as effective in the interracial conflicts. Moreover, he reasoned, we have a reservoir of religiously motivated people of good will who have been working with NCCJ in communities, who have attended workshops, conferences, and programs sponsored by the Conference. The majority of these people were in positions of influence in their communities. Why could not this network be utilized in the struggle that was threatening to tear the country apart? All that was required was a change in the priorities for programming. If an all-out effort were mounted in every office in the country, it was sure to have an impact.

His next task would be to locate as many people as he could find on the staff and on the Boards to discuss the idea of shifting into high gear in all NCCJ offices to deal with racial issues. He remembered all too vividly his experiences in the mid-fifties when he had produced the first three pamphlets on equal opportunity in the workplace for minorities and the controversy that raged in the NCCJ upon the publication of that material. That had been a valuable lesson for him. This time he would have to prepare the ground before he attempted any action. Every invitation to speak, each conference, workshop or program attended, he made an opportunity to speak to the regional Director and, where possible, Board members.

The passage of the Civil Rights Act in 1964 was going to be helpful because NCCJ's role as persuader was established and the law's enactment would make it much less difficult to persuade people. Lyndon Johnson won election as President by a landslide because people seemed to accept the concept of the "Great Society." The Supreme Court gave school busing its imprimatur. NCCJ was ready to help complete what Lincoln had called in his Gettysburg Address more than 100 years earlier, "the great unfinished task before us." David felt it was indeed "America's Unfinished Business."

As an example of other regions, he used the response of the NCCJ staff and Board in Los Angeles after the Watts debacle. In cooperation with the Chamber of Commerce in that city, the NCCJ set up a whole series of half-day conferences, attended by more than 200 top business and labor leaders, to discuss what could be done about improving the situation in Watts. They talked about tough problems, such as the hardcore unemployed, the training of the so-called untrainable, and the employment of persons with arrest records. (Fifty percent of the hard-core unemployed from Watts had an arrest record.) As a result of these sessions, some 30,000 persons from Watts were subsequently employed by the representatives of business and industry who attended these NCCJ institutes under the umbrella of the Labor-Management program of the organization.

In the Police Community Relations program of NCCJ, David saw a wonderful way to help communities that did not have human relations training programs in their police training academies. Circumventing the ever-present plea that there was no money available for "frills" like human relations training, the NCCJ offered trained staff to conduct classes at the academies, without charge to the police department. That allowed non-traditional police approaches to minority problems and free discussion in the classes with the police officers and the instructor, more often than not a minority person or a woman. Many police officers during these sessions were sensitized to their own attitudes to minorities and helped to see the role of such attitudes in causing poor performance in on-duty situations where a racially-charged issue might arise. In addition, the university community throughout the United States was urged to offer courses for credit in the field of Police-Community Relations. David and NCCJ's national program staff members encouraged regional Directors to offer scholarships to make it possible for police officers and minority community leaders to attend. When such people met on neutral ground, in an informal college setting, with an opportunity to eat together and talk during the breaks in the daylong sessions, David reasoned, they might be better prepared to solve a potentially explosive situation on the street. Certainly it was preferable to waiting for another Watts to erupt. David knew the NCCJ had much to learn about techniques, attitudes, and pitfalls. He did not underestimate the difficulty of the job, but he felt the educational approach had to be tried.

When David set up his office on the eighth floor of the Building for Brotherhood, next door to Dr. Brown, it was clear that he had a bit of catching up to do. Work had been going on in his absence, and he needed to know which colleagues were doing outstanding or innovative programming. On top of a pile of material to be read was an attractive green booklet with a note from the Vice-President in charge of Programming for Youth asking that he give it his attention

because it represented an opportunity for NCCJ to make an impact
in a hitherto untried program area involving work with the recently
created Job Corps program. David was pleased to learn that a proposal to fund the program across the country was under consideration. The "how-to-do-it" booklet bore the intriguing title, *Hospitality*.

David was interested to learn that the program's creator was a
new staff member who had come aboard during his absence in
Pakistan to serve in the Long Island region. Her name was Lili Reiss.
He was impressed by the simple device she had used to create a
program that obviously had national dimensions. As coordinator of
her area's youth work and education committee, she had involved
twenty-seven families from the affluent community of Oyster Bay
in extending hospitality over a weekend to thirty-four trainees from
the Kilmer Job Corps at Camp Kilmer, New Jersey.

Her purpose, as explained in the well written and documented
booklet produced by the Job Corps Agency in Washington, D.C.,
was to build a bridge:

> *Not the usual kind of bridge built of steel girders and steel cables,
> but one made of Understanding People who 'care' about the fate
> of our young men and women. Just how important this 'bridge' is
> to the young people in our society who are unprepared to meet the
> challenge of providing for themselves and ultimately for their
> families can best be understood in human terms. When we become
> aware that these young people not only do not represent a small
> segment of our society, but also represent a big stake in our future
> society, then we must realize that this is a community problem as
> well as an individual one.*[16]

It was a program idea that David felt would create hope in the
Black and other minority communities. Perhaps it would help to
avert other potential Watts situations. He thought, "I'm sure she will
be at the reception the staff is going to attend to welcome me back.
I'll make a point of speaking to her." It was his practice to encourage
creativity among the staff. "It is a gift, and NCCJ needs that kind of
gifted person on staff if we are going to make any headway with the
problems we are attempting to solve."

One of David's reasons for returning to the NCCJ was the realization that, before the U.S. Information Agency and other American
overseas agencies could sell the concept of democracy and human
rights abroad, the American people had to make it work at home.
For himself, the best way he saw of accomplishing the job was to
work through an organization that had demonstrated its commit-

ment for nearly four decades. That, however, did not mean that the Conference was monolithic. He had learned that, to his pain, on more than one occasion. There were places in the country where staff members and individual Board members took issue with NCCJ policies, but, like the rest of the United States, somehow managed to achieve a stance that seemed fair and conducive to interreligious freedom and interracial justice. David felt that people in the United States adhered to what he considered was the American Ethic. People were acculturated to do the decent thing "because it is right."[17]

Another area that troubled him was the absence of proper representation for the Eastern Orthodox Churches among the top lay leadership of NCCJ. He began to explore ways to remedy that situation. To his surprise, he found some Board members opposed because they feared that, if such a step were taken, other religious groups would request a National Co-chairman. He suggested a change in the by-laws to effect a remedy and hoped that he would be heard so that the matter would be brought up to the Board for consideration.[18] By November of that same year David was relieved to see the Board adopt the idea. His dear friend, Archbishop Iakovos of the Greek Orthodox Church of North and South America, was asked to assist the Conference in finding a National Co-chairman to represent the Eastern Orthodox Churches on the Board of NCCJ. The Archbishop proposed several candidates, and David was content.[19]

In the year following his return, David began to think about changes necessary, in his opinion, to make the operation of the organization reflect the changing times. For example, he was troubled by the erosion of staff salaries because of inflation, and, while money was not the primary motivation for many staff members, he knew they had families to feed and support. Well-qualified people were being forced to leave the work they cherished and take better-paying positions—in universities, government agencies, business, and industry. It was a distinct loss because the Conference needed their skill, talent, and experience. He attempted to discuss these matters with Dr. Brown who usually replied by reminding him that when he entered service with the NCCJ his salary was $3,000 per year, and compared to that the staff was well paid. Discouraged, David had to acknowledge that, while he felt he had to keep trying, the conversations were producing very little new thinking. Brown was simply not prepared to give high priority to the material needs of the staff or their families.

A second problem was the increasing isolation of the NCCJ's President from his staff. He perceived the growing rift and lack of communication not only from the staff in the field across the country, but right within the National headquarters building. Brown preferred to listen to those whose thinking matched his own. This troubled David; in his travels around the country, staff members told him they felt increasingly isolated and unappreciated by the National administration in New York. Whenever he tried to open up the matter in discussion with Brown, the President pleaded a lack of time. David saw this as a potentially dangerous situation. Board members were also becoming aware of growing unrest among the staff; when they asked questions, they received the same treatment. Seriously troubled by what he saw, heard, and experienced, David consulted with Dr. Arild Olsen, who shared David's apprehensions. Dr. Olsen was the Vice-President in charge of Program Development for the NCCJ, and his work, like David's, brought him into close contact with the staff in most of the regional offices. He told David of rumors reaching him that staff people were meeting secretly to discuss their problems with one-man rule.

The two men decided that, although they could not tackle the problem head-on, they must try to introduce it for discussion at every meeting of the National staff held with the President. But they discovered, to their dismay, that the time devoted by the President to such meetings grew less and less, and over a period of months almost disappeared. His agenda was too full to meet with the National staff, according to notices that canceled meetings. David and Arild agreed that the last avenue of communication was effectively cut off.

Isolation seemed to beset as well the people he loved best. He was puzzled and disturbed by Ricky's failure to become a part of the life of the village where they now lived. She made no friends, nor did she seem to want any. He loved her poetry and always asked to read it. One day he read the lines that told him his beloved Ricky was lonely, unhappy, and not going to make any attempt to reach out to anyone. She called it her "Poem Dust."

> I have been too tired to get undressed and go
>   to sleep.
> I have been too tired to drink but have never
>   been too tired to think.
>
> I don't want too many friends.
> They borrow my books and comment on
>   my looks,

and insist
upon a kiss
When the evening ends.
If they ask how jealousy grows, tell them
Its roots are made of Selfishness,
and its stems are Pride,
and its leaves are green.

The long dead road at five o'clock remembers
my waiting.

Chimes sound
On a gloomy day,
Like
Echoes that forgot
To answer back.

The air smells
Too much like Spring,
and I am reminded
of
walking down
too crowded streets
after having had
too many cocktails.[20]

He worried that he seemed to have less time than ever for her. His problems at work made him less patient than he should be. The girls at teen age were presenting problems, and friction was developing among his three beloveds. He knew, too, that the baby was a burden and hard to manage alone, with no help in running a big house. The question was: What could he do?

Over the New Year weekend in 1968 he had time to answer some long-neglected letters that had stayed patiently in his drawer for nearly two full years. His letter began:

For months which stretched into years I've been meaning to write
you wonderful people a letter.

and continued

I love my job with the NCCJ, and I am completely enthralled by
it. If I wasn't paid to do it, I'd do it as a volunteer. Fortunately,
it pays pretty well.

He recounted his return to the United States from the Foreign Service, and added:

> *Ricky will never get over the luxury of a full-time cook, a chauffeur, a gardener, and a houseboy and laundryman.*[21]

He stopped for a moment to think. Was that the reason the house was never cleaned now? So many of his Saturdays were being spent doing house chores that could have been cared for by Ricky and the girls during the week. He knew they were teenagers, but still, they could be more helpful. Ellen was four and going to school soon; that should help things a little.

He went on:

> *Ann is fifteen and a sophomore in Scarsdale High School. Caroline is nineteen and has decided not to go to college—at least not now. This past year she has worked in a drug store, a department store, then went to Provincetown and worked in a fishery gutting fish, then a gift shop, then a leather shop, busgirl in a restaurant, waitress and finally an assistant chef in the largest restaurant in Provincetown. She returned home this October to have her tonsils out. Then she took off with her boyfriend to Nova Scotia.*[22]

He paused. His heart was heavy. While he was writing about everything as though it were a great adventure and he didn't want to burden anyone with his problems, he did know that Caroline was not happy and that all her moving about was due to her disturbance and deep unhappiness. He also guessed that many of her companions were drug users and often, when he saw her tranquil, he suspected it was due to the effects of drugs rather than good feelings about herself. Just thinking about it made his heart ache. He wasn't able to reach her anymore. If only her relationship to her mother were better, perhaps Ricky would be able to help. Then his head dropped on his arms. Poor Ricky had not found an answer to her own unhappiness, he thought wearily. She looked too thin, too tired. Their twenty-fifth anniversary was coming up. "I'll plan something that will be fun for us to do." He went on to complete the letter. He maintained his cheerful approach in a determined way as he told his news, but his mood was pure indigo and he could not shake it.

It was not going to help to be depressed, he thought, and worry was not very useful. He concluded, that at this point in time, there was little or nothing he could do about the situation at the NCCJ.

Therefore it might be better to turn his attention to an area where he could do something productive. He decided to accept an appointment from Secretary of State Dean Rusk to the United States National Commission for UNESCO. His overseas experience could be utilized in that post. He knew there was a spot open as Chairman of the Commission's Public Liaison Committee, and he could manage that volunteer assignment along with his NCCJ work, since he already had the network of contacts. He felt that the 100-member Commission served a useful function as advisor to the Government on UNESCO matters and as a link between organizations, institutions, and individuals in the U.S. and the United Nation's Educational, Scientific and Cultural Organization (UNESCO). He turned his attention to drafting a letter of acceptance.

11

Tragedy Strikes Home: Winter of the Soul's Discontent

❦

The day dawned cold and chilly. His bag was on the bed in the bedroom. He looked up to find Ricky resting quietly in the rocker by the window. He was so busy getting his things together that he hadn't noticed her slip in. Usually she slept late and he left before the household was stirring, but today was different because he would be gone for a week in New York at a staff meeting. She must have wanted to say goodbye. Her eyes looked puffy, as though she had been crying, and he knew she was not feeling well. He felt he should stop a bit and say some words of comfort. Being alone in the house with two small children was not an exciting prospect for her, but he knew that she was really not well enough to come along with him. But he was so apprehensive about the mood of the staff, and the trouble he knew was coming, that the thought died before he had a chance to consider it. He rushed to finish his packing. He always tried to be there a bit earlier than anyone else to make sure everything was in order. There was no time to talk. He must catch his train.

Her eyes followed him down to the village, with that last look of silent reproach. He shook off his despair with the situation and turned his mind to the problem of how he must act to defuse the anger he knew would be directed at the National administration of NCCJ during the next week at the Americana Hotel. Word had reached him that the staff members wanted no part of a heavily structured program. That would leave lots of time, they told him, to explore the theme of the conference, "How to Make NCCJ a More

Effective Human Relations Organization." As he watched the wintry early January landscape pass by the train window, his thoughts turned to a secret meeting held in a Baltimore hotel the weekend before. Representatives had attended from every section of the U.S. He knew, even if Brown did not, that the real focus of the conference was to be on internal human relations and not program. The theme was going to show the NCCJ at a crossroads. As a staff they would either have to have a union or an internal staff organization which would protect them from what they perceived as Brown's "one-man rule." Nothing of these developments reached David directly, but he had enough information via rumors to piece together what he felt was certain would follow. The icy landscape matched his thoughts. There would be plenty of time to air grievances and complaints. He hoped it would not result in a fractured, bitter organization and the loss of more good people. He wanted to help, but, like his problems at home, he was not sure which road to take to achieve the results he wanted so desperately: harmony and a good resolution to these dilemmas.

He had better put aside his qualms and get ready to deliver the opening speech—which had taken him two weeks to write and perfect. His aim was to set the tone for four days of productive discussion. He wanted to remind everyone of the importance of the NCCJ program, and the contribution it could make to interreligious relations and interracial justice. He glanced at the allusion in his speech to the fact that despite Vatican II and the so-called Ecumenical Revolution, Christian-Jewish relations since the Arab-Israeli crisis had never been more sensitive. He would also make the point that race relations had become a paramount concern of NCCJ.

His eyes misted over when he read the portion he had written about the martyred Martin Luther King.

Two hours later he was standing in front of his colleagues delivering his speech. He quoted what Martin Luther King had said just before his death:

> *If any of you are around when I have to meet my day, I don't want a long funeral.*
>
> *And if you get someone to deliver the eulogy, tell him not to talk too long.*
>
> *And every now and then I wonder what I want him to say.*

Tell him not to mention that I have a Nobel Peace Prize—that isn't important.

Tell him not to mention I had three or four hundred other awards— that's not important. And tell him not to mention where I went to school.

I'd like him to mention the day that Martin Luther King, Jr. tried to give his life to serving others.

I'd like someone to say that day that Martin Luther King, Jr. tried to love somebody.

I want you to say that day I tried to be right and to walk with them.

I want you to be able to say that day that I did try to feed the hungry.

I want you to be able to say that day that I did try in my life to clothe the naked.

I want you to say on that day that I did try to visit those who were in prison.

And I want you to say that I tried to love and serve humanity.

Yes, if you want to say I was a drum major, say I was a drum major for justice. Say that I was a drum major for peace. I was a drum major for righteousness.

And all of the other shallow things will not matter.

I won't have any money to leave behind. But I just want to leave a committed life behind.[23]

"Whenever I feel discouraged about the grocery bills or the life insurance payments or my personal ambitions or any of the other trivial problems that all of us fret and strain about," continued David, "I reread King's statement and—like the 23rd Psalm—am refreshed and renewed by its affirmation. It puts on the line what the *true* values of life really are and why we're here on earth and why you and I are working for the NCCJ. That's why working for the NCCJ is such a creative opportunity. Every job in the Conference is bigger than we are."[24]

He had known many of the people in the room for sixteen years. As he looked around him he thought: With the exception of my family, I feel closer to them than anyone. I pray they can do what they feel they must do without destroying what we all feel is important in this organization.

The next four days were as trying as David felt they would be. Feelings ran high. When they were done and the reports had come in from all the groups, the consensus was that a staff committee be established.

Since David and Arild and others on the National staff were panelists being asked to respond to the reports, it was comparatively simple for David to choose to speak about the recommendation for the formation of a staff committee. He began by saying: "I applaud you for trying to set up a mechanism for 'participatory democracy' in the formation of a staff committee. You could have gone the route of forming a union which many other agencies have done. But a union could never bridge the communication gap between administration and staff. In my opinion all of our regional Directors are part of the administration and management, and therefore we should be a team—not antagonists. I pledge to work with all my heart and all my mind and soul to try to see that such a mechanism for 'participatory democracy' and teamwork is put into place."

In the week that followed, it was apparent to David that while Brown would discuss the formation of the staff committee, he was not in favor of it. David often had the feeling that plans were being made to exclude him from any decision-making process. He was sure that Brown felt he had been betrayed by the very man he had brought back to help him keep control of the Conference staff. He was convinced that Brown could not comprehend that times had changed from the early days of the NCCJ, and that, unless the staff were given a role in management, the organization would suffer.

During the next two weeks Ricky seemed to be less and less willing to get up, and her condition was beginning to alarm David. He begged her to see a doctor. She replied with some spirit that she couldn't understand why he was making such a fuss over a cold and flu. "I don't need a doctor," she told him, "I will be better in a week." David knew better than to argue with Ricky once she had made up her mind; so he let the matter rest. But in his own mind he had decided, if she was not better by the end of the week, he would make her go for a check-up.

One morning he could not awaken her. He quickly called the doctor, fearing for her life. The doctor confirmed his worst premonitions; he suspected that Ricky had meningitis. The ambulance was called and came within a half-hour. David followed in the car to White Plains, leaving Ann to take care of the baby. His heart was cold; his mind raced; his knuckles grew white as he gripped the steering wheel. The tension was almost unbearable. After forty-eight hours of waiting and praying in the room adjoining the intensive care unit, David was informed that Ricky had died.

It was all over so quickly. That poor tired body and sad soul made the fight against the disease an unequal contest. The doctor had warned him that, even if she had lived, she would have been mentally and physically impaired. He was sad beyond tears. He would have to go back home and tell the children, and call the family in Troy. Ricky's twin sister Betty would be devastated. The two women had remained very close since childhood.

Life went on. After Ricky's funeral David struggled to cope with a household, a small bewildered child, and a frightened, overwhelmed teenager. He shopped, cooked, got Ann to help him with the baby, and spent half of each day calling agencies to find a competent housekeeper. Apparently it was difficult to hire a replacement for a mother. For a few days his very real problems about his work were dwarfed by the pressing needs of the children and the day-to-day problems in his home. While taking care of Ellen, Ann was losing ground in school. He discovered that small children outgrow their clothes and shoes very quickly and that they must be replaced. Finally a housekeeper was found and installed. Ann was able to get back to her studies and he was able to return to work, confident that meals would be prepared, clothes washed, and the youngest child supervised to some degree. He hoped the house would get some attention as well. Nevertheless, there were conferences with teachers, troubles to be listened to at the end of the day, and other things he could not delegate to a housekeeper. He was nearing the end of his rope, and the fatigue he felt was like an old but not very welcome friend. It was his constant companion. It was hard to concentrate on anything. Expenses were mounting.

In the evening when the children were in bed, he would light the fire to chase the bitter cold of deep winter, and take a cocktail. His thoughts were poor company, and sleep came fitfully if he went to bed too early. Some mornings he would wake up in the chair in the living room, his glass in hand, the fire out, and the grey light of a winter morning filtering through the window. He would slip up the stairs quietly because he heard the housekeeper in the kitchen. He had to change and get to work.

When he got back to the office, another shock awaited him. Dr. Olsen asked to come to his office. As soon as Dr. Olsen closed the door, David knew from the look on his face that something unpleasant had occurred in his absence. Arild quickly confirmed his perception. Because Arild had indicated his approval of the staff committee,

Dr. Brown had told him his contract would not be renewed at the end of the fiscal year. David's heart felt like a dead weight. Arild was the one voice he could count on to help convince Brown that the only course open was to forge a team, making the field staff and the National administration equally responsible for the management of NCCJ. For the first time, he thought seriously about the unthinkable. He could be faced with leaving the work he loved so much that he had given up two careers for it.

When Arild left, he decided to lunch alone in order to think. In the restaurant, he ordered a martini. Feeling more relaxed, he began to review the difficult decisions that he would be called upon to make in the not-too-distant future. His thoughts ran on: "I happen to love my work; I do a good job where I am; I am not really looking for a change. However, I am still at only $26,000 a year as Executive Vice-President. There is a good chance that, if I wait out the next three years until Brown's retirement, I will be offered the presidency.[25] The situation at home is an increasing financial drain. The house, the car, and the housekeeper just can't be managed on that slim salary." He knew he should look for a post that paid more. He also knew that if Brown considered Arild expendable when Arild was doing a magnificent job, then perhaps he too would be considered expendable. He had ordered two more martinis with lunch, and was surprised when he stood up that he was a bit unsteady on his feet. Maybe he ought not to have so much to drink at lunch.

The field staff continued to let David know of their discontent, which did little for his peace of mind. There seemed to be nothing he could do but listen. And listen he did. Lunches alone were a thing of the past, and each day brought more forcibly to his attention the real and deepening rift that was developing. "If they only knew how isolated and helpless I feel," he thought. "I am in the office right next door to the President, and I can't reach him or persuade him to do things differently. How can I possibly help them?" He joined them in pleading for the administration to begin to practice the most elementary human relations with the staff. The inequities were mounting, and no solutions were forthcoming. Discouragement caused less effective work among the dedicated staff. He too was discouraged, but could not bring himself to leave, at least not yet.

One morning he decided that he would tackle the huge pile of condolence letters that had poured in after Ricky's death. It still made him depressed to look at them and even more depressed when he had to compose a short note of appreciation. But it had to be done. Time had brought some easing. The ache was not so sharp now; the regrets less consuming. There was a short, hastily written note on the bottom of one pile. He smiled when he read it because he could recall the writer very well. She was a spirited young woman who had gone to work for the Mayor of New York when her request for equitable treatment had been first ignored and then denied by Dr. Brown.

He chuckled when he remembered their last meeting several years before. She had sat opposite him, in front of his desk, and he had asked her if she needed a letter of recommendation. Her neat blonde head held very high, and with slightly heightened color on her pale gold face, she had replied tartly, "For your information, Doctor Hyatt, I am leaving NCCJ to take a job that pays several thousand dollars more than the NCCJ is willing to pay me. I would not be leaving if I had been paid enough to support my children. I am the head of my household, you know." He had admired her ability to move on to a job that enabled her to live more comfortably. He was all too aware that her salary, like all others in the NCCJ, did not reflect her considerable abilities. He was sorry to see such a creative programmer leave the agency. He knew, too, that when she was confronted suddenly with the need to raise cash for the budget in her region—when her senior colleague was overseas—she did that with absolutely no preparation. Yes, he thought, another loss to the NCCJ, without reason. We should have been able to promote her; she had earned it.

A very independent, resourceful young woman with a strong identity and tie to the Jewish people, he recalled, and smiled again. One day when he was asked to speak at an NCCJ youth conference in Westchester, she had been in the audience. Afterwards, she came up to him as he stood on the path with Ricky and told him how much she had enjoyed hearing him speak. He knew it was not a polite question, but his curiosity made him ask why such an attractive young woman was not married. Ricky pulled at his arm, and he knew she did not think the question was diplomatic. Lili had looked at him with her startling blue eyes and had answered in a way that seemed strange to him for a staff member of the NCCJ. She began, "Dr. Hyatt, I can't seem to find a proper Jewish man to marry." He must have looked quizzical, and he *was* surprised. "Does he have to be Jewish?" "Oh yes, Dr. Hyatt, you see if I have a child, it must be a Jewish child." Still puzzled, he persisted. "Why?" "Because, Dr. Hyatt," she replied with some asperity, "to paraphrase Winston Churchill, I am not here to preside over the dissolution of the Jewish people." With that she turned and left, obviously not at all pleased with the turn the conversation had taken. Later that day, upon reflection, he did recall that the whole European branch of her family had been destroyed in Austria during the Holocaust. After that thought, her position seemed more reasonable to him; and he thought it might be fun to see her now and find out how she was doing. Besides, he thought, she owes me a thank-you note. He went over to his file and pulled out the letter of recommendation she finally did ask for, a few months after she had refused it initially. He knew she had a lot of pride, and he reread the letter he had written:

> *Her record speaks for itself, and her only reason for leaving us was for a position that paid her several thousand dollars more in salary than we were at that time able to pay her.*
>
> *As a person she is a charming, thoughtful, very lovely lady whose personal attractiveness does not immediately communicate her capacity for hard and concentrated work, her ability to get things done with dispatch and efficiency, and her deep convictions regarding the brotherhood of man under the Fatherhood of God.*[26]

He glanced back at her letter which had three telephone numbers where she could be reached. At the end of her condolence note, she had written politely that she would be happy to be of any assistance she could. Well, he could do with some lively company, and it would be fun to know what had happened to her. She had apparently left the non-profit field and was now in the business world. He had so many decisions to make it would be good to talk those things over as well. He did remember she was rather astute, in a quiet way. Maybe it was time to find some diversion from his grim, grey thoughts and problems. She was just different and colorful enough to make him forget all the difficulties for a few hours. Perhaps it was time for a Second Spring.

12

Tranquil Harbor:
An Ecumenical Marriage

Except for the brightness that Lili brought into his life, that year was pretty bleak. He was having difficulties being a single parent and fulfilling the role of mother as well as father. However, David still managed to fulfill his commitment to his work, even though his duties at the Conference did not diminish as his duties at home increased. He usually averaged trips to thirty cities a year; as a concession to his difficult situation at home, in 1970 he visited only nineteen. At the same time the faulty system of field supervision at NCCJ gave him many a sleepless night.

When David had worked under Dr. Lewis Webster Jones, Dr. Brown's predecessor, the supervision of the field offices had been the responsibility of five divisional Vice-Presidents. Many faults developed in that system, not the least of which, in David's opinion, was the tendency on the part of some Vice-Presidents to "ride herd" on the regional staff without diplomacy, understanding, or tact. Indeed, sometimes, having too little to do, they became difficult over minute matters. As a result, some senior regional Directors, who had been in the work longer than their superiors, found them overbearing. To solve these problems, Dr. Jones eliminated the entire supervisory structure, giving the Vice-Presidents the choice of keeping their titles and taking other posts in the NCCJ without the power or responsibility of supervision.

In 1967 David shared his concerns with Dr. Brown about what he perceived as a serious flaw in the NCCJ supervisory structure. He urged consideration of a stronger and better organized system of field supervision, assistance, control, and evaluation than had been the case since 1960, when the old system was abandoned. Ten years had elapsed, and it was clear to both David and Dr. Brown that nothing was wrong with the idea of divisional supervision, only with the method of handling it. Brown had done nothing to alter anything or replace the system; he and David compensated for it by visiting as many cities and offices as they could. Each visit was usually combined with speaking engagements arranged by the regional Director.[27]

David was deeply troubled that, although he had made concrete suggestions at the end of 1967 and again near the end of 1970, there was still no response. The problem continued without remedy. Added to that was David's distinct discomfort when the Board of Trustees, during the meeting at the end of November, asked about the status of the Staff Representative Advisory Council and was told that the SRAC was in a state of supended animation.[28] Discouragement was David's daily fare.

But then a cheerful thought chased away his gloomiest mood. He was going to have dinner with Lili at their favorite haunt, a lovely Italian restaurant where the waiters, who knew them by sight, responded to the arrival of these two lovers with the offer of a secluded table and a bottle of their best Lambrusco. There was a ritual for these evenings—two different dinners shared and a shared tortoni for dessert. For a few hours David was away from his cares about both home and work. He knew that Lili made a great effort to distract him and to be amusing. Her lighthearted subterfuge was a success as far as he was concerned. He quite frankly enjoyed the way other men looked at her when she came in, and laughed when she told him after his late arrival one evening about the Texan who refused to believe that she was waiting for someone else.

Because he remembered her feelings, voiced years before, that if she married it would be to a Jewish man, he did not feel it wise to discuss too soon the future and his plans for their marriage. Time took care of that matter for them. Lili, always practical and experienced as a single parent, was very aware of his responsibilities and limitations regarding his children. More and more he found himself asking for and getting some very sound advice about rearing the two girls still at home with him. They began to talk about his plans to enlarge the house, with a view to a place for the older children if they should visit. He also found it easy to talk about his work because so few explanations were needed. From her four years on the staff at NCCJ, Lili knew the entire cast of characters. Her quiet, astute evaluations were often very close to the mark, and she often supplied a truly intuitive point of view that he found, on reflection, to be very helpful in making decisions.

Although she was exciting to him mentally and physically, the quality he valued most was her serenity—which made him feel rested at the end of even the most frustrating and difficult day. One evening he asked if she would visit his home and meet his children. She replied that it might be fun. The following Saturday evening she arrived, dressed in a black velvet dress with white ruffles.

What followed afterwards endeared her to him because he saw a side of her that had nothing to do with the glamorous career woman he knew as Lili Reiss.

David introduced Lili to the small scrap of humanity that was his five year old, and then stated it was time for them to leave for the restaurant to have dinner. Ann, his older daughter, was to return to baby-sit for the evening. Lili looked up and asked, in a deceptively soft voice, if the child had been given her dinner and if she had had a bath. David guessed not. Lili then smiled and asked him to make the reservation for an hour-and-a-half later. She took the little girl's hand and asked for directions to the bathroom. A few minutes later David was watching Lili in her velvet dress, ruffles rolled away from the bath water, on her knees in front of the bathtub, bathing his child. He noticed that she held her head very high, a common gesture when she was disturbed, and also that she impatiently brushed away a tear. After asking for the little girl's nightgown, Lili handed it to David with the request that he dress her for the night while she went to the kitchen to see what was available for the child's dinner. A few minutes later, when David and Ellen Cleve came into the kitchen, they found a place set and a simple meal prepared. When David commented that the girls did not eat salad, Lili smiled and suggested that he walk in the garden for a few minutes. On his return, the salad along with the rest of the dinner had disappeared from Ellen Cleve's plate. Small Ellen was chattering away about how good it was. David could scarcely believe his ears; it usually took an act of Congress to make this child touch a vegetable. He was a veteran of many a lost battle in that department. Ann arrived to baby-sit, and David drove off with the enigmatic, glamorous, miracle-working Lili beside him. He wanted to know her secret.

"Well, if you must know," she said, "it goes something like this: A bumble bee has never heard that, according to engineers, it cannot fly. I have never heard that little children decide whether or not they are to eat vegetables. I just assume that they do, and then they assume it too." When Ann heard the story, she whispered to David in an awed voice, "She must be a magic lady." David was inclined to agree, for more than one reason.

When summer came again, the old house became a beehive of activity. The children and their friends were bribed by Lili's delicious meals to try their hand at cleaning and painting. The house was given a coat of white paint from cellar to third floor attic playroom. Lili asked David if she could bring her mother to visit the family and the house. David knew it was time for this if he planned to marry Lili, as they would have to ask her blessing.

In talking about this, Lili told David that she was having serious misgivings about their marriage because she feared it might adversely affect his career. She felt that his work and his influence were too important to jeopardize. She had fretted constantly about this all during their courtship. She pointed out that not only would he be the first Catholic president of the NCCJ, but he would be adding the additional liability of being a Catholic married to a Jew. David's answer was succinct. He told her he loved her, and if it meant losing his shot at the job he had set his heart on, then it would be lost. His language was inelegant, but Lili still got the message. He said, "I love you and if I lose the chance to be President because I marry you, then the hell with the job!"

Lili accepted his verdict and went on to tell David that she planned to ask her mother, a decorator, to redo the entire house. For weeks thereafter, David came home to find swatches of material in various rooms and mysterious talk about colors and floor plans.

David and Rachel, Lili's mother, immediately formed a bond, for they were both deeply religious. Momma was at a loss to know why David should not become a Jew. They spent many hours discussing it until Lili would laughingly intervene, as she knew that David was too polite to voice his objections. Momma accepted the inevitable graciously and loved David as a son. He watched her with admiration as she transformed the house with her gifted hands. Finished, the formerly gloomy house resembled nothing so much as a spring garden transplanted to each room. It was a wonderful summer for the entire family; in rebuilding the house, they had also built a new family. An ecumenical family.

The children helped. Larry brought his Southampton College friends to paint and plaster and picnic on the lawn. The house resembled a dormitory, complete with music. Ann's high school pals busily painted woodwork, radiators, and doors. Ellen Miriam and Marty helped in their time off from work and the Air Force. Small Ellen Cleve, not to be outdone, brought her friends who were kept busy fetching and carrying. David supervised while Lili and Grandma Ray, as the children called her, cooked delicious food which many

of the children had never had before. They took to calling Lili their
Jewish Mother and quickly learned to love her potato pancakes and
blintzes. The next spring everyone helped prepare for the Seder,
under Grandma Ray's direction in the kitchen. One was set to grat-
ing potatoes for the potato pancakes and potato kugel, another to
peeling apples for the charoses. Questions about this special meal
were the order of the day. That evening, with the table set in the
traditional holiday finery, Grandma produced the matzo cover she
had embroidered as a gift for the new family. David donned a skull
cap and prayer shawl, and Larry sat beside him on his right and
Marty on his left, to help him through the Passover Service—while
Lili sat with the three girls and Grandma close to the dining room
door. There they could make sure the food would be passed quickly
and quietly. The following weekend Grandma helped Lili prepare
Easter dinner, served after the Catholic half of the family returned
from Mass.

Summer came and the days went by uneventfully. The house was
finished, and David and Lili could enjoy some moments of well-
earned rest. Suddenly David was startled to see that she looked very
tired and thin. Her schedule during the past few months had been
grueling. She had been looking after his home as well as her own,
her family and his, and her job as well. Often she stopped by during
the week, and this meant a commute of two hours. Her weekends
for months were spent cooking for the "crews" of young people who
were helping them with the house. Often when he was away, she
took care of his grocery and milk bills, and other such details involved in running a household.

David said abruptly, "I think we should get married on Tuesday."
Lili looked up and queried quietly, "Why Tuesday?" David answered, "Because I have to be in the office on Monday." She threw
her head back and laughed until the tears rolled down her cheeks;
and finally, seeing the look of bewilderment all over his face, she
managed to gasp, "My, how romantic!" Immediately David realized
he should have arranged his proposal quite differently. Fortunately,
there had been enough high adventure and romance in their relationship to make his rather shamefaced apologies superfluous.

"Anyway, it will make the milkman very happy to see us married." It was David's turn to be amazed. What did the milkman have
to do with their marriage plans? Lili reminded him that she had been
in charge of paying his household bills for months, since his work
left so little time for such chores. He had given her the necessary
money, and she had paid with her checks. This thoroughly confused

the milkman, who each week would look at her when she paid the bill and say, "Mrs. Hyatt?" Lili would reply, "Not yet." He would leave, crestfallen. The following weekend Lili gleefully reported the milkman's response when they went through their usual little exchange. "Mrs. Hyatt?" he queried. "Yes," she replied; and then, Lili said, he gave a huge sigh of relief and responded, "Thank God!"

David felt the milkman's relief was shared by all the neighbors—who had come to enjoy the sight of the family picnicking on the lawn and Lili moving back and forth with trays of food. It had been a long time since anyone had used his carefully tended lawn. David was sure all the neighbors had hoped that Lili would stay, because of their concern for his motherless household—especially with his many absences on business. It was too small a community for people not to notice such things. People responded to the marriage of David and Lili with friendly invitations, which confirmed his thoughts. They liked Lili and admired her. She had changed the sad, silent house into a happy home.

David was to learn that the transition from "magic lady" who visited on weekends to mother was not going to take place without a few bumps for Lili or for the girls. One evening when David returned to work, Lili had a rather disconcerting tale to tell. Small Ellen had returned from her first-grade class that afternoon and had walked around Lili as she was preparing dinner and kept peering up into her face. Lili waited a few minutes to see if the child would tire of that activity. When she did not, Lili asked her what was the matter. The child replied, "You look like everyone else. *What is this Jewish?*" Lili asked her if she really wanted to know. Once sure of this, Lili sat down with Ellen and, as she later related to David, simply said, "As I see it, the Christians accept Jesus Christ as their Messiah, and the Jews do not." Little Ellen sprang out of her chair and exclaimed, "Don't try to convert me to your religion!" Lili was aghast. In her orthodox Jewish upbringing she had been told often that forcible conversion to Christianity had been the lot of the Jews. Therefore, it was not only not her intention, but it would actually upset her deeply, that such a suggestion could even come to the child's mind. David knew that this had been one of her deep concerns during their courtship. She had insisted on regular long conversations with a learned, scholarly Catholic priest so that she could properly rear his children without compromising her own convictions.

David soothed her and said he would speak to the child. But he could see Lili was shaken. When he explained that the last thing on

Lili's agenda was anyone's conversion, all settled into a serene routine, with Ellen Cleve going to church each Sunday morning, sent there by a happy Lili.

During the months after Ricky's death, under the care of David and the housekeeper, the children had been given so much freedom that it took a few months before Lili was able to establish some ground rules. As she told David so often, when she suggested a change, she was greeted with, "My mother did not do it that way." Rather than challenge these statements with the smaller girl, she felt it better to ask just exactly how Ricky did do it. She would make her changes a bit later. David blessed her for her understanding of the human heart. He noticed that she asked the children to call her Lili, as did her natural children. That made for another easier transition. For all her maturity, she had a girlish quality that made it possible for her, at forty-five, to adjust to this not-so-easy situation.

The second girl, Ann, had been forced into making decisions in his absence far beyond her years, and she was happy to resume her adolescence and turn the problems over to Lili. But when Lili insisted on fewer hours on the telephone, and more hours studying away from the phone in the lovely study created for Ann outside her bedroom, Ann balked. David saw that they were on a collision course. Lili was concerned, since it was Ann's junior year in high school, that her marks be good enough to go to college if she chose that direction. Ann wanted to chatter and gossip with her friends, because to her, at sixteen, it seemed more relevant. Studying for her was a "drag." David and Lili discussed the matter, but he did not interfere. Lili felt that a lot of ground, lost while Ann was trying to fill a grown woman's role in the household, had to be made up that school year. She proposed that Ann go to summer school and do more reading. Ann felt her autonomy was being taken away, and reacted accordingly. Lili said she could not allow Ann to use her study periods at school for riding around the village in her friends' cars. Ann grew still angrier. David was pleased to see Lili hold her ground, but Lili found this tug-of-war very wearing. Her natural children were past this stage in their development. Knowing how much it meant to David, Lili persisted, but took no pleasure in it. Ann's good progress was Lili's reward. David thought how good a role model Lili was for Ann, in her loving and caring for this new family with such devotion, creating such a beautiful home, and expressing such intellectual interests, musical talent, and good business sense. He thanked his Creator for his good fortune. His life was complete, his children protected and cared for, and he could once more turn his mind to his beloved mission. And it needed his attention desperately.

Daily letters and phone calls from the field staff reporting acute distress came to his attention. From all over the country news came to him of good people losing interest out of a feeling that their efforts were unnoticed and unappreciated. The financial rewards of the work were always slender, but beyond that many felt that the simple recognition of a job well done was the primary lack. Even that reward was not forthcoming.[29] David responded to this problem with a Confidential Staff Bulletin which warmly congratulated the staff who, despite the recession, had done a splendid job of gaining support for the NCCJ program.[30] He encouraged them by issuing information bulletins that served as a special recognition for good program development and for gaining funding for the needed program over and above the usual income sources.[31]

Lili suggested that as a means of improving morale he invite the staff from the surrounding states to dinner at their home. She thought it would make possible a warm, informal gathering of the staff. He looked at her, dubious, because the work of feeding thirty people at one time would be difficult enough. However, she was proposing two weekends, one after the other, so that all the staff would be included. Finally, she persuaded him that she could do it under the trees on their rustic patio.

The two dinners proved to be memorable for their charm, and they did indeed lift morale. Lili and the children were cook and waitresses, and created almost a picnic atmosphere. Lili, as a former staff member, understood the mood of the staff, and without saying anything David noticed she made them feel that she and David cared about them. The beautiful tables, set with china, silver and flowers there under the trees, spoke more eloquently than any words. David could see that all this care was much appreciated by the guests.

Winter came, the holidays were warm, and the family gathered in. The old house and David's heart were full. He came home from work and found Lili and the children wrapping pine garlands around the old winding staircase. The house smelled like a pine forest. The mantel was covered with cotton and miniature Santas and sleighs, gnomes, and other Christmas delights. Lili, David could see, was busy making new family traditions. Christmas Eve, after singing the carols—with Lili at the piano that she had brought with her to the house—the children announced a play that had been in secret rehearsals for months. The play depicted the Hyatt household as

Camelot. King Arthur was obviously modeled after David and Guin-
evere after Lili. Ann was Merlin, called Merlina, and Larry was Sir
Laughs-a-Lot. Little Wisp was added to give Ellen Cleve a part. The
music was taken from the musical, but the words were cleverly
composed by Marty. David's eyes filled with tears, and he could see
that Lili had turned away and was blowing her nose to hide hers.
Since she and David were the only audience, they laughed and cried
enough for a crowd.

After the holiday was over and David returned to work, he received word that Dr. Brown was retiring and that the Board was
considering his candidacy for President of NCCJ.[32] He saw a wonderful end ahead to this difficult time he had passed through.

13

The Middle East: "The Man Who Was Not Surprised by the Security Council"

♭

As David sat at his desk the first week of the new year of 1972, thinking over the challenge ahead, he was well aware that, although he was being considered seriously for the presidency of the Conference, many other staff members felt equally qualified for the post. Wanting to avoid any thought that his interest in the position was based on his own ego needs, he had taken the trouble to share his thoughts late in 1971 with George Christopher, the Eastern Orthodox Co-chairman of NCCJ. This was in response to Christopher's letter asking him about his interest in being considered for the NCCJ presidency:

> *Being blessed with a wonderful wife and family and having a bent for finding ways to be useful wherever I am, I could live happily in the years ahead without the NCCJ presidency, and I have no doubt I could find another useful post outside the NCCJ should a change of administration require it. But I would like the chance to move the NCCJ to new and greater heights, and I think as President I would have the knowledge, the down-to-earth "savvy" and the common sense and the toughness and drive and enthusiasm to get the very best out of our staff and the wisest counsel and strongest possible support out of our lay leadership.*

In another paragraph he spelled out the role of the President as he saw it:

> *The President's role in all of this, as I see it, is that of a strong leader—but a behind-the-scenes, catalytic leader—who puts the*

*job to be done ahead of his place in the spotlight. . . . The spotlight
belongs to the lay leaders; they are the strength of the NCCJ and
the President is their chief executive officer, managing the organization in their behalf and in behalf of all its supporters.*

He also felt he had to address what, in his opinion, was the most
crucial problem facing the NCCJ at that point in its history—a de-
moralized and divided staff:

*NCCJ has some internal personnel problems, but I am firmly con-
vinced that they can be healed. I have the finest of relations with
my colleagues in the field—they are, in truth, after 17¼ years, my
warmest, closest friends—and I firmly believe that the difference
between "the administration" and the staff can be ameliorated.
Closer and more understanding supervision is needed, greater communication and "dialogue" must be practiced internally as well as
in our programs for outside consumption, and mutual trust must
be developed. . . .*

He also deemed it important to emphasize that he had served three
NCCJ presidents.

*During my nearly 18 years with NCCJ, I have done my utmost to
help three Presidents make the National Conference possible, advising on policy and trying to strengthen leadership, public relations, fund-raising and program. . . .*[33]

David learned that the frustration level of the staff had reached
the pitch where they felt driven to organize a union, office by office.
The news made him heartsick, but not because he was anti-union;
in fact, all his life he had been pro-union. One of his college heroes
had been Philip Murray, head of the Steelworkers and founder of
the C.I.O. David's Actors Equity and American Federation of Radio
and Television Artists (AFTRA) union cards had insured him decent
wages and other important protection during his acting days. He
believed in the principles of trade unions. But he felt strongly that
a union in an organization dedicated to better human relations was
not the proper means to insure internal human relations and com-
munications. He thought: "We tell others how to act, how about
trying it ourselves? The 120 about-to-be unionized NCCJ professionals are actually key members of the management team; we are
all equals and the President should be simply chief among equals."
But, he realized, with Brown in his present frame of mind, it was
hopeless to pursue that line of reasoning.

David perceived that there was one avenue left open that might head off a hardening of the staff discontent into rage. It was possible to arrange a long-overdue staff conference. When he introduced the subject to President Brown, the latter cited finances as a reason for *not* holding a staff conference. David then polled the staff and gained their agreement that the conference would be arranged in the most economical way possible, with each office bearing the expense to some degree. Faced with the negation of his reasons for objecting on financial grounds, Brown reluctantly agreed to the staff conference. On February 17th David was able to send a memo giving a definite date for the conference at the end of March. The theme was to be "NCCJ in the Next Decade."

At home Lili was frantically packing her bags and urging David to do the same. In a few days they were to leave for Israel where, as guests of the government, they would tour the country and learn about its problems. Since the Six-Day War in the Middle East, David had seen strong indications that Christian-Jewish relations in the United States had been adversely affected by this Arab-Israeli conflict. Therefore he wanted to learn firsthand as much as possible about the problem—with the view to expanding the program of NCCJ in this vital area of Christian-Jewish understanding. It was gratifying that the government of Israel had taken into account how much he relied on Lili's experience and judgment, and had extended an invitation to her as well.

The two of them were a team in all aspects of their lives together. He appreciated Lili's deep involvement in his work because he so often brought problems home. While she did not provide solutions, just discussing them with someone whose discretion he could count on was a great support. He was well aware that many wives would have objected to so much talk of work-related problems during time reserved for private living. Lili, because she had been an NCCJ Director, knew the NCCJ was not just a job, but a way of life requiring full dedication.

After a ten-hour plane flight they arrived in Israel. Their itinerary, planned by the Israeli government in consultation with them, included discussions with important key political, religious, and educational leaders, as well as a survey of Israel's social, economic, and interreligious problems. The Israeli government considered them an ecumenical team. Since David was not only Executive Vice-President of the NCCJ, but also reappointed to serve another three-year term on the U.S. Commission for UNESCO—for which he was that body's Human Rights Committee Chairman[34]—great pains were taken to give them access to and time with the persons who could aid their understanding of the complex issues and problems. David was especially pleased that the Israeli government made such an effort to arrange meetings with Arab leaders in Israel as well as with Israelis.

Since David had seen the Holy Land only very briefly on a three-day leave in 1942, while serving as an ambulance driver with the British Eighth Army, he was particularly impressed and indeed often amazed by what he now saw and heard in 1972—30 years later. When he and Lili stayed at Kibbutz Kfar Blum, they saw, in the orchards and farms developed by the kibbutz, the results of nine-teen years of spartan communal life under the guns of Palestinian troops across the Lebanese border. The night before their arrival at Kfar Blum, terrorists had crossed the border from Lebanon and murdered three Israelis. Israeli soldiers had retaliated, crossing into Lebanon and emptying twenty houses before blowing them up. That night, when they were to go to sleep, their hosts asked if they preferred to sleep in the bomb shelters since there might be katusha shelling in the night. When David consulted Lili, she replied, "No, thank you, we'll sleep in our room tonight." David was always amused by this fragile, hothouse flower of his. She needed her secure, safe surroundings in order to survive; yet she cheerfully packed her bags and followed him wherever his work took him, often sleeping in hotels that did not meet her standards of cleanli-ness, and tonight sleeping with him under the guns of the Palestini-ans. He had to hand it to her. At bedtime she picked up her tousled golden head from the pillow to be kissed goodnight and inquired, "See you in the morning?" With an impish grin she closed her eyes and drifted immediately off to sleep. He had a restless night, worry-ing about her safety, but he was pleased to see that she woke at 5 A.M. ready for whatever the day would bring. "She is indeed a child of her people," he thought.

When they came down from the Golan Heights (a mountain pinnacle from which, until the Israelis captured it, the Syrians had periodically shelled the Israelis in the valley below) David read in the Jerusalem *Post* that the Lebanese Ambassador to the United Nations had called upon the Security Council to condemn Israel's "incursion" across the border. David was incensed to learn that the Security Council, although it did not condemn the killing of inno-cent Israelis by Arab terrorists, had moved that Israel must with-draw from Lebanon—which it already had. He was terribly disturbed by this double standard of morality in the U.N. once again, and seemingly always, imposed upon Israel. He was quite surprised to discover that the Israelis were not at all concerned about the behavior or decisions of the Security Council; they expected it.[35]

David and Lili, with twenty-five American newsmen and broadcasters who were part of a journalists' seminar sponsored by the American Zionist Federation, were privileged to meet the Israeli Foreign Minister, Abba Eban. Eban made it clear at that meeting that Israel had no intention of giving up Jerusalem, or the Sinai Desert, or Golan Heights—the latter two serving as buffers against Israel's enemies. David's inner response was that if the day ever came when the U.N. had an effective peace-keeping force, then consideration could be given to making the Sinai buffer a demilitarized zone under U.N. jurisdiction.[36] David found it stimulating and in some cases very revealing to speak after that meeting with news media people from all over the United States. It gave much food for thought.

Other experiences followed in each of the eighteen-hour days that followed. David was quite concerned about Lili because the pace was more than enough to tire *him*, but to his relief she kept up with all the activities. They visited factories where Jews and Arabs worked together productively. Many of the Arabs crossed the Allenby Bridge on the Jordanian border each morning in order to get to work. David was so heartened by this that he asked, "With all the hostilities surrounding Israel, how is this phenomenon possible?" The Arab factory manager shrugged, smiled, and answered simply, "Life is stronger than politics." David commented that this steady stream of Arabs coming into Israel every day to earn good wages, to attain better living standards for themselves and their families, was a healthy indicator for the future of better Arab-Israeli relations.[37]

David was most interested when they met new immigrants from western Europe and the Arab countries. At an Absorption Center in Haifa, he asked an Iraqi refugee why he had come to Israel. The man replied quietly, "To escape hunger, persecution, and hanging."[38] He learned from a recent immigrant from Russia that he and other Russian Jews credited political pressure aroused by Americans for the willingness of Soviet authorities to let him and others like him leave the Soviet Union and emigrate to Israel. David was told that 10,000 had escaped Soviet tyranny that year.[39] He was amazed to learn that Israel managed to keep ahead of its immense refugee problem, and that, since 1948, the country had absorbed nearly 1.5 million Jews from all parts of the world.[40] For Lili, it was apparent to David, all these conversations had an immediacy because of the history of her own family. When they were in Tel Aviv, Lili and

David had visited the remnant of her Austrian family: one woman
and her family. During the entire trip Lili did not talk very much,
but David sensed she was feeling it very deeply. He was as well,
because in this beautiful, magic land that was the spiritual home of
three faiths, the entire tragic history of the Jews came to his attention
in a way it never had before. He saw Israel as an outpost, a bastion
of freedom—not only for Jews, but as an example for peoples everywhere.

When they returned from the east bank of the Suez Canal—with
its sand-bagged trenches, concrete bunkers, underground barracks,
and barbed wire entanglements, all of which reminded David of a
set from a World War I movie—they were very concerned and
anxious to find a cable awaiting them in their Jerusalem hotel. Their
daughter Ann had undergone surgery for acute appendicitis. They
got to the airport in record time, gratefully bade their hosts goodbye,
and departed for home. They left feeling that Israel was a land under
siege.

On his return, in addition to his speaking engagements and supervisory duties, David plunged into the work of making the staff
conference scheduled for the end of March into a useful instrument
for resolving the problems faced by the staff and administration of
NCCJ. Given the agitated feelings and discontent of the staff, he was
determined that every minute of the conference would be positive
and that nothing would occur to turn it into a large "gripe" session.
Program thrusts had to be shared. Because time was limited, he
asked staff members to accept the suggestion of the Bronx-West-
chester Director to outline and put into written form one program
that they wished to share with other Directors. Because David was
particularly concerned with new directions and innovative program
techniques, he asked the committee to build into the program a
number of "how-to-do-it" sessions in both the fund-raising and
program areas, so that new staff Directors could have badly-needed
training sessions. He also pressed for the allotment of time for giving
inspiration and new vision for the decade ahead. It saddened him
that so many people working with the Conference at that time
found the vision dimming. Although he could understand fully why
it was happening, it was painful nonetheless.

During the days after their return from Israel, Lili had assured him
every evening that Ann was improving. At the end of the month,
when they had to leave for Philadelphia and the staff conference,
Lili felt she could safely leave the children and accompany him.

During their last evening there, Lili mentioned to David that she felt his prodigious effort had paid off, that she sensed a change in the people she had spoken to. Early in April David began to receive letters bearing out her impression. The staff did not seem to remember the run-down condition of the hotel or its lack of comfort; instead the spirit of the program remained with them. Two comments restored David's soul for the next few days: "This staff conference surpassed all others to date . . . it was stimulating, refreshing, and exciting. An investment well spent, and very necessary for morale." Since the writer was Ruth Buchman of Hartford, Connecticut, a staff member for thirty years, David attributed real significance to it. The other comment, from Philip Libby, Jr., of Houston, Texas, reinforced his whole aim for the training program. Libby wrote:

> If one should lose something of the vision of what NCCJ is and does, let him attend a National Staff Conference. If he fears the parochialism of being centered in one part of our nation's geography, let him attend a National Staff Conference. The result for me is a re-freshing of my vision in our national scope, and an enlivening of my enthusiasm for its work in my assigned region.

Perry Lusk of Oklahoma City, Oklahoma, in his praise of the Conference, cited David's third reason for mounting the effort to do the training program. "This is bound to re-kindle a sense of common commitment and unity which is necessary to strengthen NCCJ in frustrating times such as these. Your leadership, along with other members of the Planning Committee, enhanced the possibility of these kinds of results."[41]

At the end of May the whole world was stunned by the atrocity in the Tel Aviv airport when 25 persons were killed and 76 wounded by 3 Japanese gunmen acting on behalf of Arab guerillas harbored in Lebanon. David wrote to all his NCCJ Board members that it was clear to him that the organization had to intensify its program on Christian-Jewish relations, particularly as affected by the Arab-Israeli conflict. He was convinced that internal education of both the staff and the Board was essential before NCCJ staff could educate the communities they served. Terrorism was a growing threat to peaceful solutions to difficult and sensitive interreligious problems. He had to stimulate people within NCCJ to provide solutions.

In September the world once more was faced with terrorist activity against Israel and its people. This time it was the murder of eleven Israelis at the Munich Olympic Games. These terrorist acts were such a regular occurrence in 1972 that Gabriel Stern, Religious News

Service correspondent in Jerusalem, sent to David a letter with an article that he had done on the Hyatts in *Al Hashimar*. The headline of the article, "The Man Who Was Not Surprised by the Security Council,"[42] was most apt, for once again David experienced no surprise, only bafflement, at the U.N. condemnation of the Israeli retaliation. He saw this action as indicative of a double standard of morality in the United Nations. This approach was completely antithetical to David Hyatt's own ethical standards and actions.

All during the first few months of 1972, David's attention was drawn to an awareness of being at a crossroads. For many years he had been moving towards a goal; now he would achieve it or lose a marvelous opportunity to live out his dream. The critical factor was to be chosen for President of NCCJ. By late May he knew that 62 letters had been received supporting his candidacy for this position. He was also aware that, despite his heroic efforts on behalf of the staff, many staff people confused his policies with those of Dr. Brown. Throughout his service in Brown's administration, David had pursued a policy of working through persuasion, even during the last few frustrating years. By June 28 he officially became President-elect; immediately the staff began to turn to him to solve their difficulties. Very aware of his superior's sensitivity and determined to maintain a decent, compassionate stance toward the outgoing chief executive of NCCJ, he refused to meet with the Staff Representative Advisory Committee in October of 1972, giving as his reason that

> there was only one President of the NCCJ, and, until I assume that responsibility, the SRAC by-laws do not make me a member of that group. Since I was never asked before, I see no reason at this point to attend, particularly since I am very sensitive about not usurping any of the prerogatives of the chief executive officer of the NCCJ until I have been legitimately given those powers.[43]

Concurrent with this refusal to elbow his way into power, David continued to work through the year with personnel managers from the private, public, and non-profit sectors to put together documentation to convince the Board of the need to change the entire salary structure of the NCCJ. The goal was to bring staff salaries into better alignment with professionals working at the same level in non-profit and government sectors. He wanted to preserve the talent in the NCCJ and attract more and better people to join the staff. It incensed him that in some cities sanitation workers were often substantially better paid than NCCJ professionals. While he understood that sanitation workers were vital to the health of a city, he also felt that the NCCJ professional was essential to the well-being of the entire community. Often the NCCJ structure in the community circumvented disaster. David recruited lay volunteers expert in personnel problems to serve on the Personnel Committee, and concurrently involved staff all over the country in the process. From this effort came a voluminous document covering potential salary ranges for NCCJ personnel comparable to salaries for teachers, school principals and superintendents with similar educational qualifications.[44] This document was sent to all NCCJ personnel because David was determined that, at the start of his term of office, salary changes were the first order of business. At the same time, being very practical, he knew that the staff would have to exercise tremendous efforts to raise the needed money. It would be his job to see to it that they succeeded in that effort.

He tried his best to help the entire staff understand that it was only a question of time before significant changes occurred; yet David discovered, to his dismay, that the press to unionize was continuing. In November it became clear that the staff intended to attend an NLRB hearing to obtain recognition for the union. They were unaware that the Executive Committee in late September had moved up his date for taking control to January of 1973. With a heavy heart he prepared to go into the NLRB hearing. At the last moment he received word that the hearing had been cancelled. Somehow word had gone out that he would assume all the duties of the chief executive officer in two months.

He met at lunch with Frank McGrath, who was to represent the staff at the hearing, and explained his position carefully, not wishing to mislead his colleagues about his plans and intentions. Apparently all the years of trust and friendship prevailed; David felt his plans for a better NCCJ could go forward without any divisiveness. He still believed that a union was not an appropriate method for the NCCJ to solve its internal problems. He had plans for a team composed of all NCCJ professionals and other staff, working together to find the needed solutions, to make the organization grow and prosper, and to be of the utmost value in the communities served by the organization.

That same evening when he and Lili talked over the day's events, he felt peaceful and hopeful—a rare and delightful sensation. He was happy to be taking the helm.

14

At the Helm

❦

As David moved on to fulfill his goals and commitments as President of the NCCJ, he encountered many roadblocks impeding the implementation of his vision of a more effective NCCJ and of better relationships among various ethnic, racial, and religious groups in the United States. But he forged ahead with a style which appeared effortless; few knew that David achieved this apparent ease by prodigious attention to details. Often this meant spending much of the night reviewing staff resumes, plotting and planning as a good corps commander would pore over maps of a terrain before a battle. This often earned Lili's disapproval because she had the old-fashioned idea that everyone needed eight hours of sleep daily! His methods worked, he often felt, because he genuinely liked people and believed in them. He understood the dissenters' reasons for their stance and wanted to enlist them on his team. He tried hard to find the strengths in people, and, sadly, when they were lacking, he would cast about for a way to compensate for the weakness he perceived. His method was to team up two people who could help each other grow.

Perceiving that his first task was to heal all the wounds of the past few years, he decided to meet with the rebel leaders in an informal, casual way while he was in Washington on UNESCO business. It proved to be a good beginning. David made two promises: first, that he would give the staff a voice by incorporating the National Staff Committee into the by-laws; and, second, that there would be a staff member with a vote on each working committee. Almost immediately David began plans for the formation of the President's Council—which would give managerial responsibility to the rebel leaders, thus channeling their energies into constructive thinking for the benefit of the NCCJ family. He also gave them an opportunity to create their own job descriptions, which he then circulated to the staff.

David was counting on the dissipation of distrust over a period of time to help him through the next tense period. At David's side during meetings were Lillian Block, Editor-in-Chief of Religious News Service, and Dr. Leonard Aries, Vice-President for Equal Opportunity Programing. Both had been in their posts for thirty years and had earned the veneration of the entire staff. This factor, combined with their ability to be scrupulously fair, totally informed, and invariably good-natured, moved the meetings along to successful conclusions.

One late winter evening at the St. Moritz Hotel in New York, David had gathered together the men he hoped would be regional field Directors and advisors to him in policy-making. As he outlined his plans, David asked them for advice and guidance, since, as he pointed out, he considered them NCCJ's foremost statesmen. Virgil Border, who, his advice ignored, had suffered for years in the Midwest, joked, "From revolutionary to statesman in such a quick jump. It makes my head swim." The rollicking laughter around the table relieved some of the tension. Virg had pointed up why these men found David's management style so difficult to digest.

It was David's intention to try to emulate his hero, Pope John XXIII, when he said that his goal as Pope for the Catholic Church was "to open a window and let in a little fresh air."[45] David felt that the NCCJ needed a little fresh air to move it into a new time in the world. It was difficult to put his ideas into words, but he expected his actions to communicate his message to his co-workers. The religious press reported some of his attitudes with headlines such as "NCCJ's President Has New Ideas."[46] Those outside the NCCJ apparently grasped his direction more quickly than those within.

In his efforts to reach the lay leadership, David asked in his inaugural address for a "non-silent, concerned majority"[47] to deal with the nation's problems. He added that this "new breed of Americans" would be men and women who cared about their fellow citizens, "ill clad, ill housed, without jobs and without hope," and were determined to change their situations. The concerned, dedicated Boards, inspired by David's pleas, responded quickly. Typical of those responses was one from Baltimore which did so much to fuel David's feeling that all he dreamed could indeed be accomplished. "Your approach to the functions of the Conference, your attitude with respect to its staff and lay members, and your obvious enthusiasm for the development of effective programming all bode well for the future."[48]

During all the pomp and ceremony of the beautiful inauguration ceremony and dinner at the Plaza Hotel in New York City, with all three of the previous NCCJ presidents alive and in attendance, small Ellen contributed a few moments of comic relief. Carefully watching her mother and father on the receiving line at the beginning of the evening, she quietly took her place beside her mother and began to greet people in a grand, grown-up manner, for all the world a miniature of Lili. She would extend her hand and say, "I am Ellen Hyatt. I am so happy you could join us." For a few moments Lili was unaware that this was happening but was mystified by very broad smiles on some people's faces as they circled off the receiving line. Then she looked over at her small helper, next at David, and burst into peals of laughter. David had some trouble keeping a decorous tone as he continued to greet guests. The older children, standing nearby, heard the sound of Lili's laughter and turned to David with questioning eyes. Then quietly they moved over to their small sister and spirited her away. David felt so proud of the two tall young men and two beautiful young women who completed his family. As he exchanged a brief glance with Lili, he saw there the same understanding, electricity and love that had been their early signal. For David it was a wonderful, full evening, with his hopes and dreams for his family and his desire to serve the world all gathered in the same room at the same time. Once more he thought, "God must have a design for my life," and a feeling of gratitude swept through his entire being.

The credibility gap that had developed in the previous administration made it imperative, in David's opinion, to keep his promises, as soon as practical, with respect to a National staff conference. He was determined to mount it as a National service to the field and to spare the regions from bearing the cost. It was also essential that he meet with small groups on a person-to-person basis before the larger staff conference. By July, having accomplished his second objective, he had a reading of what was needed and wanted by every section of the country.

Lili told him one evening that, as she was packing to go with him on another trip, small Ellen had watched her silently and finally asked, "Where are you going?" Lili wondered why the youngster never asked her father that question but seemed to accept his comings and goings. In fact, the child had gleefully announced at dinner one evening, "Oh good, Daddy is going to visit with us this weekend!" Lili's face was a study that evening, and she was very quiet. David knew that Lili was sending a message that perhaps more time was due the family; but he saw his dream—a unified, effective NCCJ—almost within his grasp. For the moment, the family would have to wait. Once again he was grateful to Lili for holding the fort in his absence, and on his return being happy, buoyant, and full of plans. She was understanding and patient, perhaps more so because she worked so often at his side. She also realized that many matters at NCCJ, during this delicately balanced period, must be worked out by David in person.

At this critical time David also offered the staff opportunities to grow in their understanding of critical program areas through a trip to Israel on a ten-day NCCJ seminar. (NCCJ was to pay the cost from donations which David helped to raise.) Twenty-five Directors could see firsthand the conditions in Israel and, at the same time, increase their skills for programming in the area of Christian-Jewish relations as they were affected by the Middle East crisis after the Yom Kippur War.[49] This caused some problems with the Executive Board; some members were still under the impression that sending trios of clergy in a single engine prop plane around the country to speak on toler- ance, as the NCCJ had done in the early 30's, was sufficient for a program of interfaith dialogue. A few Jewish Board members were also anti-Zionist members of the Council on Judaism. Therefore, David knew he had to continue to educate NCCJ from within. However, at the risk of losing touch with some dedicated NCCJ lay leaders, he persisted in bringing the staff education program into the 1970's. At the Board of Governors meeting, Ambassador Murphy, Catholic Co-chairman of NCCJ, began to question the wisdom of such staff education. David responded in defense of his thesis that Israel was a matter of conscience for the world and a reparation for the Holocaust. The Ambassador admitted during his presentation at the luncheon portion of the meeting that, while he was a consular officer in Munich in November 1921, his closest colleague was Paul Drey, a German employee of the American consulate general:

> But Paul Drey unwittingly misled me about one man and his group: Adolf Hitler. I recall the first Hitler meeting I attended with Paul; as I went out, he exclaimed: "How does this Austrian upstart dare to tell us Germans what to do? Paul and I later attended many more Nazi rallies in order to report this violent political phenome- non to the State Department. But when I asked Paul, "Do you think these agitators will ever get far?", he answered firmly, "Of course not! The German people are too intelligent to be taken in by such scamps!"[50]

Murphy made clear that he had maintained this attitude far too long.

Trips to all points of the United States made David's schedule hectic; nonetheless, he and Lili decided that they had to go to Vienna in May to meet with the International Consultative Committee of Organizations Working for Christian-Jewish Cooperation. This Committee was formally established at a meeting in Frankfurt am Main, Germany, in January 1962. The principal purpose was to provide for consultation between member organizations on matters of common concern in the field of Christian-Jewish relations. David had become increasingly aware that these matters could not be adequately understood except in an international setting. Lili's language skills proved valuable during the sessions of the Consultative Committee, but were truly indispensable when they requested permission to see the Schonau Palace Refugee Transit Camp, established for Soviet Jews fleeing to Israel. (The palace was a dilapidated old hunting lodge near the Hungarian border.)

When the Israeli Consul sent word that he could speak only German, Hebrew, and Yiddish—no English—David responded that he could speak only English but that his wife who spoke German and Yiddish possibly could interpret. Earlier Lili had promised to do this if needed, but had warned David that her vocabulary was limited. For added insurance, they took with them Monsignor A. C. Ramselaar, a Dutch priest and then President of the Consultative Committee, who spoke fluent German.

For two hours Lili, with occasional help from the Monsignor, painstakingly translated each man to the other. Exhausted, she turned to the Israeli Consul and said in German, "I may sound like a child, but I think like a woman." The urbane Consul replied in perfect English, "That is quite obvious, Madame." Lili's head went up high, her color even higher. The man had been monitoring her translations. As she told David later, the Consul was not going to risk making a mistake in English; he preferred that, if any mistakes were made, she would be the one to make them. David soothed her and said the important thing was that they had received permission to visit the camp.

Upon their return to the United States, David wrote about this experience which was so deeply moving for both Lili and him.

> *If any American could have seen these wretched, wonderful, hopeful people and talked to them as we did, he would come away with tears of pity, and then anger and outrage. . . . Mr. Brezhnev . . . was quoted as putting off American reporters who queried him about*

the status of the Jews in Russia with a cynical comment, "There is no Jewish problem, no Jewish question here. . . . Some of my closest friends from school days onward have been Jews." My wife and I, having talked to the Soviet emigrants at Schonau Palace outside Vienna, can bear witness that there are brutal, horrible, incredible Jewish problems, and that the ultimate goal of the Soviet Government is the total elimination of Judaism in Russia.[51]

The most notable response to this article came from Washington, D.C., from Rabbi Joshua O. Haberman, who wrote:

It is heartwarming in these days of crisis to hear your voice speak so clearly on behalf of freedom and humanity. We must stop the cancer of appeasement and opportunism before it is too late. Your repudiation of blackmail and terrorism lifts the spirit of all free and decent men. I am proud to be a member of the NCCJ.[52]

Before David and Lili left Vienna for home, David asked for formal admission of the NCCJ as a member of the Consultative Committee for Christian-Jewish Cooperation. The application was immediately, unanimously, and officially approved.[53]

On their return home, David's attention was drawn to those areas in the United States that were grappling with the problems of the Chicano or Mexican-American. Developing issues were tearing communities apart. David suggested to Lili that they go to the University of the Americas at Cholula, Puebla, in Mexico, to participate in a pioneer NCCJ workshop there, inaugurated by NCCJ Vice-President, Dr. J. Oscar Lee. They would spend three weeks with the NCCJ staff, along with teachers, social workers, and administrators from six states, learning what they could about the Mexican culture, history, and political structure. Once more Lili made arrangements for care of their home and children so that she could accompany him.

David was aware of a need to know more about the problems facing Mexican-Americans, so that he could continue to stimulate the staff into creating programs affecting the peaceful integration of Chicano families into communities where they had arrived as "stoop labor" for local farmers and had remained to become a part of the fabric of American life.

On their arrival in the interior, miles from Mexico City, David and Lili were appalled by the conditions of poverty and the discovery that in Mexico a child, performing poorly in the third grade, could be permanently expelled from school. In effect, this condemned that child to a life of illiteracy and chained him or her to the soil.

Lili could not comprehend or abide the lot of the Mexican woman. She told David that it would be very difficult for her to remain in an environment where she saw woman treated as beasts of burden and with so little respect. There would be small progress towards equality for anyone in that country, she told him, until the attitudes toward women changed. David agreed. He was distressed to see that Lili was fighting a losing battle with the microbes in the area. So much of the time she was distressed, physically and mentally. The contaminated water made her ill regularly, but she gamely got up each morning, attended classes and lectures, went on the field trips into archeological digs, talked to historians, sociologists, and family planners. The political scientists interested both of them, as they attempted to understand Mexican-style democracy. Every evening they did the required reading, then talked far into the night discussing program possibilities. Once more David was grateful for the partnership he was blessed with by his Creator. Lili seemed to thrive on the eighteen-hour days despite her frail constitution. She was gossamer, but gossamer mounted on a steel frame.

David returned home with a clearer understanding of why the Mexicans continued to pour into the United States, and risked and endured so much to be able to rear their children in the land that promised them a better future.

Over one weekend, as he reviewed the first few months of his presidency, David realized that he was faced with the same opportunity that faced his namesake, King David, Israel's most famous king, when he gained control of his kingdom. Instead of eliminating his former enemies, he gained the respect of nearly everyone by his magnanimity to his former foes. He gave them positions of trust. Likewise, David intended to make it his policy to employ persons on the basis of their skills and effectiveness, not because of friendship or loyalty to him. He knew there would be cynical people who would distrust his motives; however, he could only hope that in time most of the staff would come to understand that their contributions and creativity were valued and that a good working partnership based upon participatory democracy would become a reality.

Another urgent matter requiring a decision without hesitation was the need for a decent standard of living for the staff. In order to provide this, he knew he would possibly face several years of deficits. He would have to reorganize the Conference to the point where each office would show a financial gain for each year. He was also well aware that such a policy was not popular with most boards of non-profit agencies. Only if he managed to retain the respect of the Boards regarding his integrity, ability, and financial responsibility could he hope to retain the position he had worked for all of his adult life. He had to take that risk.

In early August, David, elated, hailed a landmark decision and congratulated the Elks on their convention mandate to drop a 105-year-old whites-only membership rule. He had always felt that social discrimination was one of the toughest and most poisonous forms of covert prejudice in the United States, and he was determined that the NCCJ would not rest until those cruel and insidious violations of human rights were finally eliminated. He equated those practices with the American Nazi Party and the KKK.[54] Previous Presidents of NCCJ had been overcautious about making statements and taking stands on issues publicly. David was determined that the NCCJ be clearly on record on the issues pertaining to its mission and work. While this stance often caused criticism from conservative Board members, he felt they would become accustomed to his style. He also hoped his style might attract people to the Boards who had not previously supported NCCJ because it appeared to have no convictions on vital issues. (To further this outreach, David spoke in forty cities across the country before that year was out.)

Fall came, and with it an explosion in the Middle East; on Yom Kippur, Egypt and Syria attacked Israel. David was shocked, and responded with his most impassioned plea, first in the newspapers and then in speeches. In Canada, at the annual Convention of the League for Human Rights, he said:

> I pledge to you that the National Conference of Christian and Jews—through its 70 regional offices throughout the United States and its 200 chapters, through hundreds of institutes and conferences and dialogues and discussion groups in every major city of the U.S.—will do its utmost to eliminate forever the ugly dinosaur of anti-Semitism and will also do its utmost to build bridges of understanding within the Christian community about the profound meaning to our Jewish brothers throughout the world, of Israel as a land and as a people and an essential part of the Jewish faith.
>
> The right of Israel to exist and to live in freedom and peace is absolutely irrevocable! The glorious "impossible dream" of a Jewish homeland for the oppressed and needy throughout the world must continue forever as a shining, inspiring reality! And men and women of good will throughout the world must now speak out with courage and force, and defend Israel's right to exist and to live in freedom and in peace!

I would like to close with the statement I issued on behalf of NCCJ immediately following the October 6th attack of Egypt and Syria against Israel. Here's what I said:

"In this tragic time when the very sovereignty of Israel and its right to exist is being threatened by attack, we express our deepest sympathy and strongest moral support to our Jewish brothers in America, in Israel and throughout the world.

"The present armed conflict in the Middle East constitutes the greatest peril for both Israelis and Arabs and, indeed, for the peace of mankind. We, therefore, strongly appeal for a cease-fire, trusting that both parties to the conflict will sit down to negotiate among themselves an enduring and just peace.

"As an organization of committed Christians and Jews, we express deep moral outrage that the attack on the State of Israel was launched on Yom Kippur, the day held most holy by the Jews. This assault is in itself to be deplored, but, especially on this holy day, it is a sacrilege that cannot be too strongly condemned.

"We reassert Israel's moral and juridical right to exist within secure boundaries, and no international rearrangements that emerge from the war ought to be allowed to jeopardize her existence. The emerging oil diplomacy, intensified by the domestic energy crisis, should have no place whatever in the determination of the policies of the United States toward the Middle East.

"Above all, we wish for peace. We pray that on this 25th anniversary of Israel's birth, there shall be made alive the shalom for which the world yearns."[55]

15

Shaping the Future—
NCCJ and ICCJ

Now that he had been President of the NCCJ for almost a year, David was experiencing the full significance of being head of an organization which reached into so many areas of American life— religion, race, social concerns, housing, education, women's needs, law enforcement, and jobs.

The impact of NCCJ on the international scene, by way of the Religious News Service and NCCJ's involvement with the International Council of Christians and Jews, continued as a source of pride for David. Earlier that year, at a meeting in Basel, Switzerland, he had finally persuaded the Executive Board of the International Consultative Committee of Organizations Working for Christian-Jewish Cooperation to change its name to the International Conference of Christians and Jews.[56]

The original, cumbersome name of the organization came largely in response to a warning issued by the Catholic Church to its members that they must not cooperate with an International Council of Christians and Jews. This statement sprang from the belief of the Catholic Church's hierarchy that the Council "was an 'indifferentist' organization which tended to ignore or minimize differences of religious faith and practice."[57] In 1947 there had been an abortive effort by NCCJ under the leadership of Everett R. Clinchy, then President of the Conference, to establish a World Council of Christians and Jews.[58] Because the European community was reluctant to accept American leadership, the attempt was a failure. By 1973, because of Vatican II, the climate had become more open and free in the Catholic Church, and there was no longer the need to worry about "further misunderstanding in Catholic circles."[59]

This major involvement at the international level notwithstanding, a look at David's mail at that time would have suggested that he, in fact, was spending most of his time answering individual requests for help. He read every letter—not just those concerned with large and complex issues, but also the many involving smaller, less spectacular matters that presented themselves to him on an almost daily basis. There were so many good people trying to get important projects off the ground, so many organizations where cooperation from the NCCJ was vital.

Some of the mail had piled up at the end of the previous year when he had been busy traveling, trying to cement the NCCJ into a single organization. Then, too, because of Lili's wise insistence, he had put work aside and spent the Christmas and New Year's holidays with his family. *Now* it was time to answer those letters!

The letter on the top of the pile, sent to him at the close of 1973, was from Benjamin Jaffe of the World Zionist Organization. It read:

> *I have no words to tell you how much we appreciate your effective action in the framework of the NCCJ during this Yom Kippur war. It's still too early to evaluate the various Christian reactions throughout the world, but it is very encouraging to us that friends like you did the maximum in this hour of destiny.*[60]

Elmer Winter, of the American Jewish Committee, wrote to ask if the NCCJ and AJC could work out program materials together. Neil McClusky, of Lehman College, wanted to thank David for an endorsement of the National Council on Religion in Public Education. Mr. Robert M. Neiman, a Board member from California, commended David for his letter of protest to John Scali concerning Mr. Yasir Arafat's participation in the General Assembly of the United Nations. While David had agreed with Mr. Scali that there was a need for understanding and airing the real concerns and yearnings for justice of the Palestinian people, he was also aware that Arafat headed a terrorist organization. Bearing this out, Mr. Arafat had appeared at that peaceful world assembly with a pistol strapped to his hip, and then equated Zionism with racism. David was outraged by the entire proceeding; he not only protested but induced 90% of the NCCJ offices to make a regional response. Mr. Neiman's letter concluded: "Thank you for putting the National Conference on record in this matter."[61]

Ken Kershaw of the Omaha office wrote: "I just read your 3/6/74 speech. I am moved, if not 'touched' by it—and pleased to be one of your associates." David was touched himself that a busy staff person had taken the time to read his speech, given in response to receiving the John F. Kennedy Brotherhood Award of the Jewish War Veterans. He wondered if Ken was responding in particular to his strong statement on the attitudes of the Christian bureaucracies vis-a-vis Israel, which read:

> And while many individual Christians have spoken out courageously in behalf of Israel since the Yom Kippur War, we have also heard a number of the Christian bureaucracies express, in mealymouthed platitudes, their complete misunderstanding and total ignorance of the profound meaning of Israel as a land and as a people and as an essential part of the Jewish faith to Jews throughout the world.[62]

The NCCJ had been characterized in the past as an organization content to talk rather than act. This criticism rankled sometimes, and David felt impelled to defend the NCCJ's methods. He couched one of these defense statements in an address to a youth forum in 1974. Young people in particular leveled this criticism at the Conference, as they were still being strongly influenced by the climate of activism left over from the sixties. The general attitude among the young was that no point had been made in a presentation if it did not include a demonstration. Knowing all this, David, looking at the eager faces massed below him, opened his talk with a prayer in his heart.

> That's our method: talk—talk that leads to action. And I want you to know that that kind of talk can change the world. Let me give you an example. We held an interreligious, interracial travel seminar back in 1959 that took a group of Blacks and Whites, Protestants, Catholics and Jews all over Europe and the Middle East. Two young men on that travel seminar were a brilliant and dedicated Rabbi named Israel Mowshowitz and a handsome, dynamic Black minister, the Reverend James Robinson. During their three weeks together, out of their long talks, they conceived the idea of a work program for youth called "Operation African Crossroads"—which within the next year brought more than a hundred dedicated young people like you from the U.S. over to Africa, to work for four weeks during the summer on specific work projects like erecting new schools, putting up dams, draining swamps, and building barns and houses.

The program still goes on every summer. But in 1961, President Kennedy heard about it, and, using "Operation Africa Crossroads" as a model, established the Peace Corps, which, as you know, has sent hundreds of thousands of young people like you to all parts of the world to help their brothers.

That's what talk can do; it can change the world.[63]

David knew that changes were needed in the world of the NCCJ and that he must effect them through persuasive talks with the Board. Because he believed it essential that the National Staff Committee become a permanent part of the NCCJ structure, David wanted to include it as one of the standing committees functioning within the Conference. To achieve this, David needed to convince the Board to change the by-laws to allow for the inclusion of the new committee. The next step was getting the Board to agree to a National Staff Committee consisting of nine members—eight staff members, each elected to a two-year term, plus the President. Its major purpose would be to solicit and propose to the President for appropriate action all staff recommendations dealing with matters of general staff concern. In addition, one National Staff Committee member would maintain a vote on each of the other official functional committees of the NCCJ.

Serious differences between the staff and the President were to be resolved by a three-member fact-finding body, one member selected by the Staff Committee, one by the President, and one jointly. If this body could not resolve the difference, its findings and recommendations were to be presented to the Executive Board for resolution.

David was well-satisfied with what he had accomplished. He believed that he had assured the staff a permanent and fair vehicle for improving the NCCJ. He knew the process of ratification would take some time, but he had obtained the agreement of all the key board members and was confident the measure would pass.[64] On several occasions, as an experiment, he had called National Staff Committee meetings and had also convened the group he intended to have serve as the President's Council. These meetings proved workable and productive.

Offsetting the tumult and tensions that David often encountered in the total spectrum of his work with NCCJ was the consistent warmth and inviting restfulness of his home. All the children seemed to be following paths that would lead them into positive growth. Marty, Ellie, and Ann were finishing their undergraduate work. Larry was studying at New York University's Institute for Rehabilitative Medicine, and Ellen, the youngest and still in elementary school, was learning to play the flute and the piano under Lili's watchful eye.

On weekends the children and their friends filled all the nooks and crannies of the old house. David would often find Marty and Larry playing chess for hours on end in the living room. He sensed Lili's content; with her family around her, her face shone even during the busy or hectic moments. The usually stormy Caroline also seemed to have found a quiet harbor on her miniature ranch in California. A grandson had arrived in the family, and Caroline seemed to find happiness and fulfillment in caring for her child. She was also working with other young men and women to create an alternate school in the small town where they lived. David hoped that this new-found interest would be pursued formally in a university.

Because she wanted David to be free to enjoy his family in his precious, limited times at home, Lili managed, with the help of Tom Williams, handyman and gardener, to run the house and garden without involving David at all. She had slowly assumed responsibility for so many facets of their lives. Anything that took time from his work she had gently persuaded him she could manage. He was always astounded that this gentle, kindly woman operated in a very businesslike manner, whether she was apportioning the family resources, getting the children to do their schoolwork, or keeping peace when storm clouds of teenage rebellion threatened. She was the pendulum that kept the clock of his home running. In years past he had the unfortunate experience of attempting to do what she was doing, and understood that what appeared to be effortless was the result of careful planning and very hard work.

That same year, on a lovely July 4th holiday afternoon, David was sitting under the trees on the patio, thinking about current plans at NCCJ. Lili gently chided him for thinking about his work every waking minute; she wanted him to savor this beautiful day. David, pleased with plans for the coming year, went on to talk with her about the major conference on "The Holocaust and Its Meaning for Our Times" which he had encouraged International Council to mount. After a year-and-a-half with the ICCJ, he had provided important program input; but this was to be the first conference on the Holocaust to be held on German soil—a real landmark. Dr. Bernhard Olsen, NCCJ Director of Interreligious Affairs, together with Dr. Franklin H. Littell, the oustanding pioneer leader of programming on the Holocaust in the U.S., planned to work with the twelve member nations to implement the conference. David was concerned with the means for giving a grant of $10,000 as the NCCJ's contribution towards the project; the other nations would give some support, and the German government would supply the remainder of the funds necessary for a successful program. Although the conference was still a year away, the plans were progressing smoothly.

Lili's many questions about the plans and people involved, along with many previous conversations, indicated to David the depth of her interest and satisfaction in the planned conference. The work of Rabbi Peter Levinson especially stimulated her. A naturalized American citizen, Rabbi Levinson had returned to Germany to be the spiritual leader of the remnant of the Jewish community there. As the details of the meeting advanced through the final stages and included the German Councils for the conference, David and Peter had many opportunities for sharing a task so compelling to both of them. David was especially pleased that Peter was working closely with a dedicated Christian leader in the German Council of Christians and Jews, Dr. Hannah Vogt. This liaison would insure the full participation of the leadership of the Christian religious, political, and social communities in the planning and attendance at the historic event.

Another significant concern for David right about this time was an effective response to the arrest of Soviet author, Aleksandr Solzhenitsyn. Talk and statements seemed about all David could do as President of the NCCJ. In order to prevent any further abuse to the Nobel Laureate, it was clear that world opinion had to be mobilized; the best approach for achieving this seemed to be that of depicting Solzhenitsyn as a "symbol of violated human rights." In a release David prepared and sent out through the Religious News Service Domestic Service, he attempted to reach persons of conscience. The writer's arrest shocked and revolted men and women throughout the United States. David's feelings about the importance of the issue were certainly substantiated. In his release he stated what was central to him:

> ...If some great writer like Solzhenitsyn within Germany had spoken out at the time of the Nazis, the German people might have been alerted years earlier to the crimes Hitler committed in the nefarious concentration camps.

> ...Violations of human rights anywhere in the world affect the total world community, because we are all members of the one human family.[65]

David believed strongly that the Religious News Service, with its truly unbiased news circulation about such sensitive matters as the Solzhenitsyn arrest, served a vital need in both this nation and the world. Consequently, each year, when the Service showed a deficit, he made the administrative decision to subsidize it for another year.

Since the beginning of the year, David had believed that a dialogue must be started with the Moslem community. The heightened tensions and crises in the Middle East were affecting relationships among the three religious communities, in the United States as well as in the Middle East. He saw it as a program area to be explored by the dedicated lay leadership and staff of the NCCJ. Because of exacerbated feelings on all sides, he knew that the choice of participating panel members must be done with great care, or more harm than good would come of any program. He would require good advice and must explore every facet of the program with a variety of experts. As he thought it a good idea to begin with the lay leadership, a spring Board of Governors meeting provided an excellent small forum. If the leadership understood the program, they would be more likely to support it in their own regions, David reasoned.

After David consulted with Dr. Bernhard Olsen and others, it was agreed that Dr. Muhammad Abdul Rauf, Director of the Islamic Center in Washington, DC and Dr. Marc Tannenbaum, Director of Interreligious Affairs at American Jewish Committee would be invited to serve on a panel with Dr. Olsen—to have a "Christian-Jewish-Moslem dialogue on the Middle East crisis." The program was a success and stimulated a challenging discussion. The general tone was optimistic, although there were many points of difference on facts between Dr. Tannenbaum and Dr. Rauf.[66]

In the fall David began to have talks with an inspired lay leader from Kansas City—Lorie Newhouse. This man believed that the NCCJ could make a significant contribution to peace in the Middle East by educating American leadership on the relationships of the three major faiths in that part of the world. It was his plan to organize an intercultural seminar for NCCJ's lay leadership on Christian-Jewish-Moslem relations in the Holy Land. David encouraged him to do so and offered to do all the mailings necessary to recruit the top leadership from NCCJ all around the United States. Once the plan was in motion, David knew he would be well advised to prepare his staff to program in that area, utilizing the lay leaders that would participate, six months later, in the seminar designed for them.

David was convinced that such an important interreligious, intercultural seminar would add strength and new dimensions to the NCCJ program. He was also very conscious how deeply all of the events in the Middle East affected interreligious relationships in the United States. Because he felt that Dr. Len Aries' experience would put him in a position to make the most of this opportunity to provide staff training in such a very sensitive program area, David made him responsible for its coordination. David was determined to recruit in the next few months as many Directors as could spare the time to attend the seminar. After many overseas calls and letters, plans were complete, and recruiting began for the training session with a late December target date.[67]

The title finally settled on for the program was Staff Intercultural Seminar Tour on Christian-Jewish-Moslem Relations. Although this necessitated a trip to Israel, the costs were kept low for NCCJ by contributions from an interested foundation. All the funds raised for the project were new money, personally given by Board members who expressed their gratitude for the opportunity to give staff members this tremendous experience. Most Board members who spoke to David felt it was a good investment that would enrich the program in their own regions in the years ahead. The twenty-five staff members who participated came from every corner of the United States. It was breakthrough; another window opened. It might not be as significant as the preparation in 1961 by Cardinal Bea, at the request of his hero Pope John XXIII, of a statement for study by the Ecumenical Council on Catholic attitudes towards the Jews. But it was a step toward the inclusion of yet another religious faith in the dialogue.[68]

16

New International Dimensions

🔥

As David sat by the fire one chilly Sunday afternoon early in 1975, E. B. Hayden's observation kept going through his mind:

There are circles large and circles small,
To shut men out or include them all.
The making of circles goes on and on;
But what of the circle that God has drawn?

When Lili came into the room, sensitive to his innermost thoughts to a degree he often found uncanny, she inquired if he had found a solution to the problem. Recently he had talked more and more with her about his awareness that people and events outside the United States were profoundly affecting the way Americans thought about issues. In particular, he was becoming increasingly uneasy, from his perspective on the world as a "circle God had drawn," about the way that institutions created to promote peace in the world were now being used for selfish political ends. As a part of UNESCO by virtue of his appointment to the U.S. Commission for UNESCO, he was especially upset by that organization's growing political role.

In January he had issued a statement calling for the reversal of the decision to exclude Israel from participation in the European group of UNESCO.[69] Fortunately, it now appeared that the attempt would not succeed and that the situation would be corrected at a subsequent General Conference. The United States State Department was working towards that end, according to the letter, dated February 14, 1975, which he now showed to Lili. The letter reassured him that, from the State Department viewpoint, the first vote of 30-30 at the General Conference in the fall justified a "measure of optimism."[70] David opposed abandoning the international agency, and supported restoring it to the non-political humanitarian purposes for which it had been created. The UNESCO decision "that Israel was so uncivilized that it must be banned from European regional membership and deprived of $26,000 in grants"[71] appalled him.

He also discussed with Lili the possibility of resigning from the U.S. Commission, but felt that body had behaved responsibly by opposing the action—even though it was in a minority position. David also expressed to Lili his strong conviction that, as a member of the Task Force for Human Rights of the U.S. Commission for UNESCO, he was in a position to effect some change; to resign in protest would have no effect whatever beyond the actual protest. In addition to that, David was positive that there probably had never been a time when the need for UNESCO was greater. In his opinion, this was a time for greater cultural pluralism and greater interdependence in artistic, scientific, and cultural fields. He did not want to see the work of the U.S. Commission jeopardized; it was doing invaluable work in such significant fields as education, the arts, environment, and, most important of all, human rights.

Adding to David's anxieties was his sense of a rising tide of anti-Semitism masquerading under the guise of anti-Zionism. He told Lili that there were people who insisted there was a way to make a distinction between Judaism and Israel. He did not believe it. He visualized the Jewish people and their love for God and land as parts of one tree. In his thinking it was impossible to respect Jews and their right to their own faith and in the same breath to reject their involvement with Israel and its people.

Even more disconcerting than this was a development in the financial community, the Arab blacklist of bankers. It was no more or less than inherent blackmail, designed to intimidate the American business community and thus inhibit their dealings with banking houses connected with prominent Jewish families. Bankers seeking favor with the Arabs might yield to such pressures. He knew the blacklist was already effective in Europe, where such banking houses were excluded from a series of routine international financings because of Arab pressure. The Jewish-related banking houses were also being frozen out of fund-raising syndicates. David discussed with Lili his plan to issue a statement encouraging American businessmen to follow the example of courage and integrity of financial institutions and resist Arab pressure to surrender moral principle to business advantage.[72]

Late winter and early spring proved to be an unusually challenging, demanding time for David. Lili had a serious illness, requiring hospitalization. In her usual efficient, caring way she had arranged for help to meet the needs of home and family, but this only intensified David's concern about the drain on her energy created by their family. He was aware, too, that she was finding this loss of energy and ability to cope to be quite bewildering.

In late April David flew to Little Rock, Arkansas, torn between his anxiety over Lili, who was still very weak but running the household from her bed and giving special attention to small Ellen, and his responsibility as the NCCJ President to attend the Little Rock dinner. After the dinner David had to return home immediately to be at a crucial meeting of the Finance Committee the next morning in New York City.

He hitchhiked a ride as far as Washington with Secretary of Commerce Elliot Richardson, who also had an important meeting the following morning. They flew in a small, two-engined chartered plane. Halfway to Washington the small plane began to heat up. David and Richardson, and the two aides, loosened their ties and took off their suit coats. But in spite of that the heat in the cabin drenched all of them. The cabin walls were scalding hot. The pilots calmly informed the four passengers that something was wrong with the heating, ventilating, and oxygen systems. David began to suspect that perhaps, with the track record of small private planes, he should have used a commercial carrier to return home. They came down to 7,000 feet and the plane cooled off, but the four men were still soaked through. David thought, "This is a fine kettle of fish; if I don't crash, I will get pneumonia." They landed at 3:30 A.M. From that time until 7:00 A.M., when he boarded the shuttle for New York, David kept asking himself, "Exactly what am I doing—knocking myself out, traveling all over the country, taking all kinds of risks?" The answer, he told Lili later, came so clearly: To him there was nothing more important than the work of NCCJ.

As spring progressed, David found reassurance in the many signs of Lili's improved health—tending the colorful flower beds, caring for all the family needs just as before her illness, even her customary early morning swim in the Scarsdale community pool. David himself didn't feel ready for that! Even more significant were her enthusiastic plans to accompany him to Israel with the NCCJ leadership group for the Intercultural Seminar on Christian-Jewish-Moslem Relations in the Holy Land. She talked over her ideas with David at every opportunity.

On June 15 David and Lili greeted every member of the NCCJ group, as they boarded the plane for Israel. These 84 people represented the mosaic of America David loved so well—indigenous leaders, mayors, city planners, successful business people, White, Black, American Indian, Christian, Jew. They came from all walks of life. It was a telling way to carry interfaith diplomacy to the Holy Land.

For David and Lili, Jerusalem was always a magic place. From their hotel on the hill overlooking the city, they watched the sun glitter on the Dome of the Rock before sinking out of sight. The hotel had recently passed from Arab into Israeli hands; but all the "chambermaids" were still men, since Moslem women were not allowed to do such work or come into contact with Westerners. Lili found it difficult to discourage the men from remaining in the room when she came in to change. Apparently ladies with golden hair were a novelty in that part of the world! She needed all the skill of a seasoned diplomat in order to get some privacy. She told David she was still recovering from "culture shock!"

In preparing the leadership group for the days to come, David told them that "there is no substitute for firsthand insights and face-to-face dialogue with Jewish, Moslem and Christian leaders; therefore we have allowed time with such people, so that we can learn from them and have an opportunity to share our heritage with them." Their days were filled—meeting Arab mayors, judges from the Druse religious courts, abbots, the United States Ambassador to Israel, the President and Prime Minister of Israel, educators (who lectured to them), and religious leaders from all the communities that gave Israel her identity. In the home of a Druse, who had been to America, they heard an explanation of the loyal Druse position in Israeli life. Later, that same afternoon, they sipped coffee from tiny cups, while seated cross-legged on the ground, in a Bedouin tent. David could barely keep his laughter bottled up, as he watched his brave "Sanitary Sue" sip the coffee; he knew her misgivings about how the cups were washed up. How the children would have enjoyed that sight, he thought!

The following day they were informed that the planned trip to Kalandia, a Palestinian refugee camp, was going to be dangerous because it was a known base for terrorists. Everyone elected to go. The group was escorted by Arab officials of the United Nations Relief and Works Agency. On arrival, they were astounded to see a thriving Arab village of 3,000 people. The ramshackle tents of twenty years before had been replaced by sturdy stone and concrete houses, many with additional rooms built on. Quite a few houses sprouted television antennas from the rooftops. The educational programs in Kalandia were modern. The children all wore shoes and were obviously well fed, in contrast to the barefoot Arab urchins wandering the streets of Jerusalem. There were roses growing in every dooryard. Hardly the tents pitched on sand shown in propaganda films to the American public!

Lili and David examined the dichotomy between the $40 million made available by the United States for the maintenance of the UNRWA program and the scant $2 million from all the oil-rich Arab states combined. David concluded, and Lili agreed, that the Arab governments were using the Palestinian refugees as pawns in a great propaganda game. The truth was that these refugees, by and large, enjoyed a higher standard of living than their kinsmen living in the oil-producing Arab world.[73]

The group began to explore all the areas of peaceful co-existence among the different religious faiths—in the religious area, in the economy, and in education. They were delighted to find a quiet confidence among many Jews and Arabs. The mood they observed was in contradiction to the impression often conveyed by the mass media in its emphasis on occasional incidents.[74] The group members were inspired by their visit to the Isaac Wolfson School, where Moslems, Christians, and Jews attended classes together.

David was quick to see that another myth needed exploding. He talked with a young Arab construction technician working in Jerusalem who, like the rest of his generation, had the benefit of the technical and vocational training offered by UNRWA. This young man was taking an active part in the twentieth century, and was definitely not a farmer as his father might have been. To take such people back to their old family homes and try to fit them into the lives their parents had lived would be a totally disruptive move.[75]

The problems of secure borders were graphically illustrated to the group and, as a result, everyone understood why relationships between the Israelis and their Arab neighbors were so strained. When David and Lili stood on the Golan Heights, exactly 35 miles from Damascus to the east, they looked down at the kibbutzim and were told that the Syrians had been shelling those Israeli settlements regularly for nineteen years. They inspected the well-made bunkers the Syrians had developed over that period, and wondered that they had been forced to give up the Golan. They marveled at how the Israelis had stormed up those sheer, steep cliffs and gained their objectives. Looked at from that point of view, the Israelis did not seem "intransigent."

At lunch on the final day of the trip, the people who had come together on this mission from all over the United States summed up their experiences. The American Indian, Harrison Cornelius, was hoping to convey information on Israeli agricultural methods to the American Indian communities in the Southwest. Most felt that the different groups in Israel got along on a personal level, but some could sense fear and hostility. Others saw a mirror of racial and ethnic problems in the U.S. None felt that the Mayor of Jerusalem, Teddy Kollek, had an easy job, since he had to administer the holy places of three faiths. For so many, it was the greatest experience they had ever had; it was a dream come true. David felt he too could see his own dream more clearly. It was still shining in front of him, urging him on.

Through Fr. Edward H. Flannery, a dear personal friend, David and Lili had made arrangements to stop in Rome for a talk with Fr. Peter M. de Contenson, Director of the Vatican Office for Catholic-Jewish Relations in the Secretariat for Promoting Christian Unity, and Msgr. Charles Moeller, his superior. (Ed Flannery was working in Washington as the Executive Director of the Secretariat for Catholic-Jewish Relations of the U.S. Catholic Bishop's Conference. He is a distinguished historian and author of the landmark book, *The Anguish of the Jews.*) They were also planning a meeting with Fr. Cornelius Adriaan Rijk, the first Executive Director of the Office of Catholic-Jewish Relations after its founding by the Vatican in 1966.

On that hot midsummer Roman afternoon, David and Lili sat with Msgr. Moeller and Fr. de Contenson in the latter's dim, quiet office, and listened to his measured voice defending the Vatican's position with respect to Israel. David felt his impatience rise. "You see," said Fr. de Contenson, "the Vatican never recognizes a country that does not have fixed borders, and, as you know, that is the case with Israel." David held his peace, but he was not willing to accept at face value the Director's explanation because he knew the policy reflected some anxiety about Arab Christian sentiments. He suspected, however, that his impetuous Lili would not be quite so patient. He was right. She was smiling, but David recognized this as her way of disarming her listeners. Then she spoke softly, "When do you feel the situation will resolve itself—in a year, two years, five years, ten years?" The priest replied, "Ah, Mrs. Hyatt, as you know, Mother Church moves slowly; one must be patient." Lili replied tartly, not bothering to conceal her feelings, "Father, I can be patient for myself, but perhaps I find it difficult to feel that my grandchildren might be here someday asking the same questions and perhaps receiving the same answer!" The conversation continued for four hours, covering many questions of friction in the field of Catholic-Jewish relations. Msgr. Moeller, obviously ill, spoke rarely but his rare comments gave both of them insights into the workings of the Vatican and the major difficulties in implementing policy changes. As they came out into the sunshine, David and Lili shared a feeling of frustration and sadness. The problems they had discussed there were centuries old, and, from all that they heard, would become older.

They both looked forward to an opportunity to discuss the entire experience and their reaction to it with Ed Flannery, always an extremely valuable resource for David in his search for all points of view whenever he had to make a statement or take a stand on an issue. David and Ed often stayed up far into the night discussing issues affecting Catholics and world events. Lili, too, often engaged in these discussions and also welcomed his visits from Washington as an opportunity to seek guidance from him about rearing her Catholic children in their faith. Thus, Fr. Flannery reinforced David and Lili at both the professional and personal level.

Upon their return home, David was fascinated to read some interesting statistics with a bearing on the troublesome Arab refugee issue: He learned that the Arabs who had left Israel were balanced by an equal number of Jews who had to flee the Arab countries after 1948.[76] The *Wall Street Journal*, in a series on refugees, noted that there were more refugees throughout the world than ever before. Most, the article stated, no matter what hope they might have about returning to their native land, tried to make a life for themselves in their adopted country. Only the Palestinians demanded that they be given "their" land back. Why, David wondered, could they not find a life in the oil-rich Arab lands. They seemed to bring political turmoil to each country that gave them sanctuary; first Jordan, and then Lebanon—where they attacked the Lebanese Christians. It certainly would bear more study. He was glad that the NCCJ Seminar for the following year would include visits to Jordan and Egypt, as well as to Israel.

After just a short respite from the rigors of the trip to the Holy Land, David was faced with the sad knowledge that Dr. Bernhard E. Olsen was very ill. Bernie, in addition to being a world-renowned scholar in interfaith matters, was a rare and wonderful human being. The light and beauty in Bernie's spirit, cherished by his close friends, burned brighter than in most mortals. But by September, 1975, Bernie was dead, and the loss of the wise counsel he gave so generously to David left a void in his life. Bernie's wisdom and keen insights had affected the ecumenical movement all over the world. More than a decade before, his book, *Faith and Prejudice*,[77] in its probing study of Protestant Sunday school materials, had shown convincingly how many of the texts regrettably reinforced prejudices against certain ethnic and religious groups, while other materials helped to lessen these destructive attitudes. Bernie's work in this area had a consciousness-raising impact. Because he was an honored member of the NCCJ staff, the organization had been on the cutting edge of change in interfaith affairs. David knew that he would sorely miss Bernie's insights in the new program dimension of Christian-Jewish-Moslem relations. He especially wished for Bernie's presence at the upcoming Seminar scheduled for June 14–28, 1976, in Egypt, Jordan, and Israel.

The first Intercultural Seminar proved a success. Furthermore, since lay leadership had initiated it and paid for it, the entire program cost NCCJ little beyond the promotion expenses. Almost all of the Seminar participants subsequently either sponsored programs or spoke at conferences and institutes in order to bring about better understanding among Americans of the interreligious and political problems in the Middle East. These positive responses, along with the high quality of the Seminar itself, brought David real gratification. However, to quell any thought that the program was not even-handed in its study of the Arab-Israeli conflict, Lori Newhouse and David decided to study and travel in both Egypt and Jordan, as well as Israel, in the upcoming trip.

As they scheduled and planned details for the 1976 Seminar, the Jordanians seemed quite cordial. However, they were jeopardizing the entire project by their continuing refusal to grant entry visas to the Jewish members of the NCCJ group. David finally resorted to a less-than-diplomatic approach to the official with whom he was negotiating by stating bluntly that, if *any* members of the group were unacceptable, all members would withdraw. A few days later the Jordanians backed down and issued visas to all, regardless of religious affiliation.

Their arrival at the luxurious Intercontinental Hotel in Amman, Jordan, on the blistering hot Friday afternoon of June 18th, gave the NCCJ leadership, David and Lili included, an abrupt and uncomfortable introduction to the world of Islam. The electricity had failed all over Amman, and indeed over most of Jordan. None of the elevators worked; all the luggage had to be carried to the rooms on all seven floors of the hotel. That evening the menu for dinner was pork chops—strange fare, as Moslems do not eat pork! David and Lili informed their hosts at the hotel that neither did the observant Jewish members of the Seminar group. After this complaint, vegetarian meals were quickly prepared for them. David wondered aloud to Lili later if there were possibly any connection between his firm conversations with the Jordanian Consulate concerning the visas and the hotel's obvious oversight about the menu.

David and Lorie Newhouse were concerned about another incident, this time in Egypt. On Wednesday evening the NCCJ group was asked to assemble at Shepheard's Hotel in Cairo, where they were to be greeted by Egyptian officials as well as the American Ambassador. Neither the American nor Egyptian officials ever appeared. No explanations were given; no apologies sent. Such an experience intensified the inherent difficulties of the Seminar. Middle Eastern tensions were clarified in the minds of the Seminar members as they grasped just how sensitive and fragile any working arrangements were between the Arabs and Israelis. If they, an American delegation of religious and community leaders, received such treatment, having given no apparent offense, how much more likely it was to occur in contacts with those people viewed as traditional adversaries.

On the Sunday they crossed the Allenby Bridge from Jordan into Israel, they observed the tensions from the Israeli side. (Lili told David later she would never forget that day as long as she lived.) The heat was intense as they disembarked from the buses driven by Jordanians. Their luggage was removed from the buses, as it had to be transferred to Israeli buses on the other side of the customs station. Without enough seats to go around, they sat on their bags waiting their turn to have luggage inspected and their persons searched. The search was so thorough that it included x-rays of the heels of each person's shoes, the linings of suitcases, and the cardboard tubes on hangers of the type commonly used by cleaners in the United States for delivering trousers. In addition, each person had to empty each suitcase completely, and allow customs officials to examine each article. Officials bombarded Seminar members with questions, such as, "Did you pack this yourself, or did someone who served you at the hotel pack this case?" The questions alarmed Lili. Consequently, she spoke softly to the customs people in Yiddish (to prevent the Christians surrounding her from understanding her and thus becoming very nervous), wanting to know the meaning of these procedures which to her seemed excessive for a friendly group of Americans. One replied, in Yiddish, "Madame, you have no idea the tricks these devils play on us. They hide explosives in the cardboard tubes of hangers, the heels of people's shoes, and in the linings of suitcases. We do this to avoid tragedy." Lili assumed that the "devils" were terrorists. Once she understood the urgency and the Israelis' earnest desire to speed them on their way, out of the oppressive heat and into air conditioned buses, she began to help Seminar tour members to unload their suitcases, and served as an interpreter to soothe touchy situations as they developed. She also had mounting concern about older members of the group and how they would fare spending hour after hour in the blistering heat. All she could think of, as she later discussed the whole experience with David, was to hurry the process along as best she could.

Once they were settled into the hotel in Jerusalem and the Israeli portion of the Seminar commenced, the group members became very aware of the pronounced difference in attitude of both official and non-official people, Arab and Israeli. The group, which had been both disturbed and fascinated by their experiences in the Arab world, now began to perceive the real differences in thinking and attitudes between Israel and its Arab neighbors. The NCCJ group members could then see why Israel preferred to belong to the European community in the UNESCO structure.[78]

Lectures were interspersed with meetings with both Israeli and Arab community leaders in Arab villages, as well as with Christians living in Israel—in cities, and in kibbutzim such as Nes Amin. The highlight of the trip came at the end with a meeting of the International Council of Christians and Jews at which David was elected Vice-President.

The last evening, spent in the company of people who had ties with both Israel and the United States, gave opportunity for all to talk about their experiences with others who knew the four cultures—Israeli, Arab, Christian, and the pluralistic society that is the United States. So many questions were asked, and so many complex answers given, that one group member later told David that what he learned from the trip was how much Americans had to learn about the Middle East before they could form intelligent opinions or help in any way.

On his return to work after the Seminar, David was confronted by the response of UN Secretary-General Kurt Waldheim to the anti-terrorist Israeli raid on Entebbe in Uganda, where terrorists were holding hostage the passengers on an Israeli plane hijacked in Athens, Greece. David described the Secretary-General's condemnation of Israel as "ridiculous" and was disgusted by the proposed

UN resolution of condemnation. In a news release he stated that a UN peace-keeping force should have undertaken the action taken by Israel. He feared that unless some sincere efforts were made to contain terrorists and terrorist activities, any country giving sanctuary to terrorist organizations, such as the PLO, would suffer the fate of Lebanon. Jordan, as well, had been nearly torn apart, but asserted its sovereignty and ejected the PLO. The people on the streets of Egypt and Jordan, with whom the Seminar people had talked, longed for peace. Through Abba Eban the Israelis had warned the Lebanese to assert their sovereignty against Palestinian terrorists, but Lebanon did not heed the warning in 1972. In the same statement David spoke his strong conviction that the Israelis were still the one bulwark preventing a Soviet takeover of the entire Middle East. He hoped that the American public really understood this; but at the same time he knew that most Americans were totally unaware that it was impossible to enter either Egypt or Jordan with "Israel" stamped on a passport. He also believed that, if Israel and the neighboring Arab countries could pool their technical skills and manpower, the Middle East "could become a prosperous and vital area like Western Europe."[79]

Certainly the NCCJ Seminar had been a step in opening up the eyes and minds of some Americans to the complexity, dimensions, and possibilities of the situation in the Middle East. In David's mind that was a significant accomplishment.

17

One Man's Blueprint
for NCCJ's Expansion

𝔹

At his desk in late 1976, David studied a nearly completed outside examination of NCCJ that had been requested by the Board of Directors just prior to his assumption of the presidency in 1973. He turned his attention to seeing if he could put the already obsolete document entitled *A Comprehensive Futures Study for the NCCJ* to some useful end for the organization. David discovered that the staff of the IMS (Institute on Man and Science) had used most of the resources allocated to the project to study data acquired from staff and Board members pertinent to the administration prior to his presidency. This was clearly stated in the transmittal letter for the study, sent to the National Co-chairmen by Harold Williams, President of IMS.

> *The profile of the NCCJ as it exists in 1975 is the result of many factors*, most of which have existed many years. *Thus, what we say is not to be taken as a direct reflection on NCCJ's present leadership configuration. In general, people in NCCJ are acting out roles and following implicit guidelines and norms established a decade or more ago.*[80]

Consequently, the report leveled criticism at many situations and programs already rectified in the two years of his tenure as President. In addition, the staff had indicated to David that they questioned the expertise of the people who were employed to do the study; too, the working papers seemed vague and naive.[81] David had hoped that some usable program ideas would emerge from the study, but the whole report was more critical than creative. He was also disturbed because the cost of the study by publication time had risen to twice the original estimated cost of $60,000.

The entire idea had begun with a questionable premise. Dr. Everett R. Clinchy, former President of NCCJ, was also the head of the Institute for Man and Science, the organization commissioned to undertake the study. In a letter to David in April 1973, Dr. Clinchy stated, "Under your lead, my hope is that the NCCJ and IMS will grow together in spirit and practice. . . ."[82] "NCCJ is my first love, as far as organizations go; no event could give me greater satisfaction than to witness a working, proper bridging of IMS with NCCJ. . . . IMS needs the almost half-century momentum, the nationwide involvement of people, and the financial stability of the NCCJ."[83]

Mr. Oscar Straus, the Jewish Co-chairman of NCCJ, also served on the board of IMS and had the major burden of getting financial support for IMS—a task growing more difficult with each passing year. The support for NCCJ came from a broad business community; David feared the study was intended to prove that the NCCJ stood in great need of IMS direction for its program and future—for which it would in return become the financial backer of IMS. A bit like the tail wagging the dog.

Still, he did feel that something could be gained, and turned his attention to the report of the four NCCJ Co-chairmen dealing with the study. As he read, the necessity for working out the findings and assumptions in the study with the entire staff became very clear to him. A staff conference had already been scheduled, with the Futures Study as its main focus. It would be held the second week of the new year, when offices were generally quiet and no fund-raising dinners were on the calendar. With so many questions and grave reservations about the study, its conclusions and recommendations reached by Hal Williams and his team, a staff conference would be a positive method of salvaging whatever was useful in it.

The roads were treacherously icy that mid-January day in 1977, but Lili insisted on driving David up to the staff conference—even though she did not plan to stay beyond the reception in the evening and some of the morning work sessions. Regretting his decision to let her drive all that distance on such bad roads, David started to ask her not to return for him as planned on the last day of the conference. He stopped, because in her usual intuitive way, Lili said, "If I stay and attend all the sessions, the staff may be inhibited about what they say. If I were not to attend at all, they would say we are headed for the divorce courts, because I have always been involved as though I were a staff member. However, if I am present for the reception this evening and the morning session tomorrow, and disappear afterwards until the closing session, I will have an opportunity to greet the staff from all over the country and make them welcome without intruding. I will be there for the closing session, so there will be no feeling that I am not interested in the outcome of the deliberations." Then she smiled at him mischievously, "Do you think there is another opening at the State Department for another Hyatt?" David had to agree: She certainly plotted that strategy. He did need her, to talk to about the whole complex situation, and her driving meant that he could work on the first draft of his closing address.

The three days allotted to the conference flew by. Lili drove up again, safe and sound he was relieved to see, for the roads were even more icy than on the first trip from their home in Scarsdale to Kiamesha Lake. She greeted everyone quietly, and then took her seat where he could see her as he made his presentation to the assembled staff. David began:

> When I became President of NCCJ three-and-a-half years ago, I pledged to you to make this organization the finest human relations agency in this country, not only in its program but internally as well. And we've made some sound steps in those directions. Certainly no one could say we did not practice democracy here at this conference. There was no need for private sessions or secret caucuses. We let it all hang out. You said what you felt. And despite the many complaints about our deficiencies, I have tried and I am still trying to make NCCJ a democratic institution—not a military model but an open society, with policies democratically arrived at by group consensus, and with your President simply a chief among equals. . . . We are, I believe, truly moving toward eventually achieving the participatory democracy you all cried out for so plaintively and so angrily and so helplessly at the Americana Hotel in 1970.
>
> I stayed up until three this morning, studying carefully all of your reports. They are thoughtful and constructive and most useful, and I thank you for this splendid start. But let's agree it is only a start, just the beginning.
>
> When I agreed with our Co-chairman to undertaking the IMS Comprehensive Futures Study, I did so figuring we'd get a five-year plan out of it—a clear-cut blueprint for the future that would make my job, as your quarterback, a lot easier. After all, it was called a Comprehensive Futures Study! But it was clear that the Institute for Man and Science couldn't do this, brilliant though I think Hal Williams is—and he's here today as an observer. . . .

> *After the IMS Study was in, again looking for some easy answers, I said: Well, when we get the staff all together, they'll take the IMS data and come out with a five-year plan, that blueprint for the future I've been waiting for. Well, let's face it. You've made a great start . . . but you haven't really blueprinted. . . .*[84]

Lili later told him that, at that point, it was so important that he was able to offer them his "blueprint," his vision for NCCJ. His was there—before, during, and after the expensive, time-consuming IMS study.

David continued:

> *Because we in NCCJ are also on the front lines—*
> * *combatting bigotry;*
> * *fighting against racism;*
> * *overcoming prejudice;*
> * *working for equality and justice for all Americans;*
> * *working for "a new birth of freedom," to use Lincoln's phrase, so that we can live up to the promises of America and truly become a single nation and a united America!*[85]

He then went on to tell them about nine programs he specifically wanted to see implemented—for women, Blacks, Hispanics and minorities—in the interreligious field.

> *One. I would hope and pray we would make the denial of equal housing a cause of shame and an act of immorality, through concerted programs in all of our offices.*

> *Two. I would hope and pray that, in the next five years, we would use our negotiating and persuasive skills to open up the hundreds of social clubs and country clubs which bar Jews and Blacks and women and other minority groups. I would hope every office would do its utmost to wipe out this ugly blot in our democratic world.*

> *Three. I would hope and pray that, with over one quarter of all the Jews in the entire world enslaved behind the Iron Curtain, our stance on the plight of Soviet Jewry would be more than a statement from the President and a few scattered programs in cooperation with Sister Gillen's Task Force on Soviet Jewry, but would be a nationwide crusade involving every office to awaken Americans to the subtle but horrible holocaust the Soviet is now conducting to gradually eliminate all Jews and all vestiges of Jewish life within the Soviet's realm.*

Four. I would hope and pray that our stance on Israel's right to exist in peace and freedom within secure borders would become orchestrated in a much more concerted program—that really has an impact on the widespread Christian misunderstanding about the meaning of Israel as a land, as a people and as an essential part of the Jewish faith to Jews throughout the world.

Five. I would hope and pray that our Task Force on Women's Rights—effective and inspiring though its first steps have been these past two-and-a-half years—would be just the beginning of a whole network of NCCJ lay Task Forces for Women's Rights, with every office involved in such programs, to insure that over 100 million Americans are not denied equality because they happen to be women.

Six. I would hope and pray that we could develop a system via our network of regional offices, our regional Boards, and our regional media whereby every moral stance taken by your President could be picked up and amplified and made a subject for equally strong regional stances in the local media—as was done so successfully on the issue of equating Zionism with racism, in which every office took positive action and got a media response. Here was an out-standing example of the awakened giant of NCCJ having national impact through its 70 regional offices!

Seven. I would hope and pray that our Religious News Service—already doing great work in behalf of inter-religious understanding—could expand to reach not simply 150 daily newspapers but 500 to 1,000 such dailies, and that its TV service could be developed to a point where a half-hour weekly RNS program could be a major educational program of every NCCJ office.

Eight. I would hope and pray that . . ., in the next five years, [we] will find some new program formats and some new handles to enable us to claim our fair share of the action on both commercial and educational television. Seventy million people saw the Super-bowl game. We must revitalize our [media efforts] to this end [so that millions rather than thousands are reached by our programs.]

Nine. I would hope and pray that, in the next five years, our splendid youth . . . program, [which] reached 5,000 young people last year, could be emulated by all of our offices, and, instead of reaching 5,000 youth, we might have an impact and an influence on perhaps a quarter of a million young people.[86]

In conclusion, David said:

NCCJ never faced a greater challenge, and its program has never been more relevant nor more needed. And with the leadership of the creative and gifted regional and National staff and Boards we now have, we can meet that challenge; and in the next decade, we can do a job that is absolutely vital to the unity of this country![87]

The response from the assembled group was a standing ovation.

On the way home to Scarsdale, David was spent, tired, and in need of time to recoup his energy. He was so grateful for Lili's sensitivity, and her willingness to drive while he mulled over the staff's complaint about the need to infuse new leadership at the Board level. As usual, he mused, the staff seemed to lag behind in perceiving problems. This particular problem he had addressed the year before, by restructuring the by-laws to create the position of National Chairman of the Executive Board, and then persuading Irving Mitchell Felt, Chairman of the Board of the Madison Square Garden Corporation, to take the post. Irving Felt had ties to the sports world, the entertainment and theater world, and with major corporate leaders. With these contacts he could infuse NCCJ with a broad spectrum of new volunteer leadership.

A few weeks later David initiated what was to become an ongoing communication with the Carter administration, because of his keen gratification with Carter's courageous championship of human rights in a speech at the United Nations. In David's opinion, President Carter deserved the everlasting gratitude of the American people, as well as of the millions of enslaved and imprisoned persons behind the Iron Curtain. As he told Lili, he applauded this new day that had been ushered into American foreign policy, and the breath of fresh air in United States diplomatic relations. David also expressed to her his conviction that the new moral force that Carter had brought to bear upon international politics had probably encouraged world public opinion to be mobilized to help spare the lives of Solzhenitsyn and Sakharov. To show his enthusiastic support and appreciation for Carter's leadership, David sent a mailgram to the White House.[88]

In midsummer the Carter administration asked David for advice and counsel regarding the President's reorganization of civil rights affairs within the U.S. government. David heartily endorsed one proposal among six reorganizational options that called for the creation of a Cabinet-level Department of Human Rights, because "this publicly makes *domestic* as well as foreign human rights a major flag of the Carter Administration in a way that no other approach to this problem could possibly do."[89] David offered the name of Fr. Theodore Hesburgh as the "perfect man"[90] to become the first Secretary of Human Rights.

He told Lili that he also had suggestions of ways to avoid the fragmentation of the federal civil rights program. He strongly believed that discrimination is discrimination regardless of sex, race, ethnic origins, or age! Consequently he recommended a "central command over the federal civil rights thrust, [which] would put an end to the jungle of varying rules and policies . . . within a number of Cabinet departments as well as several other separate agencies. . . ."[91] Disturbing elements in American society indicated to David the pressing need for the Cabinet post to give added impetus and emphasis to civil rights problems.

David and Lili often discussed his dismay over the appearance of a revitalized Ku Klux Klan. Because he recognized the necessity of speaking out against bigotries in time to prevent the further germination of their poisons, he had made two very serious attempts to have an editorial to that effect put into the *New York Times*. His first attempt was in the form of a detailed letter to the editor; it was never used. David's very able Vice-President for Public Relations, Harry Robinson, phoned the paper to learn the reason for the letter's rejection and was told that it was too long to use. Then David agreed to edit the letter to the size they would consider publishing. Finally, the *Times* agreed to publish the letter, and it appeared on April 20, 1977, after over a month of negotiation.[92] Even so, David was discouraged that it took such monumental effort to alert a sleeping public, most of whom were unaware of the menace of such a movement. An investigative report in the *New York Post* called attention to the Klan's existence in New York City. An avowed Klan leader appeared on a local TV morning show.[93] David did not wish to see a return of the Klan-led religious and racial intolerance which had necessitated the formation of the NCCJ fifty years before.

Later that same year David met with the distinguished lawyer and former Congressman, Herbert Tenzer, in his office—to discuss David's continuing involvement and concern about the plight of Israel, becoming increasingly isolated by world opinion because of events she neither wished for nor could control. David also expressed to Herbert his deep concern for Israel's right to exist within peaceful and secure boundaries. Out of his desire to give aid to the alleviation of the anguish of Soviet Jewry, David had become a founding sponsor of the Interreligious Task Force on Soviet Jewry headed by Sister Ann Gillen. Herb complimented him for his leadership among those Christians who protested the detention of Jews in the Soviet Union when they wished to emigrate to Israel. David said he was particularly appalled by the "ransom system" set up by the Soviet Union for impoverished Jews wanting to emigrate to Israel. The two men also discussed the continued sponsorship by NCCJ of Holocaust conferences all over the United States; three had taken place in 1977. After the death of Dr. Bernhard E. Olsen, the annual Scholars' Conference in New York City was renamed the Bernhard E. Olsen Scholars' Conferences in his honor. David described to Herb his eventual projection of a network of Holocaust conferences held annually in every major city of the United States.

At that point Herb asked David if he would serve on the Executive Board of the America-Israel Friendship League, since it was clear that David's objectives and sympathies paralleled those of the organization which Herb had founded and forged into a major force in American-Israeli relations. David agreed to serve. Conversations with Herb always gave him new insights, as Herb was one of the foremost leaders in the Orthodox Jewish community; and one of his many major responsibilities was membership on the Board of Yeshiva University. In this way he was able to share with David the sensitivities in that community, overlooked in years past by the NCCJ.

David concluded this conversation with Herb by outlining NCCJ's commitment to continuing seminars on Christian-Jewish-Moslem relations in the Holy Land. That year's seminar would be directed by Mrs. Emily Korzenik, a lay woman studying for the rabbinate. In addition to her religious training, she had a major in history and economics—which she had taught for many years. The current seminar group combined staff and lay leadership and, David assured Herb, if past seminars were any indicator, this group would have a sensitizing and mind-expanding experience.

When David revealed to Lili his newest commitment, she reminded him that he was already an active Board member for the American Field Service. David laughingly replied, "That really is an easy job compared to serving in the American Field Service during World War II." Lili walked away, shaking her head. David knew that her misgivings stemmed from his diminishing time with the family.

This time David had no qualms of conscience because he had planned time alone with her after the ICCJ Executive Committee meeting in Luxembourg. Since Lili was an armchair archeologist, who had always wanted to go to Greece, he was going to take her there. And because he loved the theater, they would stop in London on the way home to see a few marvelous productions that the English were so adept at staging. Both of them loved London. It was like a second home.

18

Assessing NCCJ
at the Half-Century Mark

§

On New Year's Day of 1978, the fiftieth anniversary year of NCCJ, David could honestly say to himself that he found the organization in the forefront, responding to most major issues involving human rights, both in the United States and abroad. All his hard work in his five years at the helm had been well worth it. At times, he knew, his colleagues and Board members were critical of his public statements, because many of them were still more comfortable with the concept of an NCCJ that said little or nothing publicly.

David believed that NCCJ methods and responses must keep pace with the times. In 1933, when NCCJ had as its major program "The Tolerance Trio"—consisting of a Presbyterian minister, a rabbi, and a Catholic priest—who embarked on a nationwide tour of 38 cities in 21 states to promote understanding, it was a courageous action. In 1978 NCCJ programs reached and involved 900,000 people in a single day, because the times demanded more.

In April, in response to allegations based on the Study by the Institute of Man and Science the year before that David spoke out only on Israel, Don McEvoy, without consultation with David, issued to all professional personnel a detailed memo concerning David's stands on a wide variety of issues. Don, Vice-President for National Programming for NCCJ, wished to set the record straight. He wrote:

> *Here are the facts. On fourteen domestic issues: David spoke against discrimination in private social clubs; in favor of busing to achieve social desegregation; in favor of the Equal Rights Amendment; in opposition to the Holt Amendment which would have impeded school desegregation; in opposition to statements made by General*

George Brown regarding American Jews; in opposition to President Ford's defense of the rights of parents to send their children to private segregated schools in order to evade integrated public schools; to request minority representation on TV panels interviewing candidates during Presidential debates; in commendation for American businessmen resisting the Arab boycott; in opposition to an anti-Catholic cartoon in a college newspaper; in opposition to the formation of a Ku Klux Klan group in Queens; in support of American hospitality to refugees of the Vietnam war; to call for complete investigation of a cross-burning in Oregon; in favor of equal employment opportunities for minorities and women.

And on eleven foreign issues he had this to say: he opposed the inclusion of the Soviet Union in mediation of Middle East peace efforts; he opposed violations of human rights in Uganda; he opposed the French release of Abu Daoud; he appealed to save the life of an American mercenary in Angola; he opposed international terrorism, and praised the Israeli raid at Entebbe and called for UN action; he supported Kissinger's statement of opposition to continued White rule in Rhodesia; he condemned the Arab boycott; he opposed the appearance of Yasir Arafat, with a gun plainly showing from his hip, at the United Nations; he supported Solzhenitsyn and urged caution in a policy of detente; he supported Soviet Jewry; he opposed UNESCO's exclusion of Israel.[94]

Don reminded the staff at the end of his memo that, until comparatively recently, the NCCJ had a President "who refused to make public pronouncements and forbade others to do so."[95]

David knew that Don was not alone in his feelings. The media coverage of NCCJ had changed markedly since the onset of his administration. Ralph King, while still Director of the NCCJ office in Pittsburgh, Pennsylvania, wrote a letter echoing Don's memo:

I want to let you know that we are getting some brief but important news coverage here in the Pittsburgh area about NCCJ. Very frankly, it has been the most consistent coverage I have seen since being in Pittsburgh, and the best national coverage since I have been with the Conference. . . .

I think you should take a bow at this point, because I feel this is due, to a large extent, to your numerous public statements on key national issues. As you know I have often bemoaned the fact to you in the past that part of our [NCCJ's] problem was the lack of a national posture. Our NCCJ leadership just never got into the race, so to speak. Now, thanks to you, I think we are moving to the top in our field, and this is where we should be.[96]

Ralph was the first Black Director on the NCCJ staff ever to be given an assignment below the Mason-Dixon line. He was then in Houston, Texas.

Early in the year, David was disturbed by the rise in the number of neo-Nazi manifestations in the United States, France, and West Germany. The reports on activities here were well documented by responsible professionals in community relations. According to Norman A. Stack, Executive Director of the Jewish Community Relations Council of St. Louis, Missouri, the city had a long record of Nazi and Nazi-like activity. Even more upsetting was the march planned by a small bunch of home-grown Nazis through the heavily Jewish suburb of Chicago, called Skokie. Many of its Jewish citizens were survivors of the Holocaust in Europe, prior to and during World War II. Indeed, Skokie had more survivors per capita than any other American city; this was a primary reason for the American Nazi decision to march there. A Nazi presence was distressing, too—for a variety of reasons—to thousands of non-Jewish residents of the area. A group of Roman Catholic and Protestant clergy issued a statement expressing their commitment "to identifying with Jewish residents in their deep distress occasioned by the Nazi presence and exercise of un-American and irreligious free speech."[97]

The program department of the NCCJ, working with the Director in the Chicago office, Mr. James Rottman, made plans for a minimum of 5,000 Christians wearing yellow stars to stroll the streets of Skokie, whenever the Nazis planned to march. David was delighted to learn that it became a nationwide program when Don McEvoy asked all the regional offices of NCCJ to give top priority to mobilizing support for a Jewish-Christian solidarity demonstration in the month of April. This was geared to answer the Nazis with a quiet affirmation of the best values of the Judaeo-Christian traditions in the United States. The national office of NCCJ contacted forty national heads of church bodies, and enlisted the cooperation of NCCJ local units to contact local church groups and seminaries. David appreciated at times like this what a force for good NCCJ could be, and rejoiced in the opportunity to serve at its helm.

On the European scene it was apparent to David that remedies were not so easily found. According to Justice Minister Hans-Jochem Vogel, neo-Nazi propaganda in West Germany was showing a sharp increase; he complained of a flood of books, Nazi insignia, and phonograph records with speeches by Hitler and other Nazi leaders.[98] David intended to discuss the problem with his good friend and colleague, Rabbi N. Peter Levinson, President of the ICCJ and Co-president of the Coordination Council of the Societies for Christian-Jewish Cooperation in West Germany.

Peter was fifty-seven, and he had escaped the Nazi regime by fleeing to America from Germany in 1941 with his parents. His main concern in Germany was that a whole generation of German youth did not have any knowledge or understanding of the Holocaust. In Peter's opinion, expressed to David a year earlier, this youthful group was particularly vulnerable to anti-Semitic, neo-Nazi propaganda. "[The] reluctance to face the past is a factor in the rise of anti-Semitic movements that exist in West Germany today. [The Holocaust] is something they cannot accept, so they just deny it.[99] For example, there is no word in German for the attempted extermination of the Jews, similar to "Holocaust."

In France the situation was quiet but consistently bad, according to Henry Bulawko, the leader of the umbrella group of French Jewish organizations. He said the Jewish community had "long periods when acts of anti-Semitism were received silently—just with contempt; and other times . . . when people get fed up and make things public."[100]

Later in the spring, when David discussed a projected trip to Vienna with Lili, she confessed to mixed feelings about going. Vienna, once the most Jewish city in Europe and a center of Jewish culture, was left at the end of the Holocaust with a very small Jewish population. Still, she confessed to David, she loved the opera and the Volkoper there, and so many of the customs reminded her of her parents and her childhood home. She also had mixed feelings because, while there, David would take on another responsibility, that of President of ICCJ. This meant that he would spend even less time with his family because, even though the position was an honorary one and a labor of love, he would spend as much time and effort on it as it required. Ruefully, David had to admit to himself that she was right on the mark in her appraisal. He was anxious to get to Vienna because the subject of the annual ICCJ conference was neo-Nazism, and it was being co-sponsored by the Action Combatting Anti-Semitism in Austria and ICCJ.[101] When the time came to leave for Vienna, Lili was ready, despite her misgivings. They both looked forward to meeting friends from all over the world, all caught up in working on Jewish-Christian relations in their respective countries.

Milton Ellerin, who worked within the Trends Analyses Division of the Domestic Affairs Department of the American Jewish Committee, had prepared a background paper for the ICCJ conference on neo-Nazism. After reading the paper, David looked forward to an opportunity to discuss it further with Milton Ellerin. Milton and his wife were a part of the American delegation to the Vienna conference. This would provide David the desired opportunity. The picture presented in the paper was not comforting; it was apparent that NCCJ had still a big job to do. The opposition of bigots to the showing of the film *Holocaust* certainly bore witness to that.

At the end of the Conference, the annual meeting and election of officers took place. David was elected the first American President in the organization's history.[102] Serving with him were Ellen Roth of Switzerland, Kurt Pordes of Austria, Jean-Paul David and Mme. Claire Huchet-Bishop of France, Luc Dequeker of Belgium, Peter Jennings of England; Joseph Emanuel of Israel; Willem Zuidema and Msgr. A. C. Ramselaar of Holland.[103]

For David the day was very significant because it was possible, after months of work with Rabbi Levinson, to announce that the ICCJ had acquired a permanent home, a gift of the West German government. It was the home of Martin Buber in Heppenheim. The West German government offered the property free of charge, and would provide funds for its upkeep and maintenance. Previously, the organization had been headquartered in London, on a tenuous basis, as a guest of the British Council.[104] Now, in David's opinion, the organization could go forward, with its own headquarters providing a solid base.

David returned to his NCCJ work, and Lili returned to undertake the whole complex task of moving the family to New York City. For some time Lili had been building a strong case for such a move, citing the demands on David of the long daily commute and the pressure on her of at least three trips weekly by car into the city to meet him for business-related social functions. For her this was an additional drain, after meeting the demands of home, family, and her own job.

Once David was somewhat convinced of the desirability of a move into the city, Lili arranged for him to see several apartments; none of them gave him the slightest desire to exchange their lovely home in Scarsdale for city living. Lili almost succumbed to the defeat showing in every line of her body as they walked down Central Park West. Suddenly she said, "Let's go into that house." David stared at her in amazement, and rather impatiently asked, "Why?" Lili pleaded with him to humor her just this once; then they would stop looking and stay in their house. They walked into the lobby of the apartment building, not knowing if it were a rental or a cooperative, and asked if there were any apartments for sale. After looking them over rather guardedly, the superintendent answered cautiously, "One, and the lady is home." The owner allowed them to see the apartment which, like the whole building, must have been a handsome place in its day—very early 1920's—but now showed signs of wear and age. Lili, with design talent inherited from her mother, could see beyond the deterioration to the creation of a beautiful home. Her vision prevailed and over the noisy objections of the children, who were very happy with the old family homestead, a deposit was put on the apartment; and the house was put up for sale. David never failed to laugh when he thought of how the whole move evolved from Lili's uncanny sixth sense.

Over the next few months Lili coped with all the givens of moving—sorting out and discarding many things stored in the attic over the years they had lived there, showing the house, finding a school in New York for Ellen who had become interested in drama. Their son, Larry, was having serious problems related to his Vietnam experience; this added an enormous strain to Lili's already very demanding life.

At the same time David was as busy as ever at work, with some deep concerns about the upcoming 1980 Oberammergau Passion Play making special claims on his time and thought. Various Board and staff members had expressed their concerns about the script. This script, written in 1860, depicted Jews as Christ killers and "shylocks." It was not surprising that it had received much praise from Hitler. David saw no defensible reason for using such a script when an earlier version, first used in 1750, characterized Satan as the villain.

David's plan of action was to mobilize American public opinion, so that American tourists in Germany would boycott the performances. He also planned to involve the member countries of ICCJ in an orchestrated protest as well, if Oberammergau insisted on using the offensive script. As he stated publicly,

> The Second Vatican Council denounced anti-Semitism and absolved Jews of any blame for the crucifixion of Jesus.
>
> We hope the town council realizes its error and instead uses its 1750 version—which makes Satan the heavy—and like the New Testament portrays the Jews as divided over Jesus.[105]

In mounting its campaign against the anti-Semitic script, the ICCJ appointed Sister Katherine Hargrove of Manhattanville College, Pur-

chase, New York, and a national Board member of NCCJ to visit
Oberammergau for the purpose of negotiating with the town council there to "reconsider the recent decision to revert to the old script."[106]
Both the Anti-Defamation League and the American Jewish Committee also played major roles in this undertaking. As a result of
their conversations, some changes were made in the script—which
made it somewhat more acceptable.

With David's support and encouragement, another major project
in that period sprang from the initiative and vision of Dr. Harry
Robinson, NCCJ's Vice-President for Public Relations. In conjunction with the research firm of Louis Harris and Associates, he developed a program to determine the shape and extent of racial and
religious prejudice and discrimination in America in 1978. Such an
in-depth survey seemed an appropriate undertaking in NCCJ's fiftieth
anniversary year. By measuring and analyzing White and Black
attitudes toward the minority Spanish-speaking groups, as well as
those toward Jews and women, the survey would provide a comprehensive inventory of social attitudes. It would thus document the
changes in both White and Black feelings since the civil rights movement had become a central issue in the United States fifteen years
before. At that time the Harris firm had conducted a landmark study
for *Newsweek* magazine.[107] Not only had Harry conceived the idea
for the study, he had been enterprising enough to get corporate
support from such major firms as Exxon, Mobil, Ford Motor Company, Hoffman Laroche, Mutual of Omaha, Arthur Anderson, Barn-
hill-Hayes, Inc., and Northern Natural Gas. David was well pleased
with Harry's undertaking. He firmly believed that this new tool
would be instrumental in creative planning for an even more profitable
future for NCCJ—an organization born out of a crisis of hatred and
bigotry, which went on to mobilize the knowledge of social scientists and educators and the moral dynamism of people of good will
toward working together for the common good.

Late in August David received a call at home, from Washington,
D.C., asking him to speak to Sargent Shriver (brother-in-law of the
late President Kennedy.) Mr. Shriver asked David if he would sign
a letter which would be delivered on September 1 to President
Carter, President Anwar Sadat of Egypt, and Prime Minister Mena-
chem Begin of Israel, all struggling at Camp David toward a peaceful
solution to the problems that beset the Middle East. This letter
would be signed by people noted for their work in reconciling
differences which caused bitterness among people of the three faiths.
David was to sign as a concerned Christian vitally interested in the

peaceful outcome of the talks among the three world leaders. He was more than happy to oblige, and he commended Mr. Shriver for the effort to encourage these men in their attempt to rebuild the trust ". . . eroded by pain and war."[108]

A week later while David was in a meeting with Ernest Nives; Banco Van den Val, Executive Director of the Anne Frank Foundation in Amsterdam, Holland; and Cor Suik, Treasurer of the Foundation, to discuss the organization of an American Friends of the Foundation for fund-raising purposes, a call came for him from home. For the first time in their marriage, David asked his secretary to hold the call, promising to call back later. It proved to be a nearly complete disaster. Not wanting to alarm David, Lili had not told his secretary that she was seriously ill. The next call came from the family doctor who said he suspected Lili had had a heart attack. The movers had been at the house packing breakables, and Lili, while supervising them, had climbed the stairs once too often.

On the way home, the longest ride he could ever remember, David kept thinking he should have been home helping Lili. The steel frame under her gossamer had cracked. The burden had proved too heavy for his delicate darling, who always took on more than she could realistically do but always before had managed to do it. He wondered in anguish, why hadn't he taken her call? He tore out of the cab almost before it stopped in front of his house and dashed up the steps. Neither David nor the doctor could persuade Lili to enter the hospital. Her reason was simple. Ellen Cleve was terrified of New York. Their apartment was not ready for occupancy, and this meant they would be staying in a midtown hotel where David had found accommodations. Lili felt she had to be on hand to watch over Ellen Cleve. She promised to have all the necessary tests and follow the doctor's orders.

As it turned out, Lili was able to supervise the workmen at the apartment and also care for Ellen Cleve. Soon the Hyatts were able to move into their "house in the sky" as Lili had dubbed it. And that Thanksgiving, with his entire family around him, David offered up an even more fervent prayer of thanks to a merciful God who answered his prayers. Lili was getting stronger every day—so much so that David was going to let her risk a trip to Spain with him to celebrate the opening of the Spanish Council of Christians and Jews.

David felt that he gained several valuable insights from the trip to visit with the Spanish Council of Christians and Jews. First, it was obviously important to have such an organization in a country where, until recently, it was forbidden to mount a sign over or near a synagogue to indicate that it was a Jewish house of worship. Second, the reception given the ICCJ delegation by the Spanish clerical hierarchy was barely polite. The ICCJ group requested a study of the materials used with children in the study of religion; they received no assurance that such a study would be done.

After this experience, David admitted to Lili that sadly he had to conclude that inter-group education at every level of Spanish life would have to take place in order to eradicate centuries of anti-Semitic feelings and actions. Lili simply smiled and said that she had known more than she wished about that problem, even before she came to Spain. As a Jewish child she learned at an early age that much history had been written in two versions—one written by Christians and the other, in many cases perhaps closer to reality, by Jewish scholars and historians. When they went to see the ancient synagogue in Toledo, she told David she could palpably sense the years of history and sorrow in the walls of the place. It gave her an even deeper appreciation of what David was trying to achieve in this troubled world.

Late in that anniversary year David received from Everett Clinchy two letters reflecting David's impact on the organization. In one, dated November 16, his predecessor told him that he was doing a great job and that his "team clicks as the Penn State football team plays together this year."[109] At the end of the year Everett Clinchy wrote again to say, "As the Fiftieth Anniversary Year ends, I wish to express my appreciation of your presidency of NCCJ. All that I hear is approval of your work. NCCJ has grown in budget, extension, and influence. . . . There were a couple of times in the first decade when NCCJ almost fell apart. There were many reactionaries who wanted it to terminate. But now it is flourishing under your baton in the role of conductor."[110]

19

New Worlds, New Problems

𐤀

For several months David had been pondering with Lili about joining a United States interreligious group, led by Rabbi Israel Mowshowitz, Vice-chairman of the World Conference on Religion and Peace, on a trip to Nationalist China as the guests of the Taiwan government. After all the details for the mission had been worked out, the headlines suddenly erupted with news of a surprise move by the Carter Administration; it had decided to establish diplomatic relations with the Chinese Communist regime in mainland China. David and Lili watched the television news programs in horror and consternation as they flashed pictures showing Deputy Secretary of State Warren Christopher being roughed up by students, his eyeglasses broken, and his car shaken by an angry mob. David seriously questioned the safety of Americans in Taiwan while feelings were running so high, albeit justifiably. He and Lili weighed the advisability of canceling their plans, but decided that the people of the Republic of China, an ally of the United States for so many years, deserved to know that they still had friends among the American people. In the middle of January 1979, David and Lili, with the rest of the small party of religious leaders from different parts of the United States, boarded the China Airline jet for the long flight to Taiwan.

It was impossible for them not to see and sense almost immediately upon their arrival in Taiwan the anguish and humiliation felt by the top leadership in response to the American government's repudiation of the long-standing relationship between the two countries. This abrupt shift in policy left a bewilderment shared by all the intelligent people encountered by the party of religious leaders.

During their seven-day stay, they talked with American businessmen, many major political leaders, executives in commerce and
industry, as well as clergy of all faiths. The feeling of isolation and
rejection was uniform and unanimous—even among hotel workers,
shopkeepers and members of the press.

The interreligious group were guests at lunch of the Interfaith
Association of the Republic of China—which was far more representative of the faiths of the world than most European or North
American councils in its inclusion of Christians, Buddhists, Taoists,
Muslims, and other smaller groups. The American group expressed
surprise that there was no Jewish representation in the Interfaith
Association. Soon afterwards David learned that simply introducing
members of the Jewish international community to the key members in the Taiwanese interfaith group would not result in an invitation to the Jewish community in Taiwan to become a part of the
organization. David invited the Interfaith Association to join ICCJ,
but explained that they could not do so unless they had Jewish
participation. The Taiwanese group expressed an interest but took
no action.

Very shortly after his return from Taiwan, David sent a mailgram
to President Carter urging him to give "concrete, specific and uncompromising assurances"[111] that the United States would not allow
a military takeover of Taiwan by mainland China. He also wrote the
President of the many violations of human rights occurring
regularly in mainland China and of the real threats to religious
freedom foreseen by Taiwanese leaders should a takeover occur.
The trip left David with many keen anxieties as expressed in his
mailgram to the President, but also many lively recollections of the
lavishly warm reception granted the visiting Americans by
Taiwanese at many different levels.

Throughout 1979, and 1980 as well, David found himself caught
up not only in the creative continuation of NCCJ programs and
projects that had been initiated earlier in his tenure as President, but
also deeply exhilarated by the new challenge of the ICCJ presidency—which involved him in international affairs as well as intergroup problems on the national level. He had brought the two
organizations into a cooperative relationship when NCCJ was the
host and co-sponsor, with the sixteen-nation member ICCJ, of an
International Colloquium on "Religious Responsibility and Human
Rights, Lessons from the Holocaust for Today's Times," held in
New York City.

David accomplished this major project, without using NCCJ funds earmarked for operating costs, by procuring the needed funding from the William Randolph Hearst Foundation, the Stern Foundation, the Edith Blum Foundation, and the D.A. and R.N. Gottesman Foundation. The Conference was most rewarding, with the participation of 200 persons in key positions in 19 countries, and attendance of 80 overseas delegates. The Declaration of Conscience formulated there was entered in the *Congressional Record* by the Hon. Robert F. Drinan on June 27, 1979.[112] In its adoption of this Declaration, David felt that the ICCJ had taken a tremendous step forward in dealing with human rights problems. Until six years before, when NCCJ became actively involved in ICCJ, the latter organization concentrated only on Christian-Jewish relations, often as a way out of even more difficult human rights problems.[113]

At the Colloquium, Gerald Green, author of the teleplay and book, *Holocaust*, received the NCCJ National Media Gold Medal. The presentation cited him ". . . for his tremendous understanding of the necessity to awaken the conscience of humanity to the dangers of anti-Semitism and, indeed, all forms of religious and racial prejudice."[114] David regarded this citation as the best way to respond to growing anti-Holocaust sentiments. The NCCJ had sponsored a number of important Holocaust conferences in 1977 to counter this problem. The whole effort resulted in an invitation to David to testify at Congressman William Green's hearing on the need for a President's Commission on the Holocaust. Subsequently, Irving Greenberg, Executive Director of the President's Commission on the Holocaust, wrote David, praising his testimony and his encouragement of government matching funds for a "Yad Vashem" model institution in this country.[115]

For many years David and Dr. Franklin Littell, a professor at Temple University, had had a warm and fruitful relationship. Littell, in David's opinion, had done more than anyone else in the United States to insure that the terrible tragedy of the Holocaust would never happen again. In 1974 Littell and Dr. Bernhard Olson talked with David, expressing the need for the NCCJ to assume the responsibility for the annual Scholars Conference on the Holocaust which Littell had initiated but which was without funds. It needed a yearly NCCJ budgetary commitment of at least $5,000 to implement the program. Littell had encouraged the formation of an international team of researchers and writers to work together in an interdisciplinary approach to search out the lessons of the church struggle and the Holocaust. Because David was so impressed with the quality and importance of Littell's work, he agreed to obtain the funds essential to the successful continuation of the program. In the ten years since NCCJ and scholars like Littell had begun to awaken the academic community, the number of courses on the Holocaust offered in American colleges, universities, and seminaries had risen from no more than a dozen to 700.[116]

David had been watching the progress of the Carter Administration and admired its sensitivity and courage in taking the initiative in human rights issues, as well as in the potentially explosive situation between Israel and Egypt, by inviting the leaders of those two nations to Camp David. David was moved to send the President a message in which he stated:

> *Without your unflagging leadership, this first but most crucial step toward lasting peace in the Middle East would never have been accomplished.*

> *The people of Egypt, of Israel, and of the U.S.—indeed of the world—are in your debt for your brilliant statesmanship in bringing about this agreement. As you rightly told the Knesset, the people of Egypt and Israel deeply long for peace (Having been to both countries I know this is an undeniable fact.) and security, and you moved their leaders to override past precedents and to gamble—as you did—and keep pace with their people in the search for their anguished desire.*

> *Once again, my personal heartfelt thanks for your God-inspired magnificent work in your successful recent Middle East peace mission.*[117]

President Carter thanked him for his message in a letter dated April 2, saying: "Your support makes easier the remaining task of building a just and lasting peace throughout the Mideastern region."[118] Later that spring the NCCJ honored President Carter at the Annual Dinner held each year in Washington, D.C. David and Lili had opportunity then to congratulate the President personally on his tremendous accomplishment.

Also, in April, David and Lili participated in a national civic Holocaust Commemoration Ceremony to observe the "Days of Remembrance," sponsored by the Congress of the United States and held in the Rotunda of the United States Capitol Building. As David looked around the hall—jammed with distinguished members of the House of Representative and Senate, many invited guests, and television crews and cameras—he realized that the hard work of interpreting and communicating the lessons to be learned from the

Holocaust had indeed been most worthwhile. The short, but moving, ceremony did more to reassure him of man's ability to learn from the mistakes of the past than any other event could have. This was the opposite of "good men remaining silent while evil triumphed."

In June, Teachers College of Columbia University honored David with the Distinguished Alumnus Award for being in the "front ranks of those who seek interreligious, interracial, and international tolerance."[119] The citation noted David's writings on human rights, his service with UNESCO as Chairman of its Human Rights Committee, along with his outstanding leadership in NCCJ and ICCJ. Certainly a well-deserved accolade.

David and Lili were elated to be going on a busman's holiday to England. Sir Sigmund Sternberg had invited them to visit for a month and arranged their stay in a lovely apartment in Finchley, just twenty minutes from London. Sir Sigmund, who had visited the United States and come to know something of the work of NCCJ, felt it would be useful to have David speak in England about some of the intergroup problems encountered in the United States and some of the methods used in an effort to ameliorate them.

Both David and Lili came to have a great affection for the modest, charming, witty, and deeply thoughtful man who was their host. They found him to be a most humane person, of great wisdom and rare vision and courage. A behind-the-scenes mover who quietly got things done for the betterment of his fellow man, he rarely consented to be in the limelight, preferring to give others that spot. Lady Hazel was a perfect mate for him, always thoughtful about the needs of others. Between them they gave David and Lili a memorable experience. Very soon after their arrival, Sir Sigmund arranged a reception for David in the Jerusalem Chamber of Westminster Abbey. Lili teased David, saying that it was her understanding that to be honored at Westminster Abbey you were usually dead! David admitted to being not just honored, but overwhelmed!

At a meeting for the British Council of Christians and Jews at Bury St. Edmunds, David described in detail the NCCJ program. While there, they were put up at an old manor house supposedly visited by Queen Elizabeth I—Hengrave Hall. In the evening they strolled in the old garden and mused on the day's events. For them both it was most interesting to perceive how differently similar intergroup problems were viewed and understood in the two countries.

Upon their return to London, Sir Sigmund asked David to report to the British National Committee on the Holocaust what was being done at the National level in the United States by the President's Commission on the Holocaust. David explained that this Commission was still searching to determine its mission. He told them of the appointment of the 34-member President's Commission on the Holocaust with a Christian and Jewish membership. David also informed them of the hearings held by Congressman Green of New York in order to learn from people active in Jewish community life their sense of what should be the work of the President's Commission. He reported his own testimony, recommending a memorial of the same moving sculptural quality as the Yad Vashem Memorial in Israel, with an extensive photo exhibit and the capacity for showing films such as *The Twisted Cross*. Sir Sigmund later told David that the British Committee found the information both useful and informative.

During David's and Lili's month in England, Sir Sigmund went to great pains to assure David of opportunities to meet privately with English community leaders to share their common concerns. Lady Hazel and Sir Sigmund both concerned themselves in a very touching way with providing many pleasurable, relaxing activities— seeing restored houses, attending receptions and garden parties, and generally experiencing the flavor of life in England. At the end of the month they reluctantly left Britain with a treasure of warm memories and a sense of "mission accomplished."

The following January when Sir Sigmund and Lady Hazel visited the United States, David was instrumental in arranging for the British industrialist to receive the National Brotherhood Award of NCCJ for his personal qualities and his many contributions to humane undertakings without any thought of recognition. Both David and Lili felt that, no matter how many opportunities they might provide for this rare and wonderful couple to meet American community leaders or to enjoy some of the special qualities of life in the United States, they would never be able to repay them for their graciousness and thoughtfulness.

In February, 1980, the National Council of Churches convened a "Special Panel on the Middle East." Seventeen Jewish organizations rejected invitations to attend, claiming that the hearings were geared to an anti-Israel stance. The problem emanated from a resolution proposed the preceding November by the Antiochian Orthodox Archdiocese of North America (composed of Arab Christians) accusing Israel of violating human rights and demanding an end to U.S. aid to Israel. The NCCJ sent a telegram to NCC board members urging them to reject this resolution because it was "replete with factual errors and patently untrue allegations."[120] Out of his concern that this whole set of circumstances might mean a real bias in the presentation of Israel's position at the hearing, David consulted Dr. Carl Herman Voss, NCCJ's Ecumenical Scholar-in-Residence, to find a means of correcting the imbalance. Voss had held this position with NCCJ since 1975, and during those years he and David had developed a very special relationship. Carl, a Protestant clergyman and highly respected author, would be a strong, highly credible spokesman for the NCCJ viewpoint at the upcoming NCC panel. Carl accepted the responsibility and agreed to present a ten-page statement outlining NCCJ support of Israel as detailed by David in 1976 in a special press release and in a 1978 letter to the *New York Times* strongly denouncing the PLO and its terrorism. Nathan Perlmutter of the Anti-Defamation League of B'nai B'rith, in an expression of gratitude to David for Carl Voss' statement, wrote: "It is an absolutely splendid paper—forthright, comprehensive, unsparingly critical where necessary, and immensely supportive in its own unique loving way of Israel and the Jewish anguish with the PLO. You have performed an important service in the cause which both of our agencies hold dear. . . ."[121]

The ICCJ Colloquium and Annual Meeting, June 15 to 20, in Sigtuna, Sweden, gave David and Lili both pride and pleasure. Each year, since David had initiated NCCJ involvement with the international organization, the latter had shown encouraging, progressive growth. The fledgling Swedish Council, already able to host all the ICCJ member nations, attested to that fact. To have an ICCJ Council in Sweden was a particular triumph, in David's opinion, because, during the Holocaust period, Sweden had remained neutral. Whenever David or Lili discussed this with Swedes, the latter claimed that, even while cooperating with the Germans, Sweden was taking in Jews who fled Norway and Denmark. "Thank you, Scandinavia" later documented this information. The conference theme was, appropriately enough, "Faith after Auschwitz—The Impact of Faith and Theology in Judaism and Christianity."

The beauty of the countryside and the people, along with their wonderful hospitality, struck David and Lili immediately on arrival at the retreat house in Sigtuna. The new Council coordinated the program in a way that would have done credit to a well-established organization with thousands of members. For David the whole experience provided opportunity to see a dream achieve reality.

In September a rather shocking event pointed out to David that, despite all the input of NCCJ in Christian-Jewish relations, his work had really just begun. Like many others, he was stunned by a statement by Bailey Smith, President of the Southern Baptist Convention, that "God Almighty does not hear the prayer of a Jew."[122] It was comforting that the Hon. Brooks Hays, the former President of the Southern Baptist Convention, released a statement disassociating himself from Smith's well-publicized remark by saying, "To believe that God hears only the prayers of Christians invoking the name of Christ would be to shut out from God's love and care the largest part of the world's population, and to abrogate to ourselves alone his mercy and favor, something Jesus never intended."[123] In David's opinion this caught the essence of NCCJ's work. He had never been more proud of his old and dear friend. Brooks, at eighty, was still a towering figure, and the film of his life, *Return to Little Rock*, initiated by NCCJ and carried out by the brilliant young filmmaker, David Solomon, bore vivid witness to this.

After Smith's ill-considered outburst, David, at home with Lili, expressed his outrage at the insensitivity of the religious establishment on yet another point—the place of women in religion. In a foreword to a book by Betsy Covington Smith, entitled *Breakthrough: Women in Religion*, David had written, "The male chauvinism of our churches and synagogues is perhaps more entrenched than in most of our other establishment institutions. Indeed, this tradition that only the male can truly speak to God goes back thousands of years to the primitive roots of Judaism and has continued this day in both Judaism and Christianity."[124] In response to David's agitation, Lili one day laughingly reminded him that Orthodox Jewish men offer up daily a prayer of thanks to God that they have been created men, not women. With such an attitude built into daily prayer, she added, one could not expect too much progress. David replied ironically that males displayed such characteristics regardless of their creed or race.

David was once again deeply involved in affairs in the Middle East. His concerns for that part of the world had never been limited to Israel, but had extended to all of the people in that war-torn, ravaged area. He made available the facilities of NCCJ to the Lebanese Relief Fund Emergency Campaign, and hosted a reception with Hugh Downs and The Most Reverend Francis M. Zayek, Bishop of St. Maron-U.S., as featured speakers. The Task Force for Peace in Lebanon, of which David was a member, was broadly ecumenical and included Bishop Zayek; Dr. William Sloane Coffin of Riverside Church, New York; Dr. Muhammad Abdul-Rauf, Director of the Islamic Center in Washington, D.C.; Rabbi Amiel Wohl of Temple

Israel in New York; along with other ecumenical leaders. Together with Rabbi Wohl, David signed a letter urging people, without regard to religious affiliation or national origin, to join in this ecumenical effort to give humanitarian aid to all the victims of the Lebanese conflict. Lili supported David's efforts, along with the added demands on him, out of her own deep concerns for the Lebanese people. She saw David as a man with a heart large enough to hold all mankind, and sometimes said that she wished she had the gift for "cloning" him so the world could have all the time he wanted to give it.

20

Beyond the Horizon

❦

The year 1981 started off quite uneventfully, with David tending to necessary administrative and program tasks. At home, life was also uneventful but satisfying. All seemed to be following their own patterns—working and studying; falling in and out of love, as Lili reported from time to time about the two younger girls; and the married children enjoying their lives as couples.

This rather rare and very welcome period was marred in March by sadness at the death of Lillian Block, in the fullness of her years. Although Lillian had retired as Editor-in-Chief of Religious News Service a year earlier, David still relied on her vast store of knowledge in the interreligious field when he had to come to a decision or make a statement. Lillian's brother, Ted, wrote David to say how moved he was by the interfaith memorial service which gave all of Lillian's many friends a chance for a last goodbye to their old friend, "The First Lady of religious news." Both David and Lili felt that they too had lost a dear sister. It was time for them to seek a respite, David decided.

He and Lili had been married for ten years; now they could take the honeymoon they had missed because of family and job pressures. A well-deserved holiday in Italy, before going to work at the ICCJ meeting in Germany, seemed the ideal choice. Lili was elated by his plans. Italy, to her, meant opera, works of art, and soft Neapolitan love songs. A few weeks later, as they danced on a patio in the Villa Minani hills high above Rome, a camera flash bulb suddenly went off. A young couple, obviously honeymooners, danced close by. When Lili asked, "Accident?", the young man, shaking his head, replied, "No. We wanted your photograph because, when we are your age, we hope we will be as in love as you two are." Lili laughingly assured them they would be and reveled in this special moment.

Not too long after their return, David was sobered by the realization that one of the hard-won gains of the civil rights movement was in danger of being lost; the Voting Rights Act of 1965 was about to be emasculated. Since it was considered the single most effective civil rights law ever passed, protecting the rights of those Americans previously excluded by force, intimidation, and rigged local laws, David felt it an NCCJ mandate to prevent that eventuality. Consequently, he released a statement to the media and to the regional offices of the NCCJ, urging them to send it to their local news outlets. It said, in part:

> As President of the National Conference of Christians and Jews, an organization which has been in the continuing struggle to combat bigotry and prejudice since its inception in 1928, I am deeply disturbed at the apparent move to emasculate the historic Voting Rights Act of 1965, particularly the pre-clearance provision that gives it any real enforcement meaning. . . . The current veiled attempts to turn back the clock on equal rights, and perhaps set in force a counter-offensive against the rights won in 1965, are disturbing to all those who believe in equal rights for all Americans.[125]

David feared the negative impact, both morally and spiritually, on the minorities affected. Despair and a lack of faith and hope were the seeds that bred anarchy, in his opinion. He vowed he would continue the fight until it was won. A year later he saw his goal achieved.

He was not as fortunate with another cause for which he had fought hard—the Equal Rights Amendment. It was painful to see that, despite the gains made by and for women, so much more needed to be done before equality was achieved. As early as 1975 he had said at a conference on Women's Rights sponsored by the NCCJ, "Women's rights and human rights for all Americans are inseparable NCCJ goals." When the Equal Rights Amendment to the United States Constitution seemed doomed, he wrote:

> There is no battle in the world more important than the struggle for human rights. The current effort to constitutionally insure the rights of women is an integral part of the continuing quest for human equality.
>
> The issue of ratification of Equal Rights Amendments has awakened the country to the dimensions of the many forms of discrimination which have been imposed upon women in a male-

dominated society. It is incredible that, although 51 percent of our population is female, most are paid less for doing the same job than their male counterparts, and are discriminated against, held back, and humiliated in countless other, even more vicious and subtle, ways that are condoned within our present society.[126]

When the required number of states failed to ratify the ERA in the summer of 1982, David regretted deeply the loss of the hard-fought battle but was encouraged that the cause would not be abandoned but taken up once more, in hopes of future success.

During the Spring of 1982, David became enmeshed in controversy when President Reagan was selected as the recipient of NCCJ's highest award, the Charles Evans Hughes Gold Medal, "for courageous leadership in governmental, civic, and humanitarian affairs." The situation perplexed and disturbed him, and also strained his ability to absorb the hostility and partisanship. He responded to the criticism, unfairly directed at him, by pointing out that the award was a non-political one; it was being given to the man as a person and as the President of the nation—not as a political leader. As in most such instances, the professional executive leader of the organization does not choose the recipient of such an award; rather, selection is the province of the lay leadership. Since there was no precedent for the furor that followed the announcement of the award, David could not possibly have foreseen the deep and bitter result of the choice. He was deeply shocked by the "hate mail" and the lack of restraint shown by some staff and Board members over the issue.

The tension surrounding the dinner, with crowds of protesters surrounding the hotel, and the incredibly tight security—right down to cutting off the service in all elevators until the President was safely inside the banquet hall—made the entire affair eerie, despite the air of normalcy in the festive mood, beautiful appointments, and good music. Throughout the evening David and Lili experienced the weight of apprehension. Their first concern was that there be no repeat of the nearly fatal shooting of the President the previous year; second, that no one in the crowd of protestors be hurt or killed; and third, that no ugly incident of any kind turn a tense evening into a tragic one. Although David was heartsick at the inability of the staff and some Board members to apply the NCCJ philosophy of conciliation to this divisive issue, he in no way betrayed or revealed that this award dinner was any different in climate from those of previous years.

A month before the dinner, David decided to attempt to induce the President to show more sensitivity on certain issues in his awards dinner speech. Rather than write to the President directly, he suggested to Dr. Harry Robinson, NCCJ's Vice-President and Director of Public Relations, that he write to Mr. Aram Bakshian, Jr., in the White House speech writers office, presenting several ideas that could be incorporated into the President's speech. The President's speech that night of March 23rd indicated that, upon reflection, he had used a number of the suggestions. David had urged the inclusion of the Enterprise Zones plan relating to urban renewal; a denunciation of the PLO and terrorism, with reassurance for Israel; and a statement against anti-Semitism. At the end of the President's speech, David was glad to hear the words that too many of the NCCJ staff and Board seemed to have forgotten entirely; referring to "those outside the hall who spoke with such passionate conviction earlier this evening," the President asked, "Can't such a dialogue be carried on with decency and understanding, without a tone of hatred?"[127] The evening ended without incident. David and Lili went home, drained, but with a sense of profound relief.

That weekend Lili talked with David about her sense of a profound change in his thinking, asking him why he had chosen the day of the annual Board of Directors meeting to announce his retirement. David explained that for some time he had had a growing desire to free himself from the burdens of administration, and the twin responsibilities of raising $9 million yearly and assuring that staff could maintain a decent standard of living and have job security in this difficult economic period. What he wanted more than anything else was to devote more of his time to the central program concerns of NCCJ through speaking and writing. The demands of winning raises for staff based both on merit and cost of living, for eight out of the nine years of his tenure, had drained him of the energy needed to explore new challenges. These same problems repeated themselves year after year, without letup. Approaching his ninth year, he came to the conclusion that it was time to step down and find new ways to stretch his creative talents and inner development. Again, he reminded Lili that he had been guided throughout his life by the faith expressed in his favorite psalm, "The Lord is my shepherd; I shall not want. He maketh me to lie down in green pastures: he leadeth me beside the still waters. . . ." Even though he had no clear idea of what his Lord's "still waters" held in store for him, he told Lili that in January, 1982, without telling her, he had informed the Chairman of NCCJ's Executive Board that he would like to resign as President at the end of the fiscal year of 1982. For NCCJ that was October 1.

Even though David could not see clearly where he was going, Lili was convinced, she told him, that he was already there. For some time, she reminded him, he had been moving steadily into the international arena in both human rights programs and the scholarly realm. David conceded that perhaps she was right. The most recent example was the upcoming International Symposium on "Judaism and Christianity under the Impact of National Socialism," to be held in Jerusalem at the end of June. NCCJ was the only organization with Christian members giving financial support and sending delegates, and actually the only organization outside of Israel to be involved at any level. And on a broad, comprehensive, creative level, there was his continuing work with the International Council of Christians and Jews. Both of them admitted to great joy in thinking back to the previous summer's trip to Rome, resulting in the formation of a Council of Christians and Jews. It had been very difficult because the Roman Jewish community had always been under the shadow of the Vatican, and centuries of oppression had made both the Christian and Jewish communities very cautious in their relationships.

Both David and Lili eagerly anticipated a visit in August with another new Council of Christians and Jews, this time in Ireland. From there they would proceed to Berlin for the International Convention of ICCJ. The convention theme, "Meeting Point Berlin, Jews and Christians Between the Past and the Future," promised great challenge and stimulus. Perhaps the most awesome aspect of all would prove to be the trip, along with other convention delegates from western Europe, the United States, and Canada, behind the Iron Curtain.

As always, both of them felt ready and eager to take on yet another new adventure.

Epilogue

The ecumenical movement of the twentieth century is a singular effort at unity and peace in an age that has known neither. David Hyatt's contribution to the vision of ecumenical sisterhood/ brotherhood is perhaps best summarized by his friends and colleagues, the ones to whom the vision of a world at peace and living in hope is not a quixotic fancy. Reality to the visionary is a world where people embrace and resolve conflict, not the one in which all resolution fails. The Hyatt legacy to the NCCJ, and to the entire ecumenical movement, is one which is a beacon of light for others to follow, for those who also see reality as truly expressed in justice and love. The kingdom of God may never be realized on earth, and perhaps it is only realized by the efforts of some who believe that it can exist. But in the instant that one effort to establish God's peace is made, another dream is born that it will triumph. David Hyatt is a man of practical vision, who wished to share his vision with others, so that they too would follow with confidence a pathway which leads not only to peace and justice, but to God.

The words of others who have shared the presidential tenure of David Hyatt reflect a mutual respect in the work all believe so essential to world peace.

> *My friend, you have been a bridge-builder who never hesitated to unite people, no matter the danger or the cost. For many, you have been a lamplighter who illumined the darkened streets, so that we can rediscover each other as brothers and sisters as we walked along in life's journey toward the Eternal Father. For all, you have been a spiritual man, worthy of emulation and tribute.*
>
> —Archbishop Iakovos
> Archbishop of the Greek
> Orthodox Church of North and
> South America

Yours has been a leadership of creativity. The times are long since gone when expressions of brotherhood were courageous. What once took courage is not a cliché. You, by daring to be forthright, by taking positions on issues which some shunned for fear of being deemed "controversial," gave strength to us all—and vitality to the Conference.

—Nathan Perlmutter
National Director,
Anti-Defamation League
of B'nai B'rith

David has sensed the mood of the world. He is the personification of Teilhard de Chardin's universal man who "builds the earth." He has been an architect, a builder, a reconciler. Under his leadership, NCCJ has entered the world scene.

—Thomas Patrick Melady
Assistant Secretary for
Postsecondary Education,
U.S. Department of Education

Let me put in writing here what I have said many times to others: I was deeply saddened to hear of your plans for early retirement because I believe that NCCJ needs your leadership for the duration of the time we had anticipated—even longer. We are at a crucial stage in our history, concurrent with the critical situation of our nation and world. You have been the staying power in our organization because of your sensitivity to the human needs and desires of our staff. Having worked here for some twenty-four years, I know the great contribution you made in lifting staff morale and giving us the spirit of "the NCCJ family."

—Mary L. Chrichlow
Director, Long Island Area,
National Conference of
Christians and Jews

But surpassing these contributions, to my mind, were initiatives taken in the National Conference of Christians and Jews. Literally, with respect to Jewish-Christian relations, he turned that organization around. Before he assumed the Presidency, the Conference had never faced the problem of relations between Christians and Jews in joint efforts to solve rather the problems of the community that involved prejudice and injustice in general. The Conference was apparently reluctant to have the Jews and Christians of its membership face one another, in order to consider themselves different identities, or to do the same with respect to Jews and

Christians in the community. President Hyatt took the initiative here, and in short time the National Conference of Christians and Jews became one of the most active and important organizations dedicated to Jewish-Christian friendship and understanding in the United States. It was a major development which must be accredited for the greatest part to David Hyatt.

—The Rev. Edward H. Flannery,
Director
Continuing Education of the Clergy,
Our Lady of Providence Seminary.
Former Executive Secretary,
Secretariat for Catholic-Jewish Relations
of National Conference of Catholic Bishops

I also think you have made a unique contribution to the NCCJ's public image by your public statements on behalf of Israel, the poor, our minorities, and for basic pieces of legislation important to the advancement of human rights. Again, to my knowledge, you have led the way for the entire Conference in this vital area.

—Don Eagle
Regional Director of Arizona
and Vice-President of Field
Development for the Southwest

David Hyatt has, in sum, been willing to carry the interfaith work of Jews and Protestants and Roman Catholics beyond the purely humanitarian and patriotic areas to those matters that pertain to the Ultimate. To do this required great vision and courage, and his contribution deserves the response of great gratitude from all who value the Dialogue.

—Franklin H. Littell
Professor, Temple University,
Founder and Honorary Chairman,
National Institute on the Holocaust,
President,
National Christian Leadership Conference for Israel

Four Historically
Significant Addresses
On Human Rights and
Interreligious Understanding
1954-1982

The Sacredness of Every Human Being

An Address Before the Moline Rotary Club,
LeClaire Hotel, Moline, Illinois, Feb. 25, 1955

When I was a boy on a farm in Ohio, my folks used to pay me a nickel for every psalm I learned by heart.

One of them, which I've never forgotten, is the one that begins:

The heavens declare the glory of God;
And the firmament sheweth his handywork.

I never fully realized the meaning of those words, however, until a few weeks ago when I read Arthur Clarke's book, *The Exploration of Space.* For then I learned that our sun and our solar system are but one of a hundred billion such suns and such solar systems which form a roughly disc-shaped system known as a galaxy. And this galaxy revolves—even as the billions of solar systems within it—completing a revolution once every 200,000 years. And this great revolving galaxy is but one of many other galaxies which go on and on in outer space—beyond our knowledge and beyond our comprehension.

It's amazing and breathtaking to contemplate, isn't it?

Yet even more amazing and breathtaking is the fact that God, in his infinite creativeness, endowed every one of us—as he did the stars—with a divine spark, with a touch of himself.

We speak of the music of Mozart and the writings of Shakespeare as divinely inspired. But too often we fail to realize that all of us, even as Mozart, have the capacity to tune in upon a love and a light and a power that is far, far greater than ourselves.

Some of us saw this most vividly during the last war. It was a curious thing, but when a man faced death he almost never thought of himself. Legless men gave away their boots. Mortally wounded men ordered the doctor to care for others.

I shall never forget, as an ambulance driver in North Africa, picking up a colonel who had been terribly wounded during a raid. "Don't waste time on me," he pleaded, "this is it for me. Take care of the others! Take care of the others who still have a chance!"

I remember thinking at the time how strange it was that such power and beauty in men should show so brightly in the midst of war. But when faced with death, they became bigger than themselves. Divinity—the God in man, selflessness, brotherhood, name it what you choose—it is the most hidden and yet perhaps the deepest impulse in man. And it is there in every one of us—something sacred and holy and a part of God.

And so it follows, if this is so, that to degrade man in any way, to mistreat him or humiliate him, is to blaspheme against God.

You might say that, in essence, is what my organization, the National Conference of Christians and Jews, is in business for—to combat that sort of blasphemy.

People so often say, "Of course, we have no problems of prejudice in our town." I don't suppose there are any such problems in this city, either. And yet I'm constantly shocked by the amount of such blasphemy which continually goes on.

- *Insurance firms and banks which won't hire Jews.*
- *Restaurants which won't hire Negroes.*
- *Hotels which exclude Jews and Negroes.*
- *Real estate men who fence off areas as Black and White, Jewish and non-Jewish.*

Two years ago, looking for a house in Connecticut, I saw an ad in the paper which intrigued me. I called up the agent and asked him about it. He described the house at length, and it sounded perfect—just what we wanted. Then he said, "Of course, I assume you're not Jewish; this area's restricted."

Well, that man didn't realize it, I'm sure, but he was as guilty of Godlessness as the Communists who for the past 10 years have been carrying on a systematic program to eliminate all Jews and all vestiges of Jewish life in the satellite countries.

And when a Negro American family in a Chicago housing development must board the windows of its apartment and crouch in terror behind the couches in the living room for fear of being stoned by an angry White mob—that, too, is an act of sheer Godlessness, the behavior of Communists, a denial of the sacredness of every man regardless of race, creed or color.

The Commies, of course, are experts at this sort of blasphemy.

They're doing their utmost to wipe out the Judeo-Christian concept of "the brotherhood of man under the Fatherhood of God."

In Iron Curtain countries, as you know, all vestige of religious life is slowly being eliminated.

In Hungary, according to *Time* magazine, church bells are being used for scrap metal to build a greater war machine for Communist aggression.

In Prague, Catholic Bishop Trochta has been sentenced to 25 years in prison, following the path of Cardinal Mindzenty and hundreds of other devout Catholic churchmen who have refused to bend to totalitarian wills.

In Africa and Asia, race hatred is one of the tools the Communists are using to turn native peoples against the free nations of the West.

In Moscow, youth organizations have been ordered by government edict, and I quote: "to wipe out God." End quote.

What can we do about these blasphemies against the sacredness of man? How can we positively promote "the brotherhood of man under the Fatherhood of God"?

Albert Schweitzer, who has been called by many the greatest living man in the world today, has shown us one way to do it. He was already at 30 a great organist and theologian, when he turned his back on the dazzling rewards the world offered him in order to serve his less fortunate fellows as a medical missionary. For nearly 50 years he's devoted his life to healing, counseling, and teaching the natives of equatorial Africa.

The men of Maryknoll have shown the same devotion to the lost, the miserable, and the ill of China.

We cannot, of course, all become Schweitzers or all join up with the men of Maryknoll, but every one of us is in the position to put the principles of brotherhood into positive action in our daily lives.

- *You can do it in your business life.*
- *You can do it in your daily associations.*
- *You can do it in your clubs.*
- *And you can do it in your churches and synagogues.*

Perhaps you're thinking, "But I'm just one guy—and the problem's so big. What good can I do?"

Let me give you a few examples of what "just one guy" can do.

When Branch Rickey was a coach in a mid-west college, he took his team to play in a nearby town. But the management of the hotel where his team was to stay overnight wouldn't give one of his players a room, because the boy was a Negro. Finally, Branch Rickey persuaded the hotel management to let the boy sleep on a cot in his room.

That night the Negro boy sat on the side of his bed and cried, and pulled at one hand with the other, and said, "God, Mr. Rickey, if I could only change the color of my skin!"

The next day he took his team to St. Louis to see a major league game and the Negro boy had to sit in a separate part of the ball park.

After these two incidents, Ricky resolved that, if the opportunity ever presented itself, he'd do something about it.

When he became manager of the Dodgers, as you know, he hired Jackie Robinson. He was the first major league manager to hire a Negro player. His doctors pleaded with him not to do it. They warned him that the strain and worry of taking this step could seriously undermine his health. But Ricky pushed their warnings aside and went ahead and put Jackie on the payroll.

Both Rickey and Jackie got hundreds of threatening letters and phone calls—but they stood their ground.

In Boston, some of the boys starting making jibes and sneering at Peewee Reese for playing with Robinson. Reese was from Louisville and they figured he would react in the traditional southern way. Instead Reese just walked over, while they were jibing, and put his arm on Jackie's shoulder.

Jackie, telling the story afterwards, said that he doesn't even remember what Reese said to him at the time—but what Reese said wasn't important, it was what Peewee did. Jackie says that the effect of Peewee's action on the Boston players was like a slap in the face.

When the team first went to St. Louis, there was talk of the St. Louis team striking. But Ford Frick, President of the National League, stood behind Rickey and Jackie. He told Jackie he was for him 100%, that he had as much right as anyone else to play major league ball. And when he heard rumors about a strike, he stopped it abruptly. "I won't have any such talk," he snapped, "and I'll suspend any player who goes on strike."

Well, there wasn't any strike. And some others came through and lent their strength to Jackie's cause. Eddie Dyer, for instance— a Texan—came up to Jackie before the game, and said, "Don't worry. There isn't any problem. I'm with you 100%."

What can "just one guy" do about eliminating prejudice? Well, Branch Rickey, Ford Frick, Peewee Reese and Eddie Dyer, by a few simple actions, changed the whole course of baseball and eliminated an ugly blot on our national sports record.

Let me give you another example. Benny Goodman hired Lionel Hampton to play the vibraphone in his orchestra and Teddy Wilson to play the piano.

When he hired them, it was the first time a major orchestra leader had ever hired Negroes to play in his band. He hired them because they were the finest musicians he could find, and it seemed perfectly natural to him to hire them; he wasn't trying to be a great reformer. At the time, he didn't realize he was walking into plenty of trouble.

There were hotels that wouldn't put up his band. There were other spots where they wouldn't hire his orchestra. Or they'd try to hire it without Teddy Wilson and Lionel Hampton.

Benny Goodman wasn't looking for trouble, but everytime he ran into this sort of un-Americanism he came out fighting. And usually by arguing out the question with the hotel management or the theater managers or dance hall owners, he made them see the error of their ways.

There was a stagehand, for instance, who made some disparaging remarks about Teddy Wilson. Benny Goodman took the guy aside. "Look," Benny said, "when you make remarks like that about Teddy, it hurts Teddy real bad, and when he's hurt he can't play good. And when he can't play good, my band doesn't sound good. And when my band doesn't sound good, I can't get jobs in these theaters. And when I can't get jobs, that means *you* don't work either!"

Well, from then on, that stagehand behaved like an American.

Benny Goodman was "just one guy," but he changed the thinking of hundreds of people by standing up for Lionel Hampton and Teddy Wilson.

Some men with courage have done the same thing in business.

A Negro slave helped Cyrus McCormick build the first successful reaper in a blacksmith shop on a farm in Virginia more than a hundred years ago. Cyrus' grandson, Fowler McCormick, remembered that, and he offered Negroes equal employment opportunities in all International Harvester plants some 20 years ago.

After World War II, International Harvester decided to open plants in Memphis and Louisville. At that time Negroes just weren't hired for skilled position such as welders and crane operators in those two towns. Harvester could have followed the established employment pattern there. But instead they had the courage to stand by the rightness of their own firm's policy.

But they didn't want trouble either. So they conducted a public education campaign in each city. They published full-page newspaper ads, gave talks before city officials and groups like this one here, explaining the Company's long-standing non-discriminatory policy. And in interviews with all job applicants, they fully explained the company's policy.

A few bigots walked away when they learned the awful truth that they must work side-by-side with Negroes, but most of the job applicants said they didn't care. Today more than 900 Negroes are working alongside 4500 Whites in skilled positions in these two southern plants. There have been no incidents, no violence, and no real trouble to amount to anything.

Americanism has moved ahead another step, thanks to half a dozen businessmen at the top of International Harvester—in particular Ivan Willis, their Vice-President in Charge of Industrial Relations.

The same thing happened at Spiegel's, the famous Chicago mail order house, again thanks to the efforts of "just one guy."

His name happened to be Spiegel—and that helped a bit, of course. Back in 1944, Modie Spiegel, who was Chairman of the Board, decided it was time his company utilized Negro labor. Elmo Roper, who was also on the Board, felt the same way. In fact, Roper's employer-attitude surveys had already indicated that American business lost more than $30 billion every year because of discrimination. According to Roper, any firm that doesn't hire on the basis of merit and merit alone is not only guilty of injustice but of woeful extravagance as well.

Between the two of them, Spiegel and Roper talked the rest of the Board into inaugurating a full-fledged integration program.

Once they had talked the Board into going along, then they had to educate the executives and supervisors down the line.

They held meetings for all of the supervisory staff, pointing out that Spiegel was embarking on a program to employ Negro labor—first of all, because it was morally right, and secondly, because it was economically sound. It took more than a year to get the program underway, but it went through without a hitch.

Spiegel, who is on our Labor-Management Commission, wrote to me about it last year. "I'm proud of the success of this program," he said, "and so is everyone who had a part in it. It's paid off in profits and employee morale a thousand percent."

Well, those are just a few examples of what fellows like you and me can do about this problem. We can't all be Schweitzers or men from Maryknoll, but we can put brotherhood into action in thousands of ways in our daily life.

Every one of you can help by bringing into your businesses, into your clubs, and into your churches and synagogues, those standards of justice and fair play which are basic to our democratic system of government.

I don't want to give the impression that I feel discrimination and prejudice are the only problems we have here in America. But I do feel strongly that they are among the most important—not only nationally but internationally.

The eyes of the peoples of Europe and Asia are upon us. How we handle our intergroup relations, how we take care of our intergroup tensions, how reverently or cheaply we deal with minority groups, the extent to which we make real our national heritage and sacred ideal of "one nation under God" may very well decide whether the teeming millions abroad will cast their lot with us or succumb to the lures of the Communists.

Did you know that the 1954 Supreme Court decision abolishing segregation in the public schools made the front-page headlines all over Europe and Asia?

We do a lot of talking about combatting Communism here in this country. Well, putting the principles of brotherhood into action offers us one concrete way we can do this.

With your help and the help of thousands of other men of goodwill like yourselves, in similar communities across the country, we can eliminate for good and for all, the race riots, the name calling and the epithets, the vicious real estate restrictions against Negroes and Jews, the burning of crosses on public school playgrounds, and the closing of factory gates on workers whose color or religion is not the same as our own. And we can do it—not in the next 50 years, nor in the next 20, but within the next 5 to 10.

But that change can't be accomplished alone by passing laws making non-segregation the law of the land, nor by FEPC laws to insure fair employment. The problems of discrimination and prejudice will only be resolved as a result of a constant, widespread, and intensive program of public education—of which such laws are simply one part.

They'll only be resolved when organizations like this one—and the one I represent—have quietly and without emotionalism brought the people of this community, and all the others across the country, to a realization in their hearts and souls that *every* person—regardless of his or her race or creed or color—is a sacred human being and a child of God!

Because It Is Right!
A Searching Look at Human
Rights Today

An Address at the 32nd Annual Meeting
of the U.S. National Commission for UNESCO at the
Mayflower Hotel, Washington, D.C., October 8, 1968

On this twentieth anniversary of the Universal Declaration of Human Rights, I don't need to tell any of you here today that it is one of the noblest, most beautifully expressed, and most inspiring documents in the history of all mankind. And I don't need to tell you, either, that the gap between the preachment and the practice of that great Declaration—not only in the U.S. but in all of the so-called "civilized" nations of the world—is so colossal, it is absolutely staggering!

How have we *actually* "celebrated" its anniversary during this International Human Rights Year?

On the international front:

- *The Greek military dictatorship has tightened its stranglehold on liberty there.*
- *The situation between the Israelis and the Arabs has polarized almost beyond the point of discussion.*
- *The ruthless invasion of Czechoslovakia by Russia has almost made a mockery of the so-called East-West detente.*
- *Hundreds of thousands of people are starving in Biafra, with the casualties already more than in Vietnam.*
- *And in South Africa and Rhodesia the degradation imposed on the Blacks by a small minority of Whites grows more brutal, month after month.*

And on our own home front during this International Human Rights Year:

- *A Nobel Peace Prize winner and great human rights leader, Martin Luther King, was murdered by a paid assassin.*
- *Robert Kennedy, one of our most valiant crusaders for human rights, was killed by a deranged Arab partisan living in Pasadena.*
- *Whole sections of this city, and many others in America, were burned and destroyed by angry Black mobs in protest against the squalor and poverty of the ghettos, which the White man has imposed upon them.*
- *The UN was increasingly bypassed by our Government in times of world crisis, and in the eyes of some American leaders is actually regarded as a hindrance to effective action for peace.*
- *Our Foreign Aid Bill was slashed this year to less than $2 billion, the lowest in history, a bare one-fifth of one percent of our gross national product—an absolute disgrace for a nation as wealthy as ours, a total abnegation of our world responsibility as its richest nation to lead the fight against poverty, illiteracy, and disease.*
- *And when the report of the President's Commission on Civil Disorders, released this March, concluded that our nation was moving toward two societies—one Black, one White, separate and unequal—and suggested practical ways and means to make good the promises of American democracy to all of our citizens, these suggestions were virtually ignored by our Congress, and the riots, disorders, and violence go on.*

What does this say about America?

It says we're in one hell of a mess. It says there's a sickness abroad in our land. It says that, as Edmund Burke pointed out, all that is required for evil to take over in our fair land is for enough good men to do nothing.

Somehow we've got to turn this country around.

Somehow we've got to get this country on the move again.

In the past we made great strides as a country, both domestically and internationally, in the field of human rights.

We can be proud, for example, of the fact that, in 1941, Franklin Roosevelt's call for the Four Freedoms—for freedom of speech everywhere in the world, for freedom to worship God in one's own way, for freedom from want, and for freedom from fear—inspired and mobilized men of good will in all parts of the globe.

In the minds of millions of hungry and oppressed people, Franklin Roosevelt, by these words, transformed the entire spirit and purpose of World War II from a negative battle against Nazi aggression into a global struggle to achieve these Four Freedoms for all mankind.

We can be proud of the fact that, after the war, that great lady, Eleanor Roosevelt, in a matter of months after her husband's death in 1945, valiantly shouldered the responsibilities of trying to make his vision of world freedom a living reality in the world assembly of nations, played an important role in drafting the Universal Declaration of Human Rights, and led the fight for its adoption by the UN General Assembly in 1948.

We can be proud of the fact that the then Assistant Secretary of State William Benton, and such organizations as the AFL and CIO, the National Council of Churches, and many other organizations represented here today, had a hand in the founding of UNESCO and that the U.S. has been UNESCO's most generous contributor and still continues to give one-third of its total budget.

We can be proud of the fact that America "grew up" internationally during the nineteen forties and fifties and early sixties.

Many of you, like me, have seen our country mature from an insulated, self-concerned nation in the nineteen thirties into a nation deeply involved and deeply concerned with the freedom and the human rights and the economic welfare of other nations throughout the world community. We have seen our country help rebuild Europe from war-blighted devastation to a thriving, prosperous economy through the Marshall Plan. We stopped the Communists in Greece. Through NATO we stopped them from over-running Europe. We played a major role in transforming the United Nations from an international debating society into a splendid shield for peace—a shield for peace which effectively acted on crises in Iran, in Korea, in Egypt and Israel up until last year, in Lebanon, in the Congo, and many other places. Of these facts, the American people should be immeasurably proud.

We have given aid to underdeveloped countries in all parts of the world, helping them to help themselves; and some of them— like Japan and Greece and the Republic of China in Taiwan—are now self-sufficient, independent, and prosperous, and others— like India and Pakistan—because of our help have not only, thank God, managed to survive, but are taking important steps toward becoming viable economies. Because of these facts, too, you and I and all of our fellow Americans can hold our heads a little higher.

But today we are retrogressing in our international concerns and in our involvement in international human rights—and this must be stopped!

In our international relations, we must recapture the spirit which our late President John Kennedy expressed so magnificently in his Inaugural address, when he said: "To those people in the huts and villages of half the globe, struggling to break the bonds of mass misery, we pledge our best efforts to help them help themselves for whatever period is required—not because the Communists may be doing it, not because we seek their votes, but *because it is right!*"

Similarly, in our domestic affairs we must recognize that the credibility of our foreign policy and of our leadership in behalf of human rights within the UN, within UNESCO, and in our direct relations with other nations around the world, is largely dependent upon what we do at home.

I had the honor three years ago of serving my country as Press Attache to the American Embassy in Pakistan, on a leave of absence from the National Conference of Christians and Jews, my employer for the past 15 years. And one of the reasons I came back to the National Conference—even though my family and I loved the Foreign Service—was that we came to the conclusion that, before we could sell democracy and the concept of human rights abroad, we had to make it work at home.

I learned a lot about selling democracy and human rights during my two years in Asia. I learned, for one thing, that most of one-and-a-half billion people over there have only one concern—one square meal a day. And until the gnawing hunger in their stomachs is assuaged, until the makeshift huts they live in are replaced with decent homes, until the filthy rags on their backs can be discarded and decent, warm clothes take their place, and until their stunted, sickly children are given health facilities and some semblance of public education, they couldn't care less about theoretical democracy or so-called "human rights."

As for the 8 to 10 million out of more than one-and-a-half billion people who have some education—the teachers, the professional men, the military officers, the journalists, the civil servants, and the ruling classes—they simply do not believe that our democracy and our laws for human rights really work. And they hold up the riots in Watts and Detroit and many other American cities to prove it. When Watts exploded three summers ago, it made the front-page headlines of every newspaper in Pakistan, in India, and throughout South Asia, the Middle East, and Africa.

Let me read you just three such headlines from leading Pakistan newspapers on August 18, 1965. The Pakistan *Observer* of

Dacca screamed, "Despite Military Posts and Curfew, Negro Revolt Spreads in Los Angeles"; the Karachi newspaper *Dawn* shouted, "Another Blow to U.S. Prestige; Pravda Comments on Los Angeles"; while Karachi's *Morning News,* giving Red China equal space with Russia, used as its headline "Bloody Suppression of Negroes: Chou Slates U.S."

And you may be sure that similar headlines have been blazing ever since, in Asia and Africa, whenever America's cities erupt in racial strife!

Because of this lack of understanding of what America is trying to do, because as the greatest and most powerful nation in the world we are expected to be perfect, and because our failures are grist for the Communist propaganda mills, we've got to make the United States an absolute bastion of freedom, a showcase for racial justice and for human rights. And we must do it not only for the reasons I've just mentioned but, far more important, we must do it—as President Kennedy said—*because it is right* and *because it is just!*

And we must do it not only for ourselves but because of our children and our children's children. For how we handle our intergroup relations, how reverently or cheaply we deal with minority groups, the extent to which we make real our Pledge of Allegiance as "one nation, under God, indivisible, with liberty and justice for all" may very well decide whether the teeming millions abroad in Asia, Africa, and South America will cast their lot with the Free World or succumb to the lures of the Communists.

That's how important intergroup relations and human rights in America are today! In today's world, where 80% of the population is non-White, our world peace and freedom may very well depend on how we handle this problem!

Forgive me for using my own organization as a modest example of what just one organization can do to meet this problem.

We claim a constituency of some 200,000 contributors—corporate and individual—and a much too meager budget of only $4 million.

To celebrate the Human Rights Year and bring international emphasis to our program, we initiated three very special events:

> • *First, a human relations institute bringing together 40 Mexican and U.S. teachers and professors for a four week live-in experience at the University of the Americas this summer, with the emphasis entirely on human rights and intercultural understanding.*

- *Second, an international conference in cooperation with the Canadian Council of Christians and Jews, bringing together 200 interreligious and interracial leaders for a full week to discuss ways and means of improving intercultural, interreligious, and interracial relations.*
- *Third, right now, all day yesterday and today, 60 leaders of civic organizations from Canada and the U.S. are attending a conference at the Institute on Man and Science in Rensselaerville, New York under our auspices, to discuss the Universal Declaration and how the organizations represented at this Institute can implement human rights through intensifying their programming in this vital area.*

In addition, in cooperation with many of the organizations here today, as part of our regular programming, through 35 two- to six-week summer university workshops in human relations for 3000 teachers and civic leaders, through 20 week-long youth leadership conferences this past summer for 3000 youth, through an Equal Opportunity in Industry program for the top business and industrial leaders in 30 cities—often working with the Chamber of Commerce, the Urban Coalition, or the National Alliance for Business—through "Rearing Children of Good Will" institutes in cooperation with PTA's in more than 400 cities, through community relations programs for police in 60 cities, and through our monthly clergy dialogue programs in 70 cities, the NCCJ is trying to highlight the absolute necessity for human rights and for equality of opportunity in employment, in housing, and in education—not only for all Americans but for every human being on the face of the earth.

Now the organizations represented by the U.S. Commission for UNESCO constitute a total membership of 60 million persons, many of them top leaders in their communities.

We have the leadership right here in this group, if all 60 million persons were mobilized, to turn America around and back upon the proud and idealistic course it so nobly pursued from 1941 until recent years.

We can stop the country's drift away from idealism and back to isolationism. We can change America's present attitude of indifferentism and open hostility toward foreign aid and international involvement.

And domestically, instead of lethargy and indifference, we can move forward from the magnificent victories of the Civil Rights Act of 1964 and the Voting Rights Act and the inspiring blueprint for "A Great Society" in 1965—which that distinguished Republican journalist Henry Luce called one of the great humanitarian statements of our times—on to the practical implementation of the recommendations of the Kerner Report, which, if put into practice, could make America a pioneer, blazing new frontiers in human rights, and an example for all the world!

If all the organizations represented on this Commission—with a total membership of 60 million—could pour the utmost of their hearts and minds and souls into a nationwide, intensive, and widespread public education program in behalf of human rights, the impact could be tremendous. We could really, truly turn this country around!

And what greater reward could there be for such dedication and zeal than domestic tranquility and harmony in our streets and cities here at home, and peace throughout the world. Human rights is the key. For, to quote President Kennedy once more in closing:

"Peace, in the last analysis, is basically a matter of human rights."

The Most Important Business in America Today

An Address at the Inaugural Dinner Honoring and
Installing the Fourth President of the National
Conference of Christians and Jews, Hotel Plaza
New York, N.Y., March 29, 1973

Bless you all for your thoughtfulness, your generosity, your warm good wishes, and your heartwarming applause! How could any man be more fortunate than to have friends such as you? I thank you from the bottom of my heart!

Particularly I want to thank all of you who are participating in this program for your warm and ingratiating remarks, and I also want to warmly thank all of you who planned this affair with such love and care.

Above all, I want our wonderful national Co-chairmen—Bob Murphy, Oscar Straus and Bill May—and all of the other distinguished members of our national Board, and all of our fine staff here tonight, to know how deeply I appreciate the honor you have just bestowed upon me. I feel very humble standing before you; I promise you that I will do my utmost, with all my heart and soul, to be worthy of the trust and faith you have placed in me!

When the National Conference was founded back in 1928, unbelievable though it seems, the anti-Catholic, Jew-baiting, Black-hating, cross-burning Ku Klux Klan had 6 million un-American idiots running around the country in bedsheets; anti-Semitic restrictions in employment, in housing, in colleges and universities, and in social life were standard practice; and Blacks, both north and south, were not only continually oppressed and degraded and sometimes treated worse than animals, but were frequently lynched!

We've come a long way since then, yet we still have restrictions that fence off areas as Black and White, as Mexican-American and White, and as Jewish and non-Jewish, and despite our high-

sounding Federal and State laws regarding discrimination—
some of them on the books for more than 100 years—there are
still restrictions that block Blacks and Mexican-Americans and
Indians and Puerto Ricans and Jews from equal opportunity in
jobs and in education and in housing. And there are still hundreds
of country clubs and social clubs where Jews are barred and
Blacks enter only to be the servants of the Whites. But even
worse, our cities, because of racial unrest, have been torn apart,
by shootings, by murder, by arson, and by every other hideous
form of violent civil strife.

Three years ago the Milton Eisenhower Commission on Violence prophesied for America the fate it is already experiencing
and I quote:

> *Our cities will be composed of high-rise, high security apart-*
> *ment houses and prospering commercial areas, surrounded*
> *by squalor. And in the suburbs, behind window grilles and*
> *electronic surveillance equipment, the nervous home owner*
> *will always keep his gun handy.*

We can't let this continue in our beloved country! It means
death for America as a democracy and as a world leader. We
cannot be a divided America, torn by violence and strife! The
diversity of our people should enrich us, not destroy us!

And that's why the work of NCCJ is so urgent and why our
program must become even stronger, more intense, and more
widespread than ever before.

It is NCCJ's job to stand up implacably, with uncompromising
courage, for the principles of equality and justice and the sanctity
of the individual—which are rooted in our Judeo-Christian teaching and in our Constitution and Bill of Rights and all of its subsequent Amendments.

In our educational programming—through teaching, through
dialogue, through informational programs in the media, and through
face-to-face discussion—we must keep the lines of communication open; we must prevent the polarization of differing groups;
and finally we must reaffirm this nation's faith in cultural pluralism
and we must bring us all together toward our ultimate goal of a
single nation and a unified America.

And that's why NCCJ has to face, head-on, in its educational
programs, the toughest human relations problems in America and
the world today.

We have to deal, head-on, in our programs, with the fears and hatreds toward police that often develop among minority groups; and similarly, we must deal with the harsh prejudices against minority groups sometimes found within the police establishment and heightened by the sniping and murder they've had to face from some members of these groups.

And that's what our programs for police and community leaders are all about and why their tough, hard-hitting dialogues in our 12 national week-long institutes and in our local programs in 70 cities are so important. For it's the only way that our police officers and community leaders, particularly in the inner cities, will ever find any mutual understanding of their deep-rooted problems.

We've got to deal honestly and forthrightly with human rights in our schools and colleges, and face up to the problem of quality integrated education, yielding neither to the pressures of ethnic protectionism nor of racial separatism. And we've got to face up to the blunt fact that quality education simply does not exist in our ghetto areas.

And that's what our 35 two- to six-week accredited human relations workshops for teachers and educators in colleges and universities every summer, and our national educational conferences of opinion leaders, are all about. For the 3,000 teachers and administrators who participate in those workshops and conferences every year are right now—every day—incorporating that human relations teaching into the curriculum of their daily classroom work and into the administration of their schools. And, in the immediate years ahead, we must extend this workshop program not only to more teachers and school administrators but also to thousands of our finest young undergraduate college students, who will be the leaders of this country tomorrow!

We have to face up to the terrible alienation of many of our youth—who have rejected the establishment, and old-fashioned family morality, and the discipline of school and college life. Through institutes and conferences involving thousands of youth and parents and teachers, we've somehow got to bridge the generation gap, so that our most precious moral and spiritual values are not lost to this country.

And that's what our Rearing Children of Good Will program for youth and adults is all about, and why it must be extended far beyond the more than 4,000 young high school leaders and hundreds of parents and teachers who are now deeply involved in these institutes in all parts of the country.

In the field of equal opportunity in industry we must spread to a much larger audience the know-how we've gained from our national week-long institutes for business and labor leaders at Cornell and California State and the University of Oklahoma and other major universities, and from our regional programs in more than 30 cities. For, despite the fact that American corporations and labor unions, on the whole, have done an increasingly splendid job of trying to eliminate discrimination within business and industry, NCCJ's hard-hitting programs concerned with such problems as the employment of the hard-core unemployed, the training of the so-called untrainable, the upgrading and promotion and housing of minority employees, and the employment of ex-offenders, are still vitally needed by both business and labor, and must be greatly expanded in the immediate years ahead.

In the interreligious field, we are right now dealing with such rugged problems as Christian-Jewish relations—as they are affected by the Middle-East crisis, and the ignorance and misunderstanding of many Christians about the profound meaning of Israel as a land and as a people to the Jewish community throughout the world.

And we're also tangling with such difficult problems as the tensions which have developed between the Black and Jewish communities, and the interreligious hostilities threatening to erupt over the abortion issue and over Key 73.

And we're also dialoguing on a continuous basis on such sensitive issues as the teaching about religion in the public schools, and Sunday business-closing laws which discriminate against those whose Sabbath is Saturday, and the use of prayer in the public schools, and Federal and State aid to parochial schools.

These and dozens of other tough human-relations and church-state problems, if allowed to fester and grow malignant, could polarize Christians and Jews, and turn Protestant-Catholic relations into bitter hostilities like those now so tragically plaguing Northern Ireland.

And that's what NCCJ's ongoing Christian-Jewish dialogues, in more than 70 cities, and our hundreds of interreligious institutes and conferences are all about—to bring light and understanding rather than heat and anger to these problems.

Somehow, in the 70's, we've got to develop a new breed of men and women in this country—not a silent majority, but a concerned majority, if you will—who care deeply, to a point where it hurts them inside, about the fact that millions of their fellow citizens are ill-clad, ill-housed, without jobs, and without hope—a new breed of Americans, with a new sense of conscience and a new sense of consciousness, who are completely aware of the bitter, shattered feelings of others who have been deprived and discriminated against, and who are determined to do something about this!

I'm sure every one of you, every once in a while—just as I have—has questioned and wondered about what life was all about, about why we are here, about what our job really is here on this earth if we are to become in truth what God has asked us to become—sheaths for his light, temples of his love, and expressions of his will in all that we think and feel and say and do and are.

And I am sure that all of you—just as I—have come to the conclusion that, at the final count, all that really matters in life is how we have lived; at the final count, all that really matters in life is whether we have obeyed that great Commandment of all the world's great religions to love God and to love our fellow man; all that really matters in life is our search for God and our expression of him in the good we have done for our fellow man. And everything else—material acquisitions, self-aggrandizement, worldly honor and glory—are like chaff that the wind blows away.

What really counts is the courage we demonstrate, the moral strength we exert, the good we do for this country and the world, and the commitment we make to the sanctity of God and the sacred rights of our fellow men!

I call on you tonight to join me in making that commitment through NCCJ! Through its work with youth, with police, with business and labor leaders, with clergy, and with parents and teachers, the National Conference is doing a quiet educational job that is absolutely vital to the future of this country. We have a program designed as no other in this country to strengthen our national unity, to bring about interreligious understanding and interracial justice, and to help finally to make real that pledge of allegiance to which we all subscribe but have yet to live up to, that pledge of "one nation under God; indivisible, with liberty and justice for all!"

That's what the National Conference is in business for—to make real that pledge; and I submit to you that it is the most important business in this disturbed country of ours today!

And that's why I say to all of you here tonight that you can stand up and hold your heads high and be proud of your share in the work of the National Conference!

We must do more, much more! Every problem we ignore, as our history has shown, will return to plague our children tomorrow; and by contrast, every program of the NCCJ is a creative opportunity to do something today about the human relations problems America now faces. And every one of our programs is bigger than we are. The only limitations to the good we can accomplish are the limitations of ourselves. NCCJ has never faced a greater challenge; its program has never been more relevant; and with the help of the creative, gifted, and brilliant lay leadership and staff we now have, we can meet that challenge; and in the next decade we can do a job that can change this country profoundly.

I firmly believe that more than ever we have the power to become a crucial force in this country's struggle for national unity and for freedom and for justice and for equality for all Americans.

I firmly believe that, with the leadership NCCJ has—indeed, with the leadership right here in this room, we have the capacity to wipe out anti-Semitism for good, to make anti-Catholic and anti-Protestant feeling a medieval ghost, and to make racial prejudice the extinct, hideous ugly dinosaur it deserves to become. In its attack on prejudice and discrimination, the National Conference must double, even triple, the force of its program—and there can be no neutral ground!

Discovering Fire for a Second Time!

An Address Before Delegates from 30 Councils of the British Council of Christians and Jews at Hengrave Hall, Bury-St. Edmunds, England, July 28, 1979.

My dear wife, Lili, and I appreciate deeply the warm welcome that all of you have extended to us. It is a joy for us to be with you!

We are also most grateful to your distinguished national treasurer, Sir Sigmund Sternberg, and his charming and wonderful wife, Lady Sternberg, for all the warm and most generous hospitality they have extended to us.

The U.S. National Conference of Christians and Jews has had a close relationship with the British Council ever since World War II. Indeed, only four weeks ago Sir Sigmund Sternberg and Lady Sternberg, Rev. Peter Jennings, Dr. Caesar Aronsfeld, and a number of others from England, represented the British Council at a five-day International Colloquium in New York City, jointly sponsored by my organization and the International Council of Christians and Jews. Sixteen nations are now a part of that International Council, and all of you here today can be proud of the fact that your organization played a major leadership role in the formation of this Council.

The theme of this New York colloquium was "Religious Responsibility for Human Rights: Lessons from the Holocaust—Directions for Today." More than 150 people attended and more than 80 came from Great Britain, Europe, Israel, Canada, and South America. It was a great conference, and you can be proud of the distinguished delegation you sent to represent your country!

I've been asked to speak to you today about my organization—the U.S. National Conference of Christians and Jews—and tell you about its program.

Like your organization, mine also has its roots in the great

195

commandments of both the Old and New Testaments. These great commandments, as you know, tell us that: "Thou shalt love the Lord, thy God, with all thy mind and with all thy heart and with all thy soul and with all thy strength—and thou shalt love thy neighbor as thyself."

These great commandments, in other words, call for equality and justice and freedom for every single God-created and God-centered person on this earth and, furthermore, they call upon every one of us who is a Christian or a Jew to make it a sacred obligation to work for these human rights for our fellow men and women.

And that's what my organization, like yours, is in business for—to eliminate prejudice and discrimination and to secure these sacred human rights of equality and freedom for every American.

Now let me tell you about our program. Every summer we hold more than 20 week-long youth conferences for more than 4000 young high school leaders, who will be America's leaders tomorrow.

Every summer we play a role in assisting some 35 accredited-university workshops in human relations for 5000 teachers, who will put this new training to work in their classrooms this coming fall.

Throughout the year we hold 12 to 15 national institutes on police-community relations on university campuses, for more than 5000 police officers.

Every year we hold more than 30 institutes, usually at major universities, on equal opportunity in industry, involving top business, labor, and civic leaders of our country.

Over the past 10 years we've held conferences in every major U.S. city on "The Holocaust and Its Lesson for Today's Times," to insure that the unspeakable, awful murder of six million of our Jewish brothers and sisters by Nazi tyrants is never, ever, forgotten by our children or our children's children.

These conferences and seminars have ranged in length from one day to a full week. Some have been strictly for scholars; some for the general public; and some for teachers, to acquaint them with methods of teaching about the Holocaust.

We found too few of our young people knew anything about the Holocaust. My daughter's junior high school history textbook had a one-line reference to the Holocaust. And, to further compound the problem, there have been more than 40 books published, denying that the Holocaust ever existed and claiming it is yet another Zionist plot.

In New York City, our seminars and emphasis on the Holocaust led the New York City Board of Education to require a specific number of hours of teaching about the Holocaust during high school; and likewise in Philadelphia.

Many of you, I'm sure, saw the historic television series on the Holocaust written by Gerald Green. I'm proud to say that the NCCJ gave a national award to Mr. Green.

I'm sure that the TV series, however, would never have developed except for the fact that the NCCJ, and other organizations like B'nai B'rith and the ADL and the AJC, had awakened the public and our national leaders to its importance by our prior programming on the Holocaust.

In America, that TV showing was a landmark occasion; 120 million Americans saw the telefilm and wept.

In Germany, 23 million Germans—one-third of the entire population of the West German Republic—also saw it and wept, as well as 72% of all television viewers in France.

In early 1978, a small group of madmen, psychopaths, and idiots, who called themselves the American Nazi Party, threatened to stage a march through the town of Skokie, Illinois, a suburb of Chicago. These Nazi monsters deliberately chose this town for two reasons: first, because it was dominantly Jewish, and secondly, because its 30,000 citizens included more than 8,000 survivors of the Holocaust—obviously an intentional move of harassment.

Efforts were made to block the march by law, but the courts ruled that, in the interest of free speech, the Nazis had the right to march.

How could we make a response to this threat of a march?

We decided that, if the Nazis did march, there should be an overwhelming Christian protest. Remembering King Christian, who, when told by the Nazis that every Jew in Denmark must wear an armband with the Star of David on it, responded: "If you do that, I'll be the first one to wear the armband," the NCCJ ordered black armbands with the yellow Star of David on them. And the NCCJ mobilized the Christians in Skokie, as well as the Jews; and they were all prepared—when the Nazis marched—to stand silently on the sidewalks by the thousands, wearing these armbands and bearing witness to Jewish-Christian solidarity. Credit for this brilliant idea goes to Don McEvoy, who is our very able Senior Vice-President for Program Development.

As it turned out, the Nazis backed off when they learned of our plan—they never did march—just as they backed off when King Christian stood up to them.

But there were threats of similar small kook-type Nazi demonstrations in many other parts of the U.S. So the NCCJ, through its 70 regional offices, organized what we called Christian-Jewish Solidarity Days in more than 100 communities where we had chapters. Just to cite one spectacular example of what happened: in Little Rock, Arkansas, the Catholic bishop led a parade of more than 1,000 Christians and Jews from his cathedral through the streets of Little Rock to the leading Reform temple, there to be welcomed by the rabbi and his congregation; and at the synagogue all of the marchers and the congregation then participated together in a commemorative service on the Holocaust. The march and the service made front-page headlines. And this sort of program went on all across the U.S.

The program was such a success last year that we decided to try for a nationwide observance of the Holocaust this spring. We called for a Holocaust Remembrance Day—either a Sunday observance in Christian churches with a joint Christian-Jewish worship, or a Christian-Jewish Solidarity Day.

The week of April 22 to 29 was subsequently officially declared by Congress to be the national week of "Remembrance of Victims of the Holocaust."

This moved President Carter to establish a National Presidential Commission on the Holocaust to find and recommend an appropriate memorial for those who perished in the Holocaust. This Commission—of 34 outstanding Christians and Jews—is headed by the distinguished writer and scholar, Elie Wiesel, and includes persons of such stature as Father Hesburgh, President of Notre Dame University, and Dr. Robert McAfee Brown of the Union Theological Seminary.

During the Week of Remembrance, President Carter led a Civic Holocaust Commemoration Ceremony in the Rotunda of the Capitol Building attended by congressmen, senators, Cabinet members, and many others. Lili and I had the honor of being invited, and attended.

The President, Elie Wiesel, former U.N. Ambassador Arthur Goldberg, and others, all spoke movingly, and the ceremony was given nationwide press and TV coverage.

The NCCJ's efforts at establishing a Holocaust Remembrance Day in Christian churches was equally rewarding. More than 10,000 churches responded to our challenge, and we now are certain that Christian-Jewish Solidarity Day in Commemoration of the Holocaust will become a national annual observance.

You may ask: Why all this emphasis on the Holocaust *now*? The Holocaust occurred more than 40 years ago.

The answer is: It was beginning to be forgotten. It was neglected or not mentioned in our children's history books. Forty books, as I mentioned earlier, have been published, denying the Holocaust ever existed and charging it is a Zionist plot. And there is a terrible rise of neo-Nazism. There is just a small group of psychos in the United States; unfortunately they make headlines out of all proportion to their importance. But in Austria and Germany the neo-Nazis are on the rise, and you have your problems with them here in Britain.

As President Carter said eloquently at that Rotunda service in the U.S. Capitol Building:

> *The world's failure to recognize the moral truth 40 years ago permitted the Holocaust to proceed. Our generation—the generation of survivors—will never permit the lesson to be forgotten. . . . To truly commemorate the victims of the Holocaust, we must harness the outrage of our memories to banish all human oppression from the world. We must recognize that, when any fellow human being is stripped of humanity, when any person is turned into an object of repression, tortured or defiled or victimized by terrorism or prejudice or racism, then all human beings are victims, too."*

When I attended the Jewish sabbath services held here this morning, I was struck by a similar beautiful statement from the Jewish prayerbook:

> *Whoever destroys a single human soul destroys an entire world . . . . And whoever sustains a single human soul sustains an entire world.*

In terms of implementing President Carter's appeal, I think you can all be proud of the participation of the British delegation to our June 11-14 International Colloquium on "Religious Responsibility and Human Rights: Lessons from the Holocaust—Directions for Today." This was co-sponsored by the U.S. National Conference and the ICCJ, and we were the hosts and found the funding.

I have already mentioned the wonderful participation of Sir

Sigmund and Lady Sternberg, Peter Jennings, Caesar Aronsfeld, and others from Britain.

The important thing was that 16 nations spent six days, all told, of concern with the problem of what lessons could be learned from the Holocaust, and that it was not only concerned with the past but *with the future!* And the important thing that you should know is that this Colloquium and the ICCJ Annual Meeting committed the 16 nation-members, as never before, to the total dimensions of human rights beyond simply Christian-Jewish relations—even though that is still one of the world's greatest human rights problems.

Let me read a few excerpts from the Declaration of Conscience to which the ICCJ committed itself, and to which you, as members of the British Council and as important members of the ICCJ, are also committed:

> *. . . We have become acutely aware, in our investigations and our deliberations, that the lessons of the Holocaust have not been learned.*

> *The genocide inflicted upon the Jews a generation ago is being repeated in other nations, and inflicted on other peoples. Once again the religious communities of the world stand silent and unmoved.*

> *We speak together as Christians and Jews on the basis of our commitments to those principles and precepts which are inherent within both Judaism and Christianity, and which compel us to involved concern for the welfare of all our brothers and sisters in the human family.*

> *We decry the fact that the great silence continues. Even as Hitler was encouraged by the world's lack of outrage and protest at the massacre of the Armenians, today's oppressors seem to have been emboldened by the world's silence to the reality of the Holocaust.*

> *We confess our own participation in this conspiracy of apathy, and pledge together that we shall lift our voices and commit our bodies and our resources to active resistance to every expression of human tyranny.*

> *We call for the immediate release of all prisoners of conscience, the alteration of immigration restrictions in the Western nations so that victims of oppression may find safe haven and a new beginning of life, and the development of positive educational programs in every nation to instruct the world's*

> *children in the lessons of the Holocaust and to instill within
> them the sensitivity to the conditions of others that will in-
> spire them to actively resist all forms of tyranny and all
> violations of human rights.*
>
> *We affirm the fundamental right of every person of every
> country, every color, every class, and every creed, to free-
> dom of conscience and the expression of the dictates of that
> conscience, to freedom of religious belief, and the right to
> practice that religion . . ., to freedom from hunger, poverty,
> and the deprivation of adequate housing and medical care,
> to freedom of self-identity and cultural tolerance . . ., to free-
> dom of migration from any nation which violates these rights
> and full participating citizenship in the nation to which they
> move.*
>
> *. . . Never again will we remain aloof and uninvolved when
> any member of the family of humanity reaches out to us for
> help.*

This is what the British Council and the NCCJ, as a part of the International Council, is committed to! Can you think of anything more important than this commitment?

Now let me turn to the subject of Israel. Ever since the Yom Kippur War in Israel, we've held a nationwide series of conferences and seminars on Christian-Jewish relations as affected by the Arab-Israel crisis, and we often deal in these conferences with the apathy and deep misunderstanding of many of my Christian brothers (I happen to be Catholic) about the profound meaning of Israel, as a land and as a people and as a very essential part of the Jewish faith, to the Jewish community throughout the world.

In addition, in the past six years, NCCJ has conducted ten seminar tours on the theme: "Christian-Jewish-Moslem Relations in the Holy Land," bringing more than 400 of our leaders and 60 of our professional staff of 120 to Israel and, in some cases, also Egypt and Jordan, giving them a firsthand view of the situation there.

Afterwards, these people, of course, are used as speakers and interviewed on radio and TV and in the press in their local communities, further spreading an understanding of what Israel is all about.

We have also spoken out in the press and on radio and television concerning Israel.

When Arafat, the notorious head of the murdering terrorist

PLO, was welcomed by the UN, we protested his appearance to both Secretary-General Waldheim and to President Carter. You'll recall, when Arafat actually made his appearance, he came with a pistol visible in his hip pocket, which in itself was a symbol of his peaceful intentions.

When the UN Assembly voted to equate Zionism with racism, we not only protested nationally, but nearly every one of our 70 offices echoed statements to the press and on radio and TV labeling such an equation as a vicious propaganda lie. The nation-wide impact of that media campaign was one of our finest efforts.

Just 15 months ago, following the PLO's horrible sneak attack upon a public bus, killing 36 people and injuring 76 in early April of 1978—one of 14 such attacks in the past 8 years—I wrote a letter to the editor of the *New York Times* which appeared on April 10th—and the same letter was sent to, and published by, more than 100 other newspapers across the U.S.

Unfortunately, what I wrote still applies to the present. The letter on the editorial page of the *New York Times* was headlined *"The Issue Is Still Israel's Right to Exist."* That's really still the issue, and here is what I said:

> *I write this as a Catholic concerned about the survival of my Jewish brothers and sisters in Israel, and the preservation of human rights in the Middle East.*
>
> *Those at the very top level of our Government, who deplore the so-called 'intransigence' of present Israeli leadership regarding its terribly precarious security and call upon the Begin Government to hand the West Bank over to the Palestinians, are simply not facing up to a number of frightening facts, particularly frightening facts to any Israeli who has had his country invaded three times in the last 25 years. These facts should make it clear to any reasoning human being that such a move, without safeguards of great magnitude backed by U.S. guarantees of force, could jeopardize not only peace in the Middle East but world peace itself. The shocking and utterly damaging facts are these.*
>
> *The PLO would obviously be the new ruling elite of a Palestinian government of the West Bank, for it is, unfortunately, still deemed by a majority of the Arab world and other governments, and a majority of the U.N., as the authentic voice of the Palestinians.*
>
> *The West Bank, under PLO police-state rule, would very soon become a Soviet-dominated, Soviet-armed satellite next door to Israel—not unlike Castro's Cuba. When tiny Cuba,*

*a full 90 miles away from our coast, appeared to be threaten-
ing the giant, powerful USA simply by the presence of Soviet
arms—although there were no Cuban guerrillas invading our
country, blowing up our buses or killing our children—we
mounted a major military solution to the problem. What would
stop the PLO from continual terrorist incursions? What guar-
antees to date does Israel have from the U.S. or the U.N. for
its future security? What is left except self-protection through
retaliation, such as its invasions of Lebanon?*

*The PLO was driven from Jordan by King Hussein after its
members attempted to assassinate him and destroy his government. They then retreated to Lebanon and proceeded to
turn that beautiful country into a battleground between Moslems and Christians, and they have virtually destroyed Lebanon.*

*Is not the lesson clear? With the PLO occupying the West
Bank, would not its next victim be Israel? And would not the
inevitable result be another Middle East War?*

*The most recent madness of the PLO in killing 35 people
and injuring 76 in a sneak attack upon a public bus is but one
of 14 such PLO attacks in the past eight years. Israelis
cannot easily forget the thousands of its people who have
been murdered, maimed, and injured by these terrorist as-
saults. To speak of establishing a Palestinian state next
door to Israel to be headed by such murderers is sheer
madness.*

*Every thinking American must be aware of the relentless
Soviet pressure in the Middle East, but too few Americans
appear to realize that it is our (U.S.) arms and Israel's guts,
to put it bluntly, that have prevented and continue to prevent
a Soviet takeover of the whole Middle East. Israel is the one
bulwark against Soviet aggression in the Middle East, a point
too little emphasized in discussing U.S.-Israeli relations. The
sons and daughters of Israel who are now giving their flesh
and blood to keep the Soviet Union at bay, and to insure the
freedom and peace and sovereignty of Israel, deserve the
applause of the entire free world.*

*Neither our Government nor any other has yet suggested
any credible means of guaranteeing Israel the necessary
safeguards for the true peace it so fervently desires and
prays for. The paramount issue is still Israel's right to exist
in peace and freedom behind secure boundaries.*

*As the minimal first step toward achieving a real peace, let
all to whom captured territory is to be returned first recognize Israel and her right to exist. Then let the U.S. and others
who truly believe in democracy and freedom guarantee the*

necessary stringent military enforcement steps to insure Is-
rael's genuine security and peace, and Israel will no longer
be intransigent but will welcome such an accord.

As I said earlier, this statement reached more than 100 newspapers, and was widely quoted on radio and TV.

"Through all of these programs and many others, our basic aim
is to undergird and reinforce the moral and spiritual values of our
country, to strengthen our national unity, to bring about interreligious understanding and interracial justice, and finally to help
make real the words of our national Pledge of Allegiance—a pledge
that we, as a people, shall become "one nation, under God, indivisible, with liberty and justice for all!"

The great Catholic philosopher, Father Teilhard de Chardin,
once wrote: "Some day, after we have mastered the winds, the
waves, the tides, and gravity, we will harness for God the energies of love; and then—for the second time in the history of the
world—man will have discovered fire."

May all of us, in the years ahead, through such wonderful organizations as the British Council of Christians and Jews and the
NCCJ and the International Council of Christians and Jews, similarly devote our lives to stirring mankind into discovering fire for
the second time!

Notes

1. David Hyatt, *Return To Battle*, (Unpublished autobiographical novel, 1944) p. 243.

2. Phyllis H. Gardiner, *The Hyatt Legacy, The Saga of a Courageous Educator and His Family in California*, (New York: Exposition Press, 1959) p. 301.

3. David Hyatt, "The Religious Roots of Human Rights" (Address presented at the 1978 Convention of the National Association of Human Rights Workers) Nashville, Tennessee, October 15, 1978.

4. Elmo Roper, *The High Cost of Discrimination* (The National Conference of Christians and Jews, 1954, p. 18).

5. Ibid.

6. Peggy Mann, "Prelude to Holocaust," *The Washington Post*, April 16, 1978, pp. B1, B2.

7. David Hyatt, "Brotherhood: A Moral Imperative!" (Address presented at Dallas University) Dallas, Texas, February 26, 1960.

8. U.S., Information Agency, *Legacy of a President*, ed. Wesley Pederson, 1963, p. 108.

9. Ibid.

10. Fred Remington, "Operation Understanding," *The Pittsburgh Press*, n.d.

11. Office of the White House Press Secretary, "Remarks of the President to the Officers of the National Conference of Christians and Jews," President John F. Kennedy, November 21, 1961.

12. Letter from Brooks Hays, Special Assistant to President John Kennedy, May 28, 1962.

13. Memorandum from Lewis Webster Jones, The National Conference of Christians and Jews, Re Director of Public Information, March 13, 1963.

14. *Pakistan Morning News*, October 11, 1963.

15. *Report of the National Advisory Commission on Civil Disorders*, Otto Kerner, Chairman, March 1, 1968, p. 19.

16. *Hospitality*, Lillian Reiss, Paul Evans, Donald Kurth (Kilmer Job Corps Center, Edison, New Jersey, 1965) p. 30.

17. David Hyatt, "Because It Is Right: A Searching Look at Human Rights Today" (Address at the 32nd Annual Meeting of the U.S. National Commission for UNESCO) Washington, D.C., October 8, 1968.

18. National Conference of Christians and Jews, *Minutes of the Board of Governors*, April 22, 1968.

19. National Conference of Christians and Jews, *Minutes of the Board of Trustees*, November 17-18, 1968.

20. *Diary*, Lenore Wade Hyatt, 1968-1969.

21. Letter to Margaret and Ted Reynolds, Austinberg, Ohio, January 1, 1968, from David Hyatt.

22. Ibid.

23. David Hyatt, "Drum Majors for Justice" (Address before National Conference of Christians and Jews Staff Conference) New York City, January 6, 1970, p. 78.

24. Ibid.

25. Letter to William Cantor, The Howard Sloan Agency, 545 Fifth Avenue, New York, NY, November 13, 1970, from David Hyatt.

26. Letter of Recommendation for Lillian Reiss from David Hyatt, July 11, 1968.

27. National Conference of Christians and Jews, Confidential Memorandum. Subject: Supervision of Field Offices. To: Sterling Brown from David Hyatt, December 7, 1967.

28. National Conference of Christians and Jews, Meeting of Board of Trustees, Waldorf-Astoria Hotel, New York City, November 22-23, 1970, pp. 5 and 6.

29. Letter to David Hyatt, Building for Brotherhood, 43 West 57th Street, NY, NY 10019 from Don Eagle, November 31, 1971.

30. National Conference of Christians and Jews, Confidential Staff Bulletin, Subject: Special Gifts, Extension Membership and Direct Mail Renewal Campaigns, May 25, 1971.

31. National Conference of Christians and Jews, Confidential Staff Bulletin, Foundation and Government Grants, June 1, 1971.

32. Letter to David Hyatt, National Conference of Christians and Jews, Inc., 43 West 57th Street, NY, NY 10019, from George Christopher, President, Christopher Commercial Corp., 55 Stonecrest Drive, San Francisco, California 94132, December 14, 1971.

33. Letter to Mr. George Christopher, Christopher Commercial Corp., 55 Stonecrest Drive, San Francisco, California 94132 from David Hyatt, December 27, 1971.

34. "Dr. Hyatt Reappointed to National Commission," *Scarsdale Inquirer*, Thursday, October 21, 1971.

35. "Head of National Conference of Christians and Jews Is Impressed with Israel," *The Detroit Jewish News*, June 30, 1972.

36. Nancy Ann Rella, "Israel Trip Gives Area Couples New Insight," *The Reporter Dispatch*, White Plains, NY, March 16, 1972.

37. David Hyatt, "Life Is Stronger Than Politics," *Scarsdale Inquirer*, April 27, 1972.

38. Ibid.

39. "Greater Efforts Are Urged for Understanding of Israel," *Religious News Service*, March 6, 1972.

40. David Hyatt, "Life Is Stronger Than Politics."

41. Comments on The National Conference of Christians and Jews National Staff Conference at Sylvania Hotel, Philadelphia, March 26-29, 1972.

42. "The Man Who Was Not Surprised by the Security Council," *Al Hamishmar*, July 6, 1972.

43. The National Conference of Christians and Jews, Memorandum, The Staff Representative Advisory Council, Detroit, Michigan, October 12-13, 1972.

44. The National Conference of Christians and Jews, Memorandum. Subject: Organizational Changes to Strengthen NCCJ. May 18, 1973.

45. Gary MacEoin, *What Happened at Rome?* (New York: Holt, Rinehart, and Winston, 1966), p. 9.

46. "NCCJ's President Has New Ideas," *Jewish News*, June 15, 1973.

47. "Non-Silent Concerned Majority," *Religious News Service*, March 30, 1973, p. 1.

48. Letter to David Hyatt, April 13, 1973, from Robert L. Weinberg, Weinberg and Green, 10 Light Street, Baltimore, Maryland.

49. National Conference of Christians and Jews, Memorandum. Subject: "Would You Like to Participate in an Intensive 10-Day Travel Seminar in Israel to Further Increase Your Understanding and Skills When Programming Re: Christian Jewish Relations as Affected by the Middle East Crisis?" December 20, 1973.

50. Robert Murphy, *Diplomat Among Warriors*, Doubleday & Company, Inc., Garden City, New York, 1964, p. 21.

51. David Hyatt, "The Vienna Transit Camp," Common Ground, Vol. xxvii, Number 4, Winter, 1973.

52. Letter to David Hyatt, October 10, 1973, from Joshua O. Haberman, Washington Hebrew Congregation, Massachusetts Avenue and Macomb Street, N.W., Washington, D.C. 20016.

53. William W. Simpson, *The International Council of Christians and Jews, A Brief History*, English edition, June, 1979, p. 8.

54. "Dr. Hyatt Cites Elks on Racial Mandate," Scarsdale Inquirer, August 2, 1973, p. 3.

55. David Hyatt, " 'The Impossible Dream' Must Continue as a Shining Reality" (Address Before the Annual Convention of the League for Human Rights of B'nai B'rith) Toronto, Canada, November 4, 1973.

56. Simpson, p. 8.

57. Ibid, p. 6.

58. *Conference*, ed. Lillian R. Block, National Conference of Christians and Jews, Summer 1947, p. 3.

59. Simpson, p. 8.

60. Letter to David Hyatt, October 31, 1973, from Benjamin Jaffe, Director, World Zionist Organization, External Relations Department, Jerusalem, P.O. Box 92: Ref. No. 42.

61. Letter to David Hyatt, December 3, 1974, from Robert M. Nieman, President, Nieman-Reed Lumber Co., Inc., 12925 Riverside Dr., Sherman Oaks, California.

62. David Hyatt (Address of Acceptance of the John F. Kennedy Brotherhood Award of the Jewish War Veterans) Temple Emanu-El, New York City, March 6, 1974.

63. David Hyatt, "Talk That Leads to Action Can Change the World," (Address to National Conference of Christians and Jews High School and World Youth Forum Joint Conference at Girl Scout National Headquarters, United Nations Plaza, February 18, 1974).

64. National Conference of Christians and Jews, Special Meeting of the Board of Trustees, 43 West 57th Street, New York City, October 28, 1975.

65. "NCCJ President Sees Solzhenitsyn's Exile a Response to Outraged World Opinion," *News from NCCJ*, National Conference of Christians and Jews, February 14, 1974, p. 3.

66. The National Conference of Christians and Jews, Inc., Meeting of the Board of Governors, St. Moritz Hotel, New York, April 25, 1974.

67. National Conference of Christians and Jews, Memorandum. Subject: Staff Intercultural Seminar-Tour On Christian-Jewish-Moslem Relations. December 10–20, 1974.

68. Gary MacEoin, *What Happened at Rome?*, Holt, Rinehart and Winston, New York, 1966, p. 11.

69. "Hits Exclusion from European Group," *Religious News Service*, January 13, 1975.

70. Letter to David Hyatt, President, National Conference of Christians and Jews, February 14, 1975, from Roy D. Morey, Deputy Assistant Secretary for International Organization Affairs. United States Department of State.

71. *Religious News Service*, January 13, 1975.

72. "NCCJ President Condemns Arab Blacklist of Bankers: Applauds Leaders Who Have Resisted Boycott Efforts," *News from NCCJ*, National Conference of Christians and Jews, Inc., February 20, 1975, p. 1.

73. "Residents Attend NCCJ Seminar in Middle East," *The Scarsdale Inquirer*, July 10, 1975.

74. "NCCJ Leader Offers 'Helping Hand' to Jews and Arabs in the Holy Land," *Religious News Service*, June 25, 1975.

75. "NCCJ Head Would Dispel Two Middle East 'Myths'," *Religious News Service*, July 3, 1975.

76. "The Phony Refugee Issue," *Kansas City Jewish Chronicle*, August 15, 1975.

77. Bernhard E. Olson, *Faith And Prejudice*, Yale University Press, New Haven, 1963, p. 14.

78. Letter to David Hyatt, President, National Conference of Christians and Jews, 43 West 57th Street, New York, October 20, 1976, from John E. Fobes, Deputy Director-General, UNESCO, Paris Office.

79. "NCCJ President Says Israeli Rescuers Did UN's Job in Freeing Hostages," *Religious News Service*, July 12, 1976.

80. Letter of Transmittal to William F. May, Robert D. Murphy, Nicholas V. Petrou, Oscar S. Straus II, National Co-Chairmen, National Conference of Christians and Jews, December 10, 1975, from Harold S. Williams, President, Institute of Man and Science, Rensselaerville, New York.

81. National Conference of Christians and Jews, Minutes, National Program Staff Meeting, September 10, 1973, p. 2.

82. Letter to David Hyatt, National Conference of Christians and Jews, 43 West 57th Street, New York, April 4, 1973, from Everett Clinchy, The Institute On Man and Science, 325 East 41st St., New York.

83. Letter to David Hyatt, National Conference of Christians and Jews, 43 West 57th Street, New York, January 1, 1972, from Everett Clinchy, The Institute On Man and Science, 325 East 41st Street, New York.

84. David Hyatt, "Some Hopes and Dreams for NCCJ for the Next Five Years" (Closing address at the NCCJ National Staff Conference) Concord Hotel, Lake Kiamesha, New York, January 13, 1977, p. 6.

85. Ibid, p. 5.

86. Ibid, pp. 3, 4.

87. Ibid, p. 6.

88. Mailgram to The Honorable Jimmy Carter, President of the United States, White House, Washington, D.C. March 18, 1977, from David Hyatt, National Conference of Christians and Jews, 43 West 57th Street, New York, N.Y. 10019.

89. Letter to Mr. Howard A. Glickstein, Director, Task Force on Civil Rights Reorganization, President's Reorganization Project, Washington, D.C. 20503, July 26, 1977, from David Hyatt, National Conference of Christians and Jews, 43 West 57th St., New York.

90. Ibid.

91. Ibid.

92. "Ku Klux Klan: Re-emergence of the 'Haters' " *New York Times*, Editorial Page

93. Ibid.

94. National Conference of Christians and Jews, Inc., Memorandum. To: All Professional Personnel, Re: Statements by NCCJ's President. April 7, 1978, p. 1/2.

95. Ibid, p. 3.

96. Letter to David Hyatt, National Conference of Christians and Jews, 43 West 57th St., New York, from Ralph D. King, Executive Director, March 14, 1975.

97. "Nazi Resurgence Is Drawing Growing Christian Response," *Religious News Service*, April 7, 1978.

98. "Neo-Nazism Spreads; West Germany Acts," *The Herald Tribune*, Paris, France, February 6, 1978.

99. "German Youth in Ignorance of Holocaust, Rabbi Says," *Religious News Service*, December 2, 1977.

100. "Reports of Anti-Semitic Incidents in France Are Rising," *The New York Times*, January 15, 1978.

101. "The Interfaith Movement," David Hyatt, *Judaism*, The American Jewish Congress and World Jewish Congress, New York, Summer 1978, p. 276.

102. "Christian-Jewish Unit Elects Head," *New York Times*, May 26, 1978.

103. "Dr. Hyatt, NCCJ Head, Named President of World Interreligious Organization," *Religious News Service*, May 16, 1978.

104. Ibid.

105. "NCCJ May Boycott 1980 'Passion Play'," *The Jewish News*, June 9, 1978.

106. "ICCJ Mobilizes Campaign Against the 1850 Version of Passion Play," *Religious News Service*, May 16, 1978.

107. National Conference of Christians and Jews Press Release for 50th Anniversary, "NCCJ Sponsoring In-Depth Survey to Document Nature of Discrimination in U.S.," December 8, 1978.

108. Letter to The President of the United States, The President of the Arab Republic of Egypt, The Prime Minister of Israel prior to the Camp David Peace Talks, September 1, 1978 from leaders of the American Christian, Jewish and Islamic communities.

109. Letter to David Hyatt, National Conference of Christians and Jews, 43 West 57th Street, New York, November 16, 1978, from Everett R. Clinchy, Little Meadow Road 27, Guilford, Connecticut.

110. Letter to David Hyatt, National Conference of Christians and Jews, 43 West 57th Street, New York, December 18, 1978, from Everett R. Clinchy, Rensselaerville, New York.

111. Mailgram to The Honorable Jimmy Carter, The White House, Washington, D.C., from David Hyatt, President, National Conference of Christians and

Jews, President, The International Conference of Christians and Jews, January 31, 1979.

112. "International Council of Christians and Jews Formulates Declaration," Hon. Robert F. Drinan, *Congressional Record*, E3292, June 27, 1979.

113. National Conference of Christians and Jews, Inc., Memorandum. Subject: 1. The Importance of Your Involvement in the International Council of Christians and Jews, 2. Lessons to be learned by NCCJ Staff from the June 11–14 NCCJ-ICCJ Colloquium and ICCJ Annual Meeting June 14–15 on Religious Responsibility, 3. Further Comments on the ICCJ, July 9, 1979.

114. "Author of 'Holocaust: The Story of the Family Weiss' Received NCCJ Award," *Texas Jewish Post*, June 28, 1979.

115. Letter to David Hyatt, National Conference of Christians and Jews, 43 West 57th Street, New York, from Irving Greenberg, Executive Director, President's Commission on the Holocaust, Suite 7233 Jackson Place, NW, Wash., D.C., April 9, 1979.

116. "Lessons of the Holocaust and Church Struggle: 1970–1980," Remarks of Franklin H. Littell at the Annual Scholars Conference in New York, April, 1981, *Journal of Ecumenical Studies* (1981) 2:369–73, XVIII.

117. Mailgram to President Jimmy Carter, White House, Washington, D.C. 20500, from David Hyatt, President, National Conference of Christians and Jews, March 15, 1979.

118. Letter to David Hyatt, President, National Conference of Christians and Jews, from President Jimmy Carter, The White House, Washington, April 2, 1979.

119. "Former Resident to Receive Award," *The Rye Chronicle*, June 14, 1979.

120. "NCCJ Viewpoint Heard at NCC Panel on the Middle East," *National News of the National Conference of Christians and Jews*, Spring 1980.

121. Letter to David Hyatt, President, National Conference of Christians and Jews, from Nathan Perlmutter, Anti-Defamation league of B'nai B'rith, 823 United Nations Plaza, New York, March 24, 1980.

122. "Brooks Hays Honored by NCCJ at Premiere of Film on Life," *Religious News Service*, October 30, 1980.

123. Ibid.

124. "NCCJ President Calls Churches and Synagogues Most Chauvinistic of U. S. Institutions," *News From NCCJ*, December, 1978.

125. "Letters to the Editor," *News From NCCJ*, July 10, 1981.

126. "Regarding Women's Rights and the Equal Rights Amendment to the U.S. Constitution," *Quotes for the Media*, by David Hyatt, President, The National Conference of Christians and Jews, 1979.

127. "Trying to Be Mr. Nice Guy," *Time* Magazine, April 5, 1982.